PHILADELPHIA REGION

KEYSTONE
TOMBSTONES

JOE FARRELL AND JOE FARLEY
WITH LAWRENCE KNORR

Mechanicsburg, Pennsylvania   USA

Published by Sunbury Press, Inc.
50 West Main Street
Mechanicsburg, Pennsylvania 17055

www.sunburypress.com

ISBN: 978-1-62006-545-7 (Trade Paperback)

Library of Congress Control Number: 2015933670

FIRST SUNBURY PRESS EDITION: April 2015

Product of the United States of America
0 1 1 2 3 5 8 13 21 34 55

Set in Bookman Old Style
Designed by Crystal Devine
Cover by Lawrence Knorr
Edited by Allyson Gard

Continue the Enlightenment!

INTRODUCTION

This volume of the **Keystone Tombstones** series focuses on grave sites that can be found in and around Philadelphia. Obviously, there are plenty of tourist attractions in this area, and we believe the final resting places of the people covered in this book warrant consideration for a visit. As a matter of fact, this volume is designed to both aid and encourage readers to make such visits.

For those of you new to the series, **Keystone Tombstones** books contain mini-biographies of famous and infamous people who have been laid to rest in Pennsylvania. We also include photos of the individuals, monuments or places important to their story, as well as the graves and the tombstones. This volume has been arranged by county to make it easier for the reader to find their way around. In addition, at the end of every chapter, we have a section we call *If You Go,* where we recommend other graves in the vicinity which you may want to visit, as well as local eating establishments and watering holes where you can refresh yourself. We've gotten plenty of positive feedback relative to these sections in the books.

As far as places to visit, the Philadelphia area is a gold mine. You have your founding fathers, most notably Benjamin Franklin. You've got great sports figures like Connie Mack and Richie Ashburn, to name a few. You have a chance to visit truly impressive graves like those of Harry Kalas and Joe Frazier. The Civil War is well represented by Winfield Scott Hancock and George Meade among numerous others. You have your politicians in Frank Rizzo and Arlen Specter. Let's not forget your entertainers like Bessie Smith, Teddy Pendergrass, and Marian Anderson. You may even decide to visit the final resting place of that business and marketing innovator, John Wanamaker. Frankly, this just scratches the surface of your choices.

Many of the cemeteries themselves are national treasures. Laurel Hill Cemetery and West Laurel Hill Cemetery are very large cemeteries with hundreds of graves of historical figures. Laurel Hill is itself a National Historical Landmark and it's graves run the historical gamut from Revolutionary War figures like George Reed to Phillies' announcer Harry Kalas and West Laurel Hill has many famous Civil War figures and famous entertainers like Dave Garroway, Teddy Pendergrass, and Grover Washington. Christ Church Burial Grounds has five signers of the Declaration of Independence including Ben Franklin.

At any rate, we found our visits to the region to be very educational and fulfilling. It is our hope that you will have similar experiences should you decide to make the journeys. While we have tried to make it as easy as possible for you to locate the sites profiled within, it is our suggestion, especially in the larger cemeteries, that you go to the office for help when you arrive. Our experience is that this can save you quite a bit of time.

So, our best wishes on your adventures. We hope you find them fulfilling. Feel free to leave some grave goods in memory of those you visit. It's always nice to come upon these on your visits. Finally, we hope you enjoy the stories about the people within, and for you travelers and readers, we encourage you to check out the other volumes in the series.

Joe Farley

CONTENTS

"The Good Earth"

PEARL BUCK

County: Bucks
Town: Perkasie
Cemetery: Green Hills Farm Grounds
Address: Off Route 313 West, follow signs to Pearl Buck Homestead

Pearl Buck won the Nobel Prize for Literature in 1938. She was the first woman to be awarded this honor. Her novel, "The Good Earth," was the best-selling fiction book in the United States in both 1931 and 1932. In 1932, it was named a Pulitzer Prize winner.

She was born Pearl Sydensticker, on June 26, 1892, in Hillsboro West Virginia. Buck's parents were missionaries. As a result, she grew up in China. As a matter of fact, she learned how to speak Chinese before she was able to speak English. When she was 19, she left China to attend Randolph-Macon Women's College in Virginia. There, she studied psychology.

She graduated Phi Betta Kappa in 1914. That same year, she returned to China as a Presbyterian missionary. In 1917, she married John Lossing Buck, another missionary, who specialized in agriculture. Immediately after the wedding, the couple moved to Nanhsuchou in the very rural Anhwei province. The community was very poor and it was here that Buck began gathering information she would use in writing "The Good Earth" and many other stories involving China.

In 1920, the Bucks moved to Nanking, where they both had obtained teaching positions at a local university. The couple's first child, a daughter who they named Carol, was born that same year. The child was profoundly retarded. In addition, because a uterine tumor was discovered during delivery, Buck had a hysterectomy. The bad luck continued as Buck's mother died in 1921.

The Bucks returned to the United States in 1924. During this period Buck earned a Masters degree from Cornell University. The following year they adopted a daughter who

Pearl S. Buck

they named Janice. In the fall of 1925, they returned to China.

In 1927, a battle known as the "Nanking Incident" began. It involved forces under Chiang Kai-shek, those supporting the communists, and Chinese warlords. Several westerners were killed. Buck and her family, including her father, hid in a hut with a poor Chinese family. They spent a terrifying day in hiding before being rescued by American

Here lies Pearl Buck returned to the good earth in a beautiful grave on the property where she did most of her writing.

gunboats. Later, the Bucks moved back to Nanking for a short time. However, because of the dangers that remained, they left China for good in 1934.

Buck's marriage, though it lasted for 18 years, was never a happy one. In 1935, she and her husband divorced. Through her writing, Buck had met John Walsh who was a publisher for the John Day Company. This company published her first novel, "East Wind, West Wind," as well as "The Good Earth." In 1935, after her divorce became final, she married Mr. Walsh.

By this time, Buck had bought a farmhouse, known as Green Hills Farm, in Bucks County, Pennsylvania. It was here she and her second husband lived. Over the course of time, they adopted six more children. The farm itself is now on the Registry of Historic Buildings and approximately fifteen thousand people visit each year.

Back in the states, Buck became active in many causes, including civil rights and women's rights. In 1942, she and her husband created the East West Association. Its purpose was to encourage a cultural exchange between Asia and the West. She was angered that adoption services of her time considered Asian and mixed race children to be unadoptable, so in 1949, she founded Welcome House. It was the first agency whose aim was to promote inter-racial adoption.

During the Chinese Cultural Revolution, Buck was described as an "American Cultural Imperialist." This was used to deny her entrance to China when President Nixon visited there in 1972.

Pearl Buck died of lung cancer on March 6, 1973. She was eighty. She is buried on the grounds of Green Hills Farm. Her grave site is easy to find as it sits to the left as you enter the property. She picked a beautiful and peaceful area in which to be laid to rest. Buck designed her own tombstone with Chinese characters that represent the name Pearl Sydensticker.

If You Go:

Green Hills farm in Perkasie is a beautiful place and it is open to the public. You can tour Buck's house and see where she did, not only her writing, but her work on the causes she adopted. Her grave is unique and very well maintained. In addition, as you drive through Perkasie, you will notice numerous shops and restaurants that you might want to visit.

"Philadelphia Saints"

SAINT KATHARINE DREXEL and SAINT JOHN NEUMANN

Counties: Bucks, Philadelphia
Towns: Bensalem, Philadelphia
Cemeteries: The St. Katherine Drexel Mission Center and Shrine,
St. Peter of the Apostle Church – National Shrine of Saint John Neumann
Addresses: 1663 Bristol Pike, 1019 North Fifth Street

Becoming a Saint in the Catholic Church is no easy task. First when a person is considered for Sainthood, a Bishop is given the job of investigating that person's life. If the Bishop concludes that further consideration is warranted, the person is declared a servant of God. Then a Church Official acts as an advocate for the candidate and attempts to prove that the candidate lived a heroic and virtuous life. The advocate collects documents and testimony that are then presented to the Congregation for the Causes of Saints in Rome. If approved, the candidate gets a new title "Venerable." Next a miracle must occur through the intercession of the candidate and said miracle must be confirmed generally by the Roman Medical Board. Once confirmed the candidate earns the title "Blessed." Unless waived by the Pope, a second miracle is required before the Pope declares the candidate a Saint. There are two Saints that lie in rest in the Philadelphia area, Saint Katharine Drexel and Saint John Neumann.

Katharine Drexel was born in Philadelphia on November 26, 1858. Her family was very well-to-do as they possessed a considerable banking fortune. Her uncle Anthony founded Drexel University in Philadelphia. Drexel had two sisters: Louise and Elizabeth. In 1887, the three sisters traveled to Rome. Due to the recent deaths of their parents, they had inherited the family fortune. On January 27th they assisted at a private mass celebrated by Pope Leo XIII; later they would have a private audience with him. At the conclusion of the audience, Katherine asked the Pontiff if he could spare a few minutes to speak with her privately, and he granted her wish. She pleaded with the Pope to send Catholic missionaries to work with American Indians.

Saint Katherine Drexel

Leo responded, "Why not, my child, yourself become a missionary." He gave Drexel his blessing and the audience ended.

In 1874, the Catholic Church in America established the Bureau of Catholic Indian Missions. It is still in existence. Upon its founding it purpose was stated as:

1. To direct the administration of those agencies as were assigned to the care of Catholic missionaries.

2. To secure, if possible, the remainder of those agencies to which Catholic missionaries were justly entitled under the terms of the peace policy.

3. To protect the religious faith and material interests of all Catholic Indians.

4. To secure the establishment of suitable schools for Indian boys and girls.

5. To secure for the Indians moral and practical Christian teachers with adequate compensation for their services and to develop a general interest in Indian education.

6. To secure means to erect school buildings, in all cases possible.

Drexel wholeheartedly supported and contributed to the bureau.

Drexel resolved to use her wealth to aid both Indian and Black Americans. In 1885 she established a school for Native Americans in Santa Fe, New Mexico. In 1889 she decided to become a nun and started her training with the Sisters of Mercy in Pittsburgh. Two years later, she founded her own order of nuns: the Sisters of the Blessed Sacrament for Indians and Colored People. The title contained the purpose of the new order to bring the Blessed Sacrament to the two races. Using her vast wealth, she founded and financed over 60 missions and schools throughout the United States. She is also credited with founding the only historically black Roman Catholic University in the nation, Xavier University which is located in Louisiana.

In 1935 Drexel suffered a heart attack, and two years later she gave up the office of superior general. She continued her devotion to the Eucharist and to the two races her order was established to help. She died at the age of 96 on March 3, 1955.

Saint John Neumann

As detailed at the beginning of this chapter, becoming a Catholic Saint is not easy and it generally takes a very long time to be canonized after one's death. For example the only other American born Catholic Saint, Elizabeth Ann Seton, died in 1821 and was not declared a Saint until 1975. In Drexel's case, during her lifetime, people were already calling her a Saint and these people included Bishops and Archbishops. Bishop Joseph McShea, who preached at her funeral, said "I think she was a Saint. I am convinced she was a Saint and have no knowledge of any other dedicated woman, lay or religious, no personal knowledge, that would exceed her in sanctity."

There was still the need for miracles before Drexel could be named a Saint. George and Bea Gutherman lived in Bensalem where they raised a family that included eleven children. In 1974 one of their sons named Bob was hospitalized with a very serious ear infection. The infection was life threatening, and even if the boy survived he was expected to lose his hearing. The family prayed directly to Drexel for help, and their son's fever disappeared as did the infection. In addition, the documented inner ear damage healed. In 1987 the Roman medical board declared the case to be a miracle and attributed the cure to Drexel. In 1994 the story of a young girl named Amanda Wall provided the second miracle. Wall had been born deaf, but after family and friends prayed directly to Drexel, she was able to hear. In 2000 the church found that Wall's cure was due to the intercession of Drexel. As a result Drexel, was canonized on October 1, 2000. Her feast day is celebrated on March 3, the anniversary of her death. Her body lies under the main alter in Saint Elizabeth Chapel which is part of the Saint Katharine Drexel Mission Center and National Shrine.

John Neumann was born on March 28, 1811, in Prachatitz, Bohemia. He began his education at the village school when he was six years of age. From the beginning, it was clear that he was both intelligent and eager to learn. He grew to love the natural sciences and studied intently in that area. He also showed his spiritual side at a young age, becoming an altar boy at the age of ten.

Neumann entered the seminary in 1831. He had a driving ambition to become a priest. By 1835 he had passed the examination making him eligible to receive Holy Orders, the catholic sacrament one receives upon entering the priest-hood. Unfortunately for Neumann, his Bishop had decided that at present there would be no ordinations as Bohemia already had a more than sufficient number of priests.

By this time Neumann could speak eight languages including English. Neumann decided he would go to America where there was a need for priests and missionaries that spoke German. He arrived in America with the hope of being ordained. He met with Bishop John Dubois who then governed the Diocese of New York. The Bishop was in charge of a huge territory that included all of New York and New Jersey. Neumann must have made the right impression because he was ordained on June 25, 1836 in the old Saint Patrick's Cathedral on Mott Street in New York City.

Bishop Dubois sent Neumann to work with German immigrants in the area of Niagara Falls. His parish contained about 400 Catholics that lived in an area covering nine hundred square miles. At the time, most of the area would have been described as the frontier. He began travelling the countryside by horse to minister to his flock. He would visit the sick, teach the catechism to children and train others to teach it when he left. A number of churches were built including Saint Peter and Paul Catholic Church in Williamsville, New York. Neumann founded this church and served as its pastor for four years.

By 1840 Neumann came to believe that the spiritual direction he required could only be supplied by an established religious order. After receiving permission from Bishop Dubois, Neumann joined the Redemptorist Fathers in Pittsburgh. In 1842 he took his vows in Baltimore, Maryland and became a full member of this congregation. He was then stationed at Saint James Church in Baltimore, but he continued his practice of travelling long distances to minister to German settlers. In 1847 he was appointed Provincial Superior of the United States Redemptorists. On February 10, 1848 Neumann became a United States citizen. At this point in time he was stationed at Saint Alphonsus Church in Baltimore where he wrote catechisms in both German and English.

In 1852 Pope Pius IX appointed Neumann to the post of Bishop of Philadelphia. At the time of his appointment, Philadelphia was the largest Diocese in the United States. As

Monument in Philadelphia honoring Saint John Neumann.

was his practice, Neumann travelled frequently in order to visit parishes scattered throughout the large area he now headed. He became the first bishop in the country to establish a catholic school system. This system became the model for the parochial school system. New churches were built at an ever quickening pace. As a matter of fact, during his first three years as bishop a new church was opened each month. His programs were popular throughout the diocese, and he became known as the "Little Bishop."

In 1854 Neumann travelled to Rome at the invitation of the Pope. He was present on December 8th when Pope Pius IX issued his declaration of the Dogma of the Immaculate Conception. He took advantage of this trip to Europe to visit his father who he had not seen in 28 years. Upon his return to Philadelphia, Neumann founded a new order of nuns: the Sisters of Saint Francis, who dedicated themselves to teaching and nursing. Neumann had a history of using nuns to spread the faith. Back in 1847 he had welcomed a group of nuns from Munich known as the School Sisters of Notre Dame to America. He provided them with teaching assignments in Philadelphia, New York, Pittsburgh and Baltimore.

Here is the tomb of Saint Katherine Drexel.

On January 5, 1860, while running errands Neumann suffered a stroke, collapsed and died on a city street in Philadelphia. He was only 49 years old. In those 49 years, he had established 80 churches and contributed to the establishment of ten orders of nuns.

Despite all his good work, the need for miracles that could be attributed to Neumann remained. On July 8, 1949, J. Kent Lenahan was crushed between a car and a utility pole as a result of an automobile accident. His skull was crushed and while in the hospital his fever rose to 107 degrees. There was little hope that he would recover. His parents obtained a piece of a cassock that had been worn by Neumann. They placed the piece on their son, and within a few hours his temperature dropped to 100 degrees. In addition his injuries began to heal. Five weeks later, he walked out of the hospital without assistance. The church declared his recovery a miracle and gave the credit for it to Neumann.

Michael Flanigan was six years old in 1963 when it was discovered that he had Ewing's Sarcoma, a lethal form of bone cancer. The doctors gave the boy six months to live. His parents began taking the boy to Neumann's shrine, and after several visits the boy began to recover. By Christmas of 1963, all signs of the cancer had vanished. In 1975 the church declared Michael's cure a miracle and attributed it to the intercession of Neumann. As a result Neumann was canonized in 1977 by Pope Paul VI.

Neumann was buried unembalmed in a wooden casket beneath the floor of Saint Peter of the Apostle Church. His

Final resting place of Saint John Neumann beneath an alter at Saint Peter of the Apostle Church in Philadelphia.

body was exhumed in 1902 so that the required inspections for sainthood could be completed. His remains at the time were found to be intact, and after the inspection the body was returned to the original grave. In 1962 Neumann's body was again exhumed and a face mask was placed over the skull. The body was then placed in a glass coffin and placed under the alter in the Saint John Neumann Shrine which had been constructed on the lower level of the Saint Peter of the Apostle Church.

If You Go:
Keystone Tombstones Volume One contains stories on a number of famous people buried in the Philadelphia area including Benjamin Franklin, William Anderson, Harry Kalas, Frank Rizzo and Bill Tilden. Should you make the trip you might want to pick that volume up and visit some of those graves as well. There are plenty of Philadelphia gravesites in this volume as well including Richie Ashburn, John Wanamaker, Bessie Smith, Bert Bell, and in the Chapter titled "Philadelphia Sinners" several reputed mafia figures are profiled. Philadelphia is a historical Mecca, and you can find plenty to do there including making visits to Independence Hall and the Constitution Center. It goes without saying that there are numerous great places throughout the city where one can stop for refreshments.

Tom Gola in 1958.

"A Philly Legend"

TOM GOLA

County: Bucks
Town: Newtown
Cemetery: Washington Crossing National
Address: 830 Highland Road

He is widely considered to be one of the best college basketball players in the history of the city of Philadelphia. After his death, the Philadelphia Daily News said he wasn't years ahead of his time as a player, he was decades ahead. The former La Salle coach Speedy Morris said, "He was Magic Johnson before Magic Johnson." John Wooden called him, "the greatest all around player ever." His name was Tom Gola. Wilt Chamberlain said, 'When I was growing up you whispered the name Tom Gola. He was like a saint."

Gola was born in Philadelphia on January 13, 1933. He was the oldest of seven children born to Ike and Helen Gola. His father was a Philadelphia policeman. He grew up in an Olney rowhouse located close to the Incarnation of Our Lord parish gym. It was there he honed the skills that would make him a Philadelphia legend. Gola's parents were both under six feet tall, a height he reached while he was still in elementary school. By the 8th grade Gola's Incarnation team had won a state and a national championship.

Gola entered La Salle College High School as a highly touted six foot freshman in 1947. Within a year he had grown to a height of 6'5". He also lived up to his advanced billing on the basketball court. He could play any position, was a great rebounder and for four years he set Catholic League scoring records. Despite his size he was very quick and athletic (he also was a track star). At the conclusion of his high school career he had scored 2,222 points and in his final season he was named the league's top player.

By the time Gola graduated, he had over 60 scholarship offers from schools all over the country including North Carolina and Kentucky. Temple's coach actually offered scholarships to several of Gola's high school teammates in an attempt to attract the young star. Gola decided to stay in Philadelphia and attend La Salle University. The decision would further his already lofty reputation in the City of Brotherly Love.

Gola made an impact in college immediately. As a freshman he led La Salle to a record of 25-7. His team won the then very prestigious National Invitational Tournament held in New York City. That first year he averaged 15 points and 15 rebounds per game. The following year Gola led La Salle back to the NIT but an ankle injury kept him out of the tournament, and La Salle lost by a single point to St. John's in the opener.

1954 would be a banner year for Gola and La Salle. The team went 26-4 and reached the finals of the NCAA tournament. In the final La Salle beat Bradley 92-76 winning the national championship. Gola was named the outstanding player in the tournament. That same year he was named the National Player of the Year. For the season he averaged 23 points and 21.7 rebounds per game. New York Knicks coach Joe Lapchick stated that Gola was "ready to start in the NBA."

As a senior in 1955 Gola led La Salle back to the NCAA championship game. Here they were matched up against the University of San Francisco which was led by K. C. Jones and Bill Russell. Gola scored 16 points in his final game, but La Salle came up short.

During his college career Gola played in 115 games and averaged 20.9 points and 19 rebounds. His rebound total of 2,201 remains the most by any college player ever. Standing at 6'6" he was a forward who could shoot, score, rebound and defend. In addition he had the ball-handling skills of a guard. It is little wonder that the Philadelphia Warriors exercised their territorial rights and selected Gola in the 1955 NBA draft. The move paid off immediately as the Warriors went from last to first and won the NBA title in 5 games against the Fort Wayne Pistons. While Gola let the scoring duties up to Paul Arizin and Neil Johnson he averaged 9.1 rebounds and 5.1 assists per game.

Gola was praised during his early years with the Warriors for concentrating on defense, passing and rebounding. In 1959 Johnson retired due to a knee injury but the Warriors added Wilt Chamberlin to their roster. Gola again sacrificed his own scoring opportunities for the team and the Warriors again made it to the eastern NBA finals where they would face the Boston Celtics. Chamberlin had been named Rookie of the Year and Most Valuable Player after averaging 37.6 points and 27 rebounds a game. Despite Chamberlin the Warriors could not hang with the star-studded Celtics led by Bill Russell, Bob Cousy, Bill Sharman and Tommy Heinsohn. The series went six games with the Celtics coming out on top 119-117 in game six. This was a pattern that would repeat itself as the Celtics would win eight consecutive titles.

Gola himself described his role on those Warrior teams. "We had (Paul) Arizin (see p. 37) and (Neil) Johnston when I got there. They were like the two top scorers in the league. Then Wilt came along. My job was to guard the opponent's best guard, Jerry West, Oscar Robertson, Bill Sharman and be a playmaker." Neil Johnston said, "Tom was the kind of player who might score only eight points but who would win you the game."

When the Warriors moved to San Francisco in 1962 Gola requested that he be traded. It was his hope to remain close to home, and he got his wish when he was sent to the New York Knicks. Gola played for the Knicks for four years before retiring in 1966. In his ten seasons he averaged just a little over 10 points per game. However he did everything else so well that he was selected for five all-star teams.

Gola wasn't done with basketball as he returned to La Salle in 1968 as a coach. In his first season he had some very talented players including Ken Durrett and Fran Dunphy. That team went 23-1 and was ranked second in the country behind UCLA which was led by Lou Alcindor. Unfortunately La Salle was not permitted to participate in the NCAA tournament due to NCAA sanctions that Gola had inherited when he took the job. Gola coached one more year at La Salle where he retired with a record of 37-13.

Gola had been elected to the state legislature as a Republican in 1966. He was able to coach La Salle during this period because he only had to be in Harrisburg one or two days a week. However in 1968 he was elected Philadelphia City Controller a job that he said "was going to require all of his attention." Early in his term as Controller, he began to

battle Philadelphia's Democratic Mayor James Tate. He
filed suit against the mayor
to lift a hiring freeze and also
challenged invoices involved
in the construction of Veterans Stadium. Gola was de-
feated when he ran for
reelection in 1973 (as was
Arlen Specter) as the Republican Party was beginning to
feel the effects of the Water-
gate scandal.

In 1980, Gola became
the Philadelphia chairman
of Ronald Reagan's presi-
dential campaign. After the
election Reagan appointed
Gola to the post of regional
administrator of the United
States Department of Housing and Urban Develop-
ment. Gola made his last
foray into politics in 1982

The man that John Wooden called, "the greatest all around player ever" is buried beneath this modest tombstone.

when he ran for mayor, but he finished third in the Republican primary. After that defeat, he concentrated on running his insurance business.

On July 23, 2003 Gola suffered a head injury resulting
from a fall from a curb in Philadelphia. He was never the
same after the fall, and he passed away on January 26,
2014. He was laid to rest in Washington Crossing National
Cemetery.

Needless to say Gola was widely recognized for his athletic achievements. During his college career he was an All-
American four times and a consensus All-American three
times. In 1988 La Salle refurbished its on campus arena
and named it for Gola. The university also retired his number. He had previously, in 1976, been elected to the Basketball Hall of Fame. In addition he was elected to the Madison
Square Garden Hall of Fame. He remains one of two players
to have won an NCAA, NIT and NBA championship.

If You Go:

Washington Crossing National Cemetery is also the final resting place for two sportsmen who made their name in the world of boxing. Tony Reneal Martin was the International Boxing Council Junior Welterweight Champion in 1991. As a professional he compiled a record of 34 wins, 6 losses and 1 draw and he was only knocked out once. He passed away in 2013.

You can also find the final resting place of George A. Benton. Benton fought as a middleweight from 1949 to 1970 and compiled a record of 62 wins 13 losses and one draw. He had victories over three future world champions Jimmy Ellis, Freddie Little and Joey Giardello. When his boxing career ended he became a successful trainer. Those he trained included Joe Frazier (See page 229) and Evander Holyfield. He was with Frazier when he lost to Muhammad Ali in the "Thriller in Manilla. In addition he was involved in training Leon Spinks in 1978 when Spinks defeated Ali. Benton was named Trainer of the Year in both 1889 and 1990 by the Boxing Writers Association of America. He was inducted into the International Boxing Hall of Fame in 2001. Benton passed away in 2011.

Not far from the cemetery you can find a great spot to refresh yourself called the Green Parrot Restaurant. The Parrot features a large and varied menu, a friendly atmosphere and terrific service. The food was wonderful and we highly recommend checking it out. It is located at 240 North Sycamore Street in Newtown.

CHESTER COUNTY

"The Fighting Quaker"

SMEDLEY BUTLER

County: Chester
Town: West Chester
Cemetery: Oaklands
Address: 1042 Pottstown Pike

Smedley Darlington Butler, nicknamed "the fighting Quaker" was a Major General in the United States Marine Corps and at the time of his death, the most decorated marine in United States history. Butler was a double-winner of the Congressional Medal of Honor, one of only twenty people to ever be so decorated. He is one of three to be awarded the Marine Corps Brevet Medal and the Medal Of Honor and the only man to be awarded the Brevet Medal and two Medals Of Honor, all for separate actions. During his 34 year career as a Marine, he participated in military actions in the Philippines, China, Central America, the Caribbean, and France in World War I. By the end of his career he had received sixteen medals, five of which were for heroism. Yet his military career is only part of what makes his story so very interesting.

Butler was born in West Chester, Pennsylvania and was the Quaker son of Thomas Stalker Butler who was a lawyer, judge, and for 31 years a Congressman. During the Spanish American War, Butler left high school 38 days prior to his 17th birthday to enlist in the Marine Corps. Although he did not finish all the coursework, he was awarded his high school diploma on June 6, 1898.

In the anti-Spanish war fever of 1898, he lied about his age and received a direct commission as a Marine second Lieutenant. He fought in the Philippine-American war later that year. In 1900, he received a brevet promotion to Captain and the Marine Corps Brevet Medal for his action during the Boxer Rebellion in which he was shot in the thigh and chest. In 1903 he fought to protect the United States Consulate in Honduras from rebels. Between the Honduras campaign and his next assignment, he returned to Philadelphia and on June 30, 1905 married Ethel Conway Peters of

Smedley Butler (left) in Shanghai.

Philadelphia. The couple would have three children: a daughter Ethel and two sons Smedley and Thomas.

Butler served in Nicaragua from 1909 to 1912 and then in 1914 he earned his first Medal of Honor for the capture of Veracruz, Mexico during the Mexican Revolution. The citation says he exhibited courage and skill in leading his men.

The following year he was ordered to Haiti when Haitian rebels known as "Cacos" killed the Haitian dictator Vilbrun Sam. The Marines captured the rebel stronghold, Fort Riviere, after engaging in hand-to-hand combat. Butler's performance impressed the Assistant Secretary of the Navy, Franklin D. Roosevelt, who recommended him for his second Medal of Honor which was presented to him in 1917. That made him and Dan Daly the only Marines to receive the Congressional Medal Of Honor twice for separate actions.

During World War I, he was promoted to the rank of Brigadier General and placed in command of Camp Pontanezen at Brest, France, a debark station depot. His performance there earned him the Distinguished Service Medal of both the United States Army and Navy and the French Order of the Black Star.

After World War I, he became the Commanding General of the Marine Barracks at Quantico, Virginia. During a training exercise in 1921 he was told by a local farmer that Stonewall Jackson's arm was buried nearby. Not believing it, he had a squad of Marines dig up the spot and did indeed find Stonewall's arm in a wooden box. He replaced the wooden box with a metal box and reburied the arm. He left a plaque on the granite monument marking the place. The plaque is no longer on the marker but can be viewed at the Chancellorsville Battlefield Visitor's Center.

In 1924 Butler was asked by the Major of Philadelphia W. Freeland Kendrick to become the City's Director of Public Safety. Philadelphia's municipal government was notoriously corrupt, and Butler initially refused. President Coolidge intervened and authorized the necessary leave from the Marines. His major problem was the enforcement of Prohibition and his strong enforcement action earned him both enmity and respect. He left after two years and later stated that "cleaning up Philadelphia was worse than any battle I was ever in."

In 1927 Butler served a tour in China and returned as a Major General in 1929. In 1931 he publicly recounted a story about Benito Mussolini in which Mussolini struck a child with his automobile and refused to stop. This story caused international outrage, and Butler was arrested and court-martialed. The source of the story turned out to be Cornelius Vanderbilt Jr. who years later substantially confirmed the story. Butler was ordered to apologize to Mussolini, but he refused. Secretary of State Stimson issued a formal apology to Mussolini. As a trial approached, the case was settled by Butler receiving a reprimand. He retired on October 1. 1931.

In 1932 he ran for the United States Senate as a proponent of Prohibition but was defeated in the Republican Primary by James Davis. During his campaign, Butler spoke forcefully about the veteran's bonus for service during WW I. He spoke to the famous "Bonus Army" that marched on Washington and made camp nearby and encouraged them in their efforts. On July 28, 1932 army cavalry units led by General Douglas MacArthur dispersed the Bonus Army marchers and their wives and children by riding through Hooverville, as it came to be called, and using tear gas and burning their shelters and belongings. Butler then declared himself a "Hoover for ex -president Republican."

In 1934 Smedley Butler alleged the existence of a political conspiracy of Wall Street interests to overthrow President Roosevelt and that he had been asked to lead it. These allegations became known as the Business Plot. The allegations were never proven, but a Congressional investigation found that such an attempt was actually contemplated. (See *The Plot to Seize The Whitehouse* by Jules Archer.)

Butler became known for his outspoken views against war profiteering. In 1935 he wrote his book *War is a Racket* a condemnation of the profit motive behind warfare. His views are summarized in the following passage from a 1935 issue of the magazine "Common Sense":

"I spent 33 years and four months in active military service and during that period I spent most of my time as a high class thug for Big Business, for Wall Street and the bankers. In short, I was a racketeer, a gangster for capitalism. I helped make Mexico and especially Tampico safe for American oil interests in 1914. I helped make Haiti and Cuba a decent place for the National City Bank boys to collect revenues in. I helped in the raping of half a dozen Central American republics for the benefit of Wall Street. I helped purify Nicaragua for the International Banking house of Brown brothers in 1902-1912. I brought light to the

Dominican Republic for the American sugar interests in 1916. I helped make Honduras right for the American fruit companies in 1903. In china in 1927, I helped see to it that Standard Oil went on its way unmolested. Looking back on it, I might have given Al Capone a few hints. The best he could do was to operate his racket in three districts. I operated on three continents."

Butler fought hard to raise awareness of what the real motivating factors of war were. He tried to bring the economic implications of war to the forefront of the public conscience. "War is a racket. It always has been. It is possibly the oldest, easily the most profitable, surely the most vicious" he wrote, noting how proponents typically use God and freedom to explain the mission but never discuss the economic details:

"It is conducted for the benefit of the very few at the expense of the masses. Like all members of the military profession I never had a thought of my own until I left the service. My mental faculties remained in suspended animation while I obeyed the orders of higher-ups."

Pictured above is the grave of two time Medal of Honor Recipient Smedley Butler who showed courage on the battlefield and beyond.

In June 1940, Butler checked himself into a hospital after becoming sick. His doctor described his illness as an incurable condition of the upper abdominal tract, presumably cancer. He died in the Naval Hospital in Philadelphia on June 21, 1940. He is buried in a modest grave in Oaklands Cemetery in West Chester, Pennsylvania.

The USS Butler was named in his honor in 1942. This destroyer participated in the European and Pacific theaters during WW II. It was later converted to a high speed minesweeper. The Marine base in Okinawa is named in his honor.

His books *War Is A Racket* and *The Letters Of A Leatherneck* are still available as are many books about him. There is also a Smedley Butler Society at www.warisaracket.org.

In Soldiers' Grove, behind the Pennsylvania State Capitol Building in Harrisburg, Smedley Butler is memorialized with a headstone in the ground. All of Pennsylvania's Congressional Medal of Honor recipients are honored in this way.

If You Go:
There are a number of other interesting people buried in Oaklands Cemetery. Dewitt Clinton Lewis was a Lieutenant Colonel for the Union army who received the Congressional Medal of Honor recipient for rescuing a private.

William Hollingsworth Whyte Jr., a graduate of Princeton, was author of the 1956 best seller *The Organization Man* and a pioneer in urban planning specifically related to public life and pedestrian behavior.

Joseph Emley Borden was the winning pitcher of the first Major League Baseball game ever played. He pitched for the Boston Red Caps who beat the Philadelphia Athletics 6-5 on April 22, 1876.

Harry Dunn was an artist best known for creating the peacock logo for the NBC television network.

Samuel Barber was a two-time Pulitzer Prize winning composer whose works included symphonies, operas, chamber music and songs. His will stipulated that the burial plot neighboring his should be reserved for his longtime friend and partner Glan Carlo Menotti or at the very least have a stone inscribed "To The Memory of Two Friends." Menotti is buried in Scotland.

"You Don't Mess Around With Jim"

JIM CROCE

County: Chester
Town: Frazer
Cemetery: Haym Salomon Memorial Park
Address: 200 Moores Road

On September 20, 1973, a small commercial airplane took off from Natchitoches Regional Airport in Louisiana. The plane did not gain the necessary altitude to clear a tree at the end of the runway. All five passengers died as a result of the crash. Among them was the 30 year old singer songwriter Jim Croce.

Croce was born in Philadelphia on January 10, 1943. He developed an interest in music at a young age. When he was five, he was belting out the song "Lady of Spain" on an accordion. He attended Upper Darby High School where he would later become the first graduate named to the school's Wall of Fame. After graduation he enrolled at Villanova University in 1961. During his time at the university, he became a member of the Villanova Singers, and he also worked as a student disc jockey.

For Croce music had always been a hobby, but now he began to view it more seriously. He formed a number of college bands and performed at frat parties, coffee houses and at other universities in the Philadelphia area. He later said that his bands played anything the people wanted to hear: "blues, rock, a cappella, railroad music, anything." It was during this time that he met his future wife, Ingrid Jacobson, while he was judging a contest during a hootenanny being held at the Philadelphia Convention Hall. After they married, he converted to his wife's religion, Judaism.

Beginning in the mid-sixties Croce began performing with his wife as a duo. They started out covering other artists' songs but soon found themselves enlarging their repertoire to include their own compositions. According to Croce during this time he would put together a set list pulled from over 3,000 songs he had learned. Croce later recalled playing some pretty tough bars during this period, saying "I can still get my guitar off faster than anyone else."

Jim Croce

In 1968 Croce and his wife moved to New York City after being encouraged to do so by a record producer named Tommy West. It was in New York where they recorded their first album titled "Jim & Ingrid Croce." Following the album's release, the couple spent two years on the road in an effort to promote it. The Croce's hit the college circuit and played small clubs along the way. In all, they would travel over 300,000 miles. Despite their efforts the album was not a commercial success.

Perhaps because their record failed to do well, the Croce's grew weary of the music business and New York City. They sold every guitar they owned, save one, and moved back to the Philadelphia area. Croce worked construction jobs and as a truck driver in order to pay the bills. At the same time he continued to write songs based on people he was meeting in truck stops and at local bars.

While at Villanova, Croce had befriended a man by the name of Joe Salviuolo who was now a record producer. In 1970 Salviuolo introduced Croce to Maury Muehleisen (who would also perish in the 1973 crash) a classically trained guitarist who was also a singer songwriter. The two began performing together, with Croce backing Muehleison. Gradually these roles reversed as they discovered that Muehleison's guitar leads were the ideal accompaniment to Croce's songs.

In 1972 Croce signed a record deal with ABC records. That year he released two albums "You Don't Mess Around with Jim" and "Life & Times." The first release was an instant smash. The title song and the song "Operator" both became highly successful singles. All of a sudden Croce became a top bill concert performer. He was a very open and friendly performer who welcomed his fans backstage after a concert. Rather than listening to critics, he was always anxious to hear from those in the audience as to what they thought of his performance. For those of you who have never seen Croce perform, there are numerous clips of him on YouTube.

The song "Bad, Bad Leroy Brown" was pulled from "Life & Times" and released as a single. It rocketed up the record charts, reaching number 1 in the summer of 1973 and selling two million copies. Croce's career was booming.

Croce finished recording his third album "I Got a Name" in September of 1973 about one week before his death. The album was released on December 1, 1973. "I Got a Name" proved to be another big hit and it produced three hit singles: the title song, "Workin' at the Car Wash Blues" and "I'll Have to Say I Love You in a Song." Croce's untimely death also sparked a renewed interest in his earlier work. The song "Time in a Bottle" which appeared on his first album released the previous year reached number 1 on December 29, 1973. "Photographs and Memories" a greatest hits package was released in 1974 and proved to be a big success. To this day Croce's music receives a great deal of radio airplay. In 1990 Croce was inducted into the Songwriters Hall of Fame.

The final resting place of a great singer and songwriter who left us too soon.

Investigators of the crash that took Croce's life made the determination that it was due to pilot error. There are some who believe that the pilot, who had severe coronary artery disease, may have suffered a heart attack during the takeoff. Although Croce had recently relocated to California, he was laid to rest in Pennsylvania in the Haym Salomon Cemetery. Croce's wife Ingrid opened Croce's Restaurant and Jazz Bar in San Diego in 1985. That business is still in operation. The Croce's had one son, Adrian James Croce, (while still unborn he inspired the song "Time in a Bottle") who is an accomplished singer-songwriter. He performs under the name A. J. Croce and has released multiple CDs.

If You Go:
Should you decide to visit Croce, you are within easy driving distance of Philadelphia. Needless to say, there are numerous things to do in the city including making visits to grave sites covered in *Keystone Tombstones Volume One* as well as in this volume. The cemetery where Croce was laid

to rest is named after Haym Salomon who was a key figure during the American Revolution. Salomon was a Jewish banker who provided funds to pay for troops, as well as furnish them with food and arms. The Revolution succeeded because he and a few others like him believed in the cause and were willing to fund the effort. Salomon is buried in the Mikveh Israel Cemetery located on 8th and Spruce Streets in Philadelphia.

This is the grave of Haym Salomon a man who was key in financing the American Revolution.

"A Voice Heard Once in a Hundred Years"

MARIAN ANDERSON

County: Delaware
Town: Collingdale
Cemetry: Eden
Address: 1434 Springfield Road

She performed throughout Europe and the United States. She was a prominent figure in the struggle to overcome racial prejudice during her life time. She gave a legendary concert on Easter Sunday in 1939 on the steps of the Lincoln Memorial. For years she worked as a delegate to the United Nations Human Rights Committee. She performed at President John F. Kennedy's inauguration in 1961. She returned to the Lincoln Memorial to sing during the March on Washington in 1963. After one her performances Arturo Toscanini told her "Yours is a voice one hears once in a hundred years." Her name was Marian Anderson.

Anderson was born on February 27, 1897 in Philadelphia. Her father, John Anderson whose own father had been a slave, sold ice and coal before opening a liquor store. Her mother Annie earned money by taking care of neighborhood children. Anderson had two younger sisters Alice and Ethel. Ethel's son James Anderson DePriest became an accomplished conductor.

Anderson's family was active in the Union Baptist Church in Philadelphia. One of Anderson's aunts convinced the six year old girl to join the junior church choir. Anderson later gave her aunt credit for influencing her to pursue a career in music. When she was in her early teens, she was paid up to $5.00 to sing a few songs at various functions. She also gained the notice of the tenor Roland Hayes who provided her with guidance with her developing career.

Anderson first experienced racism when she tried to be admitted to a local music school. The young girl who handled her application shocked Anderson with the words that came out of her mouth. Anderson described the experience as being like having, a cold, horrifying hand laid on her.

Marian Anderson in 1940, by Carl Van Vechten

She said she didn't argue with the girl; instead she turned and walked out.

Anderson then pursued her music studies by receiving private lessons from Giuseppe Boghetti and Agnes Reifsynder. Her pastor along with other leaders of the black community raised money to pay for the lessons.

In 1925 Anderson won a singing competition sponsored by the New York Philharmonic. As a result, she earned the right to perform with the Philharmonic, and her appearance met with critical acclaim. Around this time, Arthur Judson, whom she met through the Philharmonic, became her manager. In the following years, she made numerous appearances in the United States, but she felt that racial prejudice was preventing her career from really moving forward. She decided to go to Europe where she launched a highly successful concert tour.

It was in 1930 that she performed for the first time in Europe. The concert took place in London, and it was a tremendous success. Because she didn't encounter the prejudice that she had in America, she spent most of the early 1930's touring Europe. In 1930 Anderson met the pianist Kosti Vehanen, and he became both her vocal coach and accompanist for a number of years. Through Vehanen, she met Jean Sibelius who heard her perform in Helsinki. The two formed a friendship, and for years Sibelius composed music for Anderson to perform.

In 1934 Anderson hired Sol Hurok to manage her career because he made her an offer that was better than the one she had with Arthur Judson. Hurok would remain her manager for the rest of her career, and he was instrumental in convincing her to return to the United States to perform. In 1935 she performed in New York at Town Hall. Once again, her concert earned numerous positive reviews. Anderson successfully toured the United States for the next four years. By the late 1930's Anderson was performing around seventy concerts a year in the states. By this time she was very famous, but that fame did not translate into acceptance everywhere in America. She was still denied service by many hotels and restaurants throughout the country. As a matter of fact, there were many times Albert Einstein acted as her host, the first time being in 1937 when she couldn't get a hotel room before a performance at Princeton University. He last hosted her in 1955 shortly before he passed away.

It was in 1939 that the Daughters of the American Revolution (DAR) refused to allow Anderson to perform before an integrated audience in their Constitution Hall. As a result of that decision many DAR members, including First

Lady Eleanor Roosevelt, resigned from the organization. President Roosevelt and others arranged for Anderson to perform in an open air concert on the steps of the Lincoln Memorial. The concert attracted a crowd of over 75,000 people, and millions of others heard it over the radio.

When World War II broke out, Anderson made it a point to entertain the troops. She did the same thing during the Korean War. In 1943 the DAR invited her to perform at Constitution Hall. She accepted the invitation and said it was no different than singing at other venues. She didn't gloat over her victory; she simply said she was happy to sing there.

On July 17, 1943, Anderson became the second wife of a man who had proposed to her when they were teenagers. His name was Orpheus Fisher, and he was an architect. After they were married, the couple purchased a 100 acre farm in Danbury, Connecticut. They had also searched for homes in New York and New Jersey and had attempted to make some purchases, but the sellers would remove their homes from the market when they found out it was a black couple that were the buyers.

In 1955 Anderson became the first African-American performer to appear with the Metropolitan Opera in New York. Afterward she was made a permanent member of the company. The following year she authored her autobiography titled *My Lord, What a Morning*. The book became a bestseller.

In 1957, she sang at the inauguration of President Dwight Eisenhower. Four years later she sang at the inauguration of President Kennedy. In 1962 she again sang for Kennedy this time at the White House. She was also very active in the civil rights movement during this period. She gave concerts to benefit the Congress of Racial Equality and the National Association for the Advancement of Colored People. In 1963 she became one of the original recipients of the Presidential Medal of Freedom. In 1965 she was chosen to christen the nuclear submarine the USS George Washington Carver. That same year she concluded her farewell tour, and her final concert took place at Carnegie Hall in April.

Back on the farm in Connecticut, she refused to be treated as a celebrity. She refused offers to move to the front of waiting lines at local restaurants. When her local

Modest grave of a woman who had a voice was heard once in a hundred years.

town lit the Christmas lights, she sang at city hall. She also performed at the local high school.

After she retired, honors continued to come her way. She received the University of Pennsylvania Glee Club Award of Merit in 1973. In 1977 she was presented with the United Nations Peace Prize. The following year she received the Kennedy Center Honors and in 1986 the National Medal of Arts award. In 1991 the Grammy's presented her with a Lifetime Achievement Award. In addition she was awarded honorary doctoral degrees from Howard University, Temple University and Smith College.

After 43 years of marriage Anderson's husband passed away in 1986. She remained in the residence until 1992 which was one year before her death. Anderson died of congestive heart failure on April 8, 1993; she was 96 years old. In 2002 the author Molefi Kete Asante listed Anderson in his book *100 Greatest African Americans*.

If You Go:

Should you decide to visit Marian Anderson you are close to Philadelphia which is an historical Mecca. We have visited many graves in this area that are included in Volumes One and Two and in our special Civil War Edition. You should also check out the If You Go section in this volume in the chapter titled *Four Founders*. It goes without saying that Philadelphia offers numerous attractions and great places to eat and drink.

"Pitchin' Paul"

PAUL ARIZIN

County: Delaware
Town: Springfield
Cemetery: Saints Peter and Paul
Address: 1600 Sproul Road

Paul Arizin, nicknamed "Pitchin' Paul," was a Hall-of-Fame basketball player recognized as one of the 50 Greatest Players in NBA History, and one of pro basketball's first jump shot specialists.

Arizin was born on April 9, 1928, in Philadelphia. He attended La Salle College High School, where he failed to make the basketball team. During his freshman year at Villanova, Arizin played CYO (Catholic Youth Organization) basketball in Philadelphia. The Villanova varsity basketball coach, Al Severance, attended one of Arizin's games and was so impressed he approached him afterwards and asked Paul if he would like to go to Villanova. Arizin answered, "I already go to Villanova."

He accepted a scholarship and played varsity basketball for the next three seasons. In his senior season (1949-50), he led Villanova to a 25-4 record and was named College Player of the Year by *The Sporting News* while leading the nation in scoring with an average of 25.3 points per game. He led the Wildcats in scoring in each of his three years with the team, averaging more than 20 points per game over 80 games. Villanova retired his #11 uniform number in 1994. But Arizin wasn't just an outstanding collegiate athlete; he also excelled in the classroom and graduated with honors.

Arizin was the Philadelphia Warriors' first pick in the 1950 NBA Draft as a territorial pick. The NBA at that time used territorial picks to help gain the support of fans in a team's home market. Before the draft, a team could forfeit its first-round pick and select any player from within a 50-mile radius of the home arena (a practice that was eliminated in 1966). Arizin was signed for a salary of $9,000.

In his first NBA season, he averaged 17.2 points and 9.8 rebounds per game, ranking among the league's top 10

Paul Arizin

According to "Philadelphia Sports," Arizin was the most underrated Philadelphia sports figure of all time.

in both categories. He would have easily been selected "Rookie of the Year" ... had that award existed at the time (it would not be created for another year, following the 1951-52 season). He led the Warriors to the playoffs in each of his first two seasons.

After his second season as a pro, the Korean War interrupted his career: he was drafted into the Marines. Arizin served in the Marine Corps from 1952 to 1954 as a bookkeeper at Marine Corps Schools in Quantico, Virginia. He

The Great NBA star Paul Arizin was laid to rest in this Delaware County cemetery.

was discharged as a sergeant in 1954, and returned to the Warriors—a team that in his absence posted abysmal records of 12-57 and 29-43.

Arizin went on to become one of the greatest NBA players of the 1950s, leading the league in scoring twice (1952; 1957). He became famous for his line-drive jump shot at a time when the game was a plodding affair featuring mostly set shots. In 10 seasons with Philadelphia, Arizin made the NBA All-Star team every year and led the Warriors to the NBA title in 1956. That championship team featured fellow La Salle College High School graduate Tom Gola (see p. 15). On December 1, 1961 in a game against the Los Angeles Lakers, Arizin scored 33 points and in the process became only the third player (joining Bob Cousy and Dolph Schayes) to reach the 15,000-point plateau.

Following the 1961-62 season, the Warriors moved to San Francisco. Pitchin' Paul had been offered a job at IBM making more money than he could earn in the NBA. He decided not to go to San Francisco and instead retired from the NBA (but would go on to play three more seasons in the Eastern Basketball League for the Camden Bullets while working for IBM).

Paul Arizin was named to the prestigious NBA 25th Anniversary Team in 1971. He was inducted into the Naismith Memorial Basketball Hall of Fame in 1978, and when the NBA celebrated its 50th anniversary in 1996 he was selected as one of the 50 Greatest Players in NBA History. He earned all of these accolades despite missing those two seasons—right in the prime of his career—due to the Korean War.

Paul Arizin died in his sleep on December 12, 2006, in Springfield (Delaware County), Pennsylvania. He was 78 years old. He is buried at Saints Peter and Paul Cemetery in Springfield.

If You Go:
See the "If You Go" section of Danny Murtaugh on page 59.

"Golf's Unknown Champion"
JOHN McDERMOTT

County: Delaware
Town: Yeadon
Cemetery: Holy Cross
Address: 626 Baily Road

He remains the youngest player to ever win the United States Open Golf Championship. As a matter of fact he won it twice and in back to back years, 1911 and 1912. He was also the first American to win it and the first to break par. His name was John McDermott.

McDermott was born on August 12, 1891 in Philadelphia. His father was a mailman, but his grandfather owned a farm that was located across the road from the Old Aronimink Golf Club. It was during a visit to his grandfather's that he first learned about the game of golf. At the time he was under 10 years old.

McDermott became a caddy, and the pro at Aronimink, Walter Reynolds, took a liking to him and taught the young boy the game. As time went on, Reynolds helped McDermott land his first job as an assistant at a golf course in Camden County, New Jersey. He later moved to the Atlantic City Country Club. It was at this club where he developed his practice routine. McDermott would begin practicing at about 5AM every morning. He would hit shots for the next three hours. At 8AM he opened the pro shop and gave members golf lessons. He would conclude his day by playing a round himself. His routine became legendary.

In 1909, at the age of 17, McDermott played in his first U. S. Open. He finished 49th. Over the next year, McDermott's game improved dramatically. The 1910 Open was held at the Philadelphia Cricket Club Course. When the tournament concluded, McDermott was tied for the lead with two Scottish brothers MacDonald and Alex Smith. In the playoff Alex prevailed, but McDermott beat his brother MacDonald by two strokes.

By 1911 McDermott had developed a confidence in his game that he was willing to express publicly. With that year's U. S. Open approaching, he told other golfers in the

Johnny McDermott with the U.S. Open trophy. Won U.S. Open in 1911 & 1912

Atlantic City locker room that the foreigners were through. He also told an assistant pro who had McDermott's clubs in tow that the assistant was carrying the clubs of the next Open champion.

The Open was held in Chicago, and once again after 72 holes McDermott found himself in a three- way playoff. This time he won the playoff by two strokes. In doing so he became the first American born Open winner and at 19 he was, and still is, the youngest to ever win the event. With McDermott's victory, the American public's interest in both the game of golf and the U. S. Open grew dramatically. It could be said that due to McDermott's victory Americans no longer viewed golf as strictly a European game. The great sportswriter Grantland Rice considered McDermott to be the greatest golfer America had ever produced.

In 1912 the Open was held at the Country Club of Buffalo. The field totaled 131 golfers which was the most ever at the time. McDermott prevailed again with a 72 hole score of 294 which included a final round where he shot 71. He had now won back to back Opens, and in doing so he also became the first player to score under par over 72 holes. Newspapers began comparing McDermott to the four time Open champion Willie Anderson (see page 188).

In 1913 two great European golfers travelled to America to compete in the Open. One was Harry Vardon who had last come to the States in 1900 where he easily took home the Open Championship. The other was Ted Ray who was the British Open champion at the time. Both were expected to be McDermott's chief competitors at the Open.

The three met prior to the Open when they played in a tournament at Shawnee-on-the-Delaware. McDermott ran away from the field beating runner up Alex Smith by 8 strokes and Vardon by 13. After the victory McDermott's confidence got him into trouble when he proclaimed, "We hope our foreign visitors had a good time, but we don't think they did, and we are sure they won't win the National Open." Later McDermott apologized for the remark, but the press in both America and England continued to report it in their stories leading up to the Open. These stories increased public interest in the upcoming event.

The 1913 Open was played at the Country Club In Brookline, Massachusetts. Despite McDermott's claim Vardon was generally considered to be the favorite. After two rounds Vardon had a share of the lead with Ray two strokes behind. McDermott shot a 79 in the second round and found himself six strokes off the pace. At the end of 72 holes there was a three way tie at the top, but McDermott was not among the three as he finished in eighth place. Instead Vardon and Ray found themselves tied with a young American amateur by the name of Francis Quimet.

Heading into the playoff most considered it to be a match between Vardon and Ray. McDermott actually did play a role in the match in that he took Quimet aside and offered some advice. He told Quimet, "just play your own game, pay no attention to Vardon and Ray." In a stunning upset Quimet shot a 72 and beat Vardon by five strokes and Ray by six.

At this point McDermott ran into some bad luck. He had invested his winnings into stocks, and those investments had gone badly virtually erasing the money he had won as a professional golfer. In 1914 he sailed to England to participate in the British Open. However he missed both a ferry and a train and arrived at the course too late to

John McDermott

qualify. Then as he was returning to America the ship he was on collided with another boat. McDermott was put into a life boat where he remained for twenty hours before being rescued. It was an experience that he was never able to put behind him.

First McDermott faced the public criticism after his comments about foreign players hit the press. This was followed by the failed effort to win his third open and his stock losses. This was followed by the shipwreck and combined they took a terrible toll on the young man. He entered the 1914 United States Open, but he displayed none of the confidence that had marked his personality. He finished in eighth place ten strokes behind the winner Walter Hagen.

In October of 1914, McDermott blacked out and collapsed at the Atlantic City Country club. His parents were notified, and he was returned home. That December McDermott resigned his position at the Country Club. His father convinced him to enter a hospital, and he spent the rest of his life in institutions. At the age of 23 his professional golfing career was over.

There were times his family took him off the hospital grounds and he would play a round of golf. In addition a six hole course was built on the grounds of the Norristown Hospital, and he played there as well. Walter Hagen visited McDermott in 1928 and played a round with him on the grounds.

McDermott's sister on occasion would take him to tournaments. At one event an assistant pro kicked McDermott out of the pro shop based on what the assistant considered strange behavior. The assistant couldn't believe it when one of the players in the tournament told him that he had just kicked out a two time winner of the U. S. Open.

McDermott was a spectator at the 1971 Open which was held in Ardmore, Pennsylvania. A golfer by the name of Arnold Palmer recognized McDermott and asked him how his game was. McDermott replied that he was hitting the ball well but was having trouble with his putting. Palmer put his arm around McDermott and said, "the only thing we can do is keep practicing."

That would prove to be McDermott's last Open. On August 1, 1971 the old golfer died in his sleep. He was close

This tombstone marks the grave of the first native born American to win the United States Golf Open Championship.

to eighty years old. He was buried at Holy Cross Cemetery in Yeadon, Pennsylvania. Some golf historians believe that, if not for his illness, he had the potential to be the greatest golfer of all time. McDermott's sister said that the only time she ever saw her brother cry was when he was informed that he had been inducted into the Golf Hall of Fame.

McDermott is portrayed in the movie "The Greatest Game Ever Played." The movie tells the story of Francis Quimet's upset victory in the 1913 Open. In one scene the actor playing McDermott issues a boastful challenge to other golfers in the clubhouse. The scene is based on the statements made by McDermott after the tournament at Shawnee.

If You Go:
Holy Cross Cemetery is large and well maintained with many interesting graves including America's first serial killer Dr. Henry Holmes and five members of the Philadelphia mafia (See *Volume Two,* Chapters 14 and 18 for those stories).

Also buried at Holy Cross is Louis Van Zeist who was the bat boy and mascot for the Philadelphia Athletics from 1910 to 1914. Due to a childhood accident his growth was stunted, and he had a hunchback. He loved sports, and one day he went to Shibe Park and asked Connie Mack (see page 273) if he could be a bat boy. Mack took an instant liking to Van Zeist and gave him the job. In the early part of the 1900s hunchbacks were considered to be good luck, and players would rub the hump before going to bat. Van Zeist became a favorite of both the A's players and their fans, so in 1910 Mack hired him for all the home games and had a uniform made for him. It appears that he did bring the team some luck as the A's won their first world championship in 1910 and then re-peated that feat in 1911 and 1913.

Louis Van Zeist

In 1914 they won the American league title. In the winter of 1915 Van Zeist was diagnosed with Bright's disease, and he passed away in March. The Athletics didn't win another pennant until 1929.

There are four Congressional Medal of Honor recipients buried at Holy Cross. William Shipman, George Crawford Platt and William Densmore received their medals for bravery during the Civil War. Philip Gaughan received his for his conduct in the Spanish American War.

Frank Hardart of the famous Horn and Hardart restaurants was laid to rest in Holy Cross. The first restaurant opened in Philadelphia in 1902. Hot entrees, cold sandwiches, bowls of soup and slices of pie awaited behind the glass doors which opened when the right number of nickels were inserted. Hardart died in 1918.

The cemetery is also the final resting place for two Hall of Fame boxers. Thomas Loughran was a Light Heavyweight Champion who is considered to be one of the most skilled fighters of all time died in 1982. The other fighter is Joseph Hagen who was the Light Heavyweight Champ from 1905 to 1912. Hagen passed away in 1942.

"America's Answer to the Ripper"
HERMAN WEBSTER MUDGETT
aka Dr. Henry H. Holmes

County: Delaware
Town: Yeadon
Cemetery: Holy Cross
Address: 626 Baily Road

One can reasonably argue that the most famous serial killer in history is Jack the Ripper. There have been numerous books written and films made about the Ripper. The actual Ripper was never found, and to this day there are numerous theories as to who he was and the suspects include members of the Royal Family. The Ripper murders began in the Whitechapel district of London in 1888, and some believe they continued until 1891. However most who have studied the case believe the Ripper was responsible for only five of the ten murders in that time frame and that his last victim was killed November 9, 1888. In contrast, America's answer to the Ripper may have tortured and killed as many as 200 people, mostly young women. He was born Herman Webster Mudgett on May 16, 1861, in New Hampshire. However, during his killing spree, he went by the name Doctor Henry H. Holmes, and that is how we shall refer to him in this chapter.

Holmes was known as a bright boy with strange tendencies. His father was a violent alcoholic, and his mother a Methodist who would read the bible to the young boy. Holmes was bullied at school, and he went through several traumatic experiences as a child. He and one of his few close friends explored a deserted house one day, and Holmes watched his friend fall to his death from a landing in the home. In addition bullies dragged him into a doctor's office and forced him into the arms of a medical skeleton. The bullies' goal was to scare him. Instead he became obsessed with death.

As he hit his teens, his fascination with death manifested itself in the killing and dissection of animals. Holmes claimed his purpose in these mutilations was medical examination. Academically he continued to do well, and in

Herman Webster Mudgett

1884 he graduated with a medical degree from the University of Michigan in Ann Arbor. While at the university, he began an unusual business pursuit that would provide funds for him throughout his life. He began taking life insurance policies out on corpses in the medical school. He would steal the corpses and mutilate them in a manner to show they had died in an accident. Then he would make his claim to the insurance company.

The infamous Murder Castle: Holmes Motel at 63rd & Wallace on Chicago's south side.

Holmes married his first wife in 1878. She bore him a son named Robert Lovering Mudgett who would go on to serve as city manager in Orlando, Florida. Holmes would marry two more times during his life without ever getting divorced. In addition he used his charm to prey on countless young women who fell for him and later died at his hands.

In 1886 Holmes moved to Chicago where he found work as a drugstore assistant. E. S. Holton, the owner of the store, was dying of cancer and his wife spent most of her time caring for her ailing husband. Holmes saw his opportunity, and he took it. When Holton died, Holmes persuaded Mrs. Horton to sell him the store. When the deal was complete, he murdered her and told those who asked about her that she had moved to California. In 1888 Holmes travelled to London where he sold skeletons to medical schools. He returned to the states in December of that same year, a time frame that becomes important later in his story.

Now that he owned a drug store that was making a good profit, Holmes began putting his plan into place. He purchased a vacant lot across the street from his store where he intended to build his "Castle." It was a three story hotel that Holmes personally designed. The ground floor featured Holmes's drugstore. The second and third floors made up the hotel and featured secret passages, concealed chambers, staircases that led to brick walls and sound-proofed rooms with peepholes in the doors. In addition several of the rooms had been fitted with gas pipes that would allow Holmes to inject lethal gases into the area at the moment of his choosing. The basement was an addition to this house of horrors. It contained a dissection chamber and pits of lime and acid as well as cremation furnaces. Holmes constructed the "Castle" by using multiple contractors. Once part of the building was complete he would either fire or refuse payment to a contractor and hire another. As a result no one could piece together what Holmes planned to do in what would become known later as "the killing house."

The building was completed in time to take advantage of the many visitors to the 1893 Chicago's World Fair. The fair itself was a tremendous success and attracted visitors from all over the country. The fair marked the appearance of the first Ferris wheel which was a gigantic machine compared to what we have today. For example, each of the 36 cars on the wheel could hold as many as sixty people. The cars were 24 feet long and 13 feet wide and weighed 26,000 pounds. The fair itself, whose buildings reflected the big dreams of the era, was known as the "White City" and even received praise from that great critic of the "Gilded Age" Mark Twain. The owner of the new hotel, which he called the World's Fair Hotel, was eager to offer housing, and in many cases more, to those who chose to visit the fair.

Holmes didn't wait for the fair to open to begin more killings. In 1890 a man named Ned Connor went to work for Holmes as a watchmaker and jeweler. He and his very attractive wife named Julia and their daughter Pearl moved into an apartment above the drugstore. Holmes gave Julia a job as a bookkeeper and then seduced her. Ned Connor found out about the affair and left his wife and daughter. By this time in 1891 Holmes was living in the "Castle." He took out life insurance policies on Julia and Pearl that

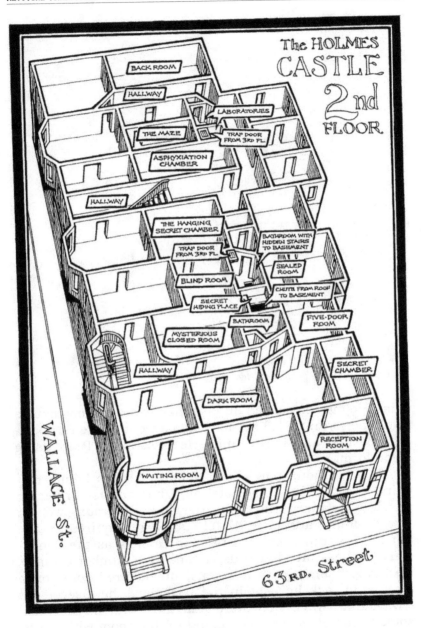

named him as the beneficiary. Around this time, Holmes began a relationship with a woman named Minnie Williams. Julia became angered by this turn of events especially in light of the fact that she was carrying Holmes's

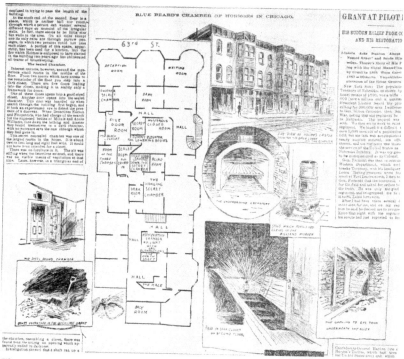

The Chicago Tribune of Sunday, August 18, 1895.

child. Holmes convinced Julia to have an abortion that he would perform. He led her to the basement where he aborted the child and killed Julia. He then killed Pearl using chloroform.

With his hotel now open, Holmes put his killing machine to work. Not only hotel staff but guests turned up missing. Holmes particularly enjoyed killing young women that he found attractive. Hotel staff were required to take out life insurance policies naming Holmes as the beneficiary. Holmes murdered his victims in a number of ways. He gassed some in their rooms, he tortured some on a stretching rack he kept in the basement, he dissected a few victims while they were still alive and he also had some fireproof rooms so he could fill the room with gases, ignite the vapors and burn the victim to death. The bodies were disposed of in his vats of acid or crematoriums. With some of his victims, he would remove the flesh and sell the skeletons to medical institutions. It is impossible to tell how many people he killed, but estimates range from 50 to 200.

When the World's Fair ended, the depression of 1893 was in full swing. With business way down at the hotel and his creditors on his back, Holmes left Chicago. He headed for Texas where he had inherited property from two sisters one of which he promised to marry. He never married her, but he did kill both sisters. He had hoped to build another Castle here, but he found that law enforcement officers were more aggressive in Texas than in Chicago so he headed back east.

In 1894, he and an associate named Benjamin Pitezel made a deal. Pitezel would take out a $10,000 life insurance policy, Holmes would find and disfigure a dead body claim that it was Pitezel and the two would split the money. Instead Holmes murdered Pitezel in Philadelphia by burning him alive to support the story of a laboratory accident. He then collected the money himself.

Pitezel had three of his five children with him at the time and Holmes took the three, a boy and two girls, through the northern United States into Canada. On the way in Indianapolis he killed the boy, cut up the body and burned it. In Toronto he put the girls into a trunk and gassed them to death. He then buried their bodies in the cellar of the house where he was staying.

Holmes had been jailed for a brief time for his involvement in a horseracing scam prior to his trip to Canada. While in jail, he told a cellmate about the plan he and Pitezel put together and he offered the cellmate $500 if he could find a lawyer that would assist Holmes with any legal questions should they arise. The cellmate found the attorney, but Holmes never paid him the $500 and as a result the cellmate told the police about the Pitezel scam. Holmes was arrested in Boston on November 17, 1894.

Following his arrest, the Chicago police searched the "Castle." In the basement they found the remains of some of Holmes's victims. They also found evidence that murders had been committed in other rooms in the hotel. Meanwhile a detective by the name of Frank Geyer was investigating the Pitezel case. He would eventually find the remains of the three children Holmes had killed during his trip to Canada. The public was satisfied that Holmes was a monster.

Holmes was put on trial in Philadelphia for the murder of Pitezel. He was convicted and sentenced to death. After his conviction he confessed to 30 murders. The Hearst newspapers paid him $7,500 (over $200,000 in today's dollars) for his confession. Holmes went to the gallows on May 7, 1896. The assistant superintendent, a man named Richardson appeared, more nervous than Holmes as he prepared the noose. Holmes turned to him and said, "Take your time, old man." Holmes neck did not snap, and as a result he died slowly. He was pronounced dead twenty minutes after the trap had been sprung.

Holmes was buried based on instructions he left behind. First cement was poured into the coffin and then Holmes's body was put in which was then covered with more cement. His body was then taken to Holy Cross Cemetery just outside of Philadelphia. The grave was dug and the coffin placed inside. Workers then filled the grave with cement. The grave was left unmarked. Holmes wanted to make sure that neither medical researchers nor relatives of his victims could get to his body.

During his stay in prison, Holmes claimed that he was possessed by the devil. Events that occurred after his execution caused some to believe it. Detective Geyer became seriously ill. The warden at the Philadelphia prison where Holmes was held and executed committed suicide. An accidental electrocution took the life of the foreman of the jury that convicted Holmes. The priest who delivered the last rites to Holmes was found dead on church grounds. Finally a fire destroyed the office of the Chicago district attorney leaving only a picture of Holmes untouched.

Recently Jeff Mudgett, Holmes's great-great grandson, has written a book about his ancestor titled *Bloodstains*. The book provides evidence that Holmes may have been Jack the Ripper. Mudgett notes that there exist records documenting Holmes travelling to London in 1888 to sell skeletons to medical schools. He was not in Chicago when the five murders credited to the Ripper took place. When Holmes returned to Chicago in December of 1888, the Ripper murders stopped. Many believe that the Ripper possessed surgical skills which Holmes certainly had. Finally

Here is the final resting place of America's first serial killer.

Mudgett had scientists at the University of Buffalo analyze letters written by Jack the Ripper and those written by Holmes while he was in prison. They reached the conclusion that the classifier performance number (97.95%) indicate that the writings of both men are similar in style. Was America's answer to the Ripper actually the Ripper himself?

When we visited Holy Cross Cemetery to photograph Holmes final resting place we had the section, range and lot number of the location of the grave. To be sure that our information was accurate we went to the cemetery office to verify it. The cemetery employee we spoke to told us, "We are not allowed to talk about that grave."

If you go:
See the "If You Go" section of "Philadelphia's Sinners" on page 68.

Danny Murtaugh with the Phillies in 1941.

"The Whistling Irishman"
DANNY MURTAUGH

County: Delaware
Town: Springfield
Cemetery: Saints Peter and Paul
Address: 1600 Sproul Road

Daniel Edward (Danny) Murtaugh was one of the most beloved and successful figures in the history of the Pittsburgh Pirates. He was associated with the Pirates as a player and manager for 29 years. He once attributed his success to "brilliant managerial thinking and dumb Irish luck." The authors don't know much about the former but are well acquainted with the latter.

Murtaugh was born on October 8, 1917, in Chester, Pennsylvania and attended Chester High School. He played Major League baseball as a second baseman for nine seasons (1941-43, 1946-51) with the Pirates, Philadelphia Phillies and Boston Braves. The three seasons he missed, he was serving in the Army as a paratrooper in Europe during World War II.

As a rookie, he led the National League in stolen bases with 18. His best season was his first with the Pirates in 1948, when he hit .290 and posted career highs in RBI (71), runs (56), doubles (21), triples (5) and games played (146). He also led all second basemen in putouts and fielding percentage.

After retiring as a player following the 1951 season, Murtaugh asked Pirates general manager and future Hall of Famer Branch Rickey for a job managing in the minor leagues. He managed the New Orleans Pelicans and the Charleston Senators before returning to the Pirates as a coach in 1956. In middle of the 1957 season, the Pirates fired manager Bobby Bragan and named Murtaugh as his successor. He would go on to manage the Pirates for parts of 15 seasons over four different terms (1957-64, 1967, 1970-71 and 1973-76).

In 1957, the Pirates finished seventh, 33 games out of first place. Just one year later, in his first full year as manager, the Pirates finished in second place with an 84-70 record. In 1960, Murtaugh's Pirates brought a World Series crown to Pittsburgh for the first time since 1925, in one of the most memorable World Series in history. The Pirates beat the mighty New York Yankees in seven games, dramatically capped off by the only Game 7 walk-off home run in World Series history. It was hit by Bill Mazeroski at Forbes Field. *The Sporting News* awarded Danny the Manager-of-the-Year award for guiding the

Danny Murtaugh as manager of the Pirates in 1973.

Pirates to a 95-win season and a world championship.

Murtaugh managed the Pirates for the next four seasons, but had to retire in 1964 after suffering a heart attack. He agreed to stay on as a part-time scout. Murtaugh was pressed to manage again in 1967 when Pirates Manager Harry Walker was fired mid-season, but then returned to the front office at the end of the season.

Murtaugh was well aware of the abundance of talent in the Pirates system when he again accepted the job as manager in 1970. That year, he led the team to a Division Championship but lost to the Reds in the National League Championship series. Murtaugh garnered his second *Sporting News* Manager-of-the-Year award, 10 years after winning his first. A year later, the Pirates were crowned World Series champs after defeating the Baltimore Orioles —led by Hall-of-Fame manager Earl Weaver—in seven games.

After winning it all in 1971, Murtaugh retired yet again and became the Director of Player Acquisition and Development for the Pirates. When Pirates manager Bill Virdon was fired in September 1973, Murtaugh was persuaded to return to managing, and amazingly won division titles in 1974 and 1975, losing to the Dodgers and Reds, respectively, in the NL Championship Series. He retired for the final time after the 1976 season, finishing his managerial

The great Pittsburgh Pirates manager Danny Murtaugh is buried beneath this modest tombstone.

career with five postseason appearances, four National League East titles and two World Series championships.

"Managing a ball club is like getting malaria," he once said. "Once you're bitten by the bug, it's difficult to get it out of your bloodstream."

Danny Murtaugh died in his hometown of a stroke at the age of 59, two months after retiring. He is buried in a modest grave in Saints Peter and Paul Cemetery in Springfield, PA.

One year later in 1977, he became just the fourth person in Pirates history to have his number (#40) retired. In 2010, his granddaughter, Colleen Hroncich, published a book called *The Whistling Irishman: Danny Murtaugh Remembered.*

If You Go:

Also buried in Saints Peter and Paul Cemetery are Hall-of-Fame professional basketball player Paul Arizin (see page 37) and a number of other noteworthy sports figures, including the voice of NFL Films for two decades, John Facenda.

After a long day of searching through cemeteries, we were happy to find Bogart's Bar and Grill at 773 W. Sproul Road in Springfield. They had great food, great spirits and great, cheerful service. The delicious food and drink revived our bodies, and the nice owner and waitress revived our spirits.

"Philadelphia's Sinners"

MICHAEL MAGGIO
ANTONIO POLLINA
ANGELO BRUNO
PHILIP TESTA
SALVATORE TESTA

County: Delaware
Town: Yeadon
Cemetery: Holy Cross
Address: Bailey Road and Leadon Avenue

"Well they blew up the chicken man in Philly last night/now they blew up his house too." These are the lyrics that open the classic Bruce Springsteen song *Atlantic City*. The song was released in 1982, a year after the violent death of Philip "Chicken Man" Testa. Testa was killed in his home by a bomb. He and at least four other reputed Philadelphia Mafia figures are buried in Holy Cross Cemetery in Yeadon.

Michael Maggio was reputedly an old time Mafia Don from the 1920's until 1959. In 1934, Maggio, who was known as the "Cheese King" because of his successful cheese business, was arrested for the murder of his second wife (Anna, 32) and son (Joseph, 21) from a prior marriage. As the story goes, Maggio suspected them of having an affair and after catching them in bed he shot and killed them both. He pleaded guilty, and was sentenced to five years, but served less than two.

Maggio is credited with sponsoring a future mob boss, Angelo Bruno, for membership in the organization. At that time, the active boss of the Philadelphia mafia family was Salvatore Sabella. Bruno was a salesman for Maggio's cheese company and put in a good word to Sabella regarding Bruno's hard work ethic. Shortly thereafter, Bruno was running several small operations for Sabella. Michael Maggio died of natural causes at the age of 69 in 1959. He is buried in a large beautiful Mausoleum with a large stained glass window.

Ruins of the Testa house.

Antonio Pollina accomplished what most people would never expect of the head of a crime family. He lived to be 100 years old. Known as "Mr. Migs," Pollina was named "don" by Guiseppe "Joe Ida" Idda shortly before Idda fled to Italy to avoided being indicted by federal authorities. Despite being named the boss, Pollina considered Angelo Bruno a rival and ordered his underboss to kill him. The underboss, Ignazio Denaro, informed Bruno and Bruno told "the Commission," a national Mafia board formed to resolve disputes among organized crime families and members. The Commission decided to remove Pollina and make Bruno the new boss of Philadelphia and advised him he could have Pollina killed for plotting against him. Bruno decided to let Pollina live, figuring the repercussion would be bad for the family. Pollina remained inactive in the mob for the rest of his life. He was a suspect in a number of murders over the years but was never convicted. He died in 1993 at the age of 100.

Angelo Bruno was born Angelo Annaloro in Sicily and emigrated to the United States in his early teens, settling in Philadelphia. After being named the new boss of the Philadelphia family in 1959, he assumed the surname of his paternal grandmother and became Angelo Bruno.

Over the next twenty years, Bruno successfully avoided the intense media and law enforcement scrutiny and outbursts that plagued other crime families. He was known for instituting order and increasing the power of the Philadelphia mob family and connections to larger more established families in New York and New Jersey. He was given the nickname "The Gentle Don" as he preferred to settle disputes in a professional, non-violent manner. He also avoided lengthy prison terms despite several arrests. His longest term was two years for refusing to testify to a grand jury. Under Bruno, the Philadelphia crime family enjoyed the most peaceful and prosperous reign. Bruno did not allow his family to deal in narcotics, preferring more traditional operations like labor racketeering, ille-

This man was known as the Cheese King he killed his wife and son (by a previous marriage) for sleeping with each other.

Known as Mister Migs this crime family head lived to the ripe old age of 100.

gal gambling, extortion, bookmaking, and loansharking. His philosophy was "make money don't make headlines." His position on narcotics, however, eroded some of his support since many factions below him felt they should have a piece of the action. Then in 1976, Atlantic City, New Jersey opened for gambling, and soon it became so lucrative that he agreed to let the New York and New Jersey families share in the profits. Bruno knew better than to try to challenge the New York families who were a lot stronger than his. This decision did not go over well with many of his underlings and further eroded his support. Several factions within the Pennsylvania family began conspiring to betray the aging Bruno.

On March 21, 1980, the sixty-nine year-old Bruno was killed by a shotgun blast in the back of the head as he sat in his car in front of his South Philadelphia home. It is believed that the killing was ordered by Antonio Caponigro (AKA Tony Bananas), Bruno's consigliere. A few weeks later, Caponigro's body was found stuffed in a body bag in the trunk of a car in New York City with about $300 jammed into his mouth and anus. The Commission reportedly ordered his murder because he assassinated Bruno without full permission. Other Philadelphia family members involved in Bruno's murder were tortured and killed.

Angelo Bruno (right)

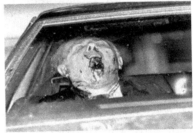

Crime scene photo of Angelo Bruno.

Philip "The Chicken Man" Testa took over as mob boss in Philadelphia after the death of Angelo Bruno. He was born in Sicily and emigrated to the U.S. and settled in South Philadelphia in

Known as the Gentle Don Bruno was killed by a shotgun blast to the back of the head. It appears that he had friends who were not so gentle.

his teenage years. He was a dour-looking man with a pockmarked face. He stood about five feet eight inches and weighed 183 pounds. He reportedly had dark emotionless eyes and a pockmarked face, which is thought to be one of the reasons for his nickname. The pockmarks are believed to have been caused by a horrible case of chicken pox with the scars never fully healing. He had a thick mustache and preferred blue-collar clothing to the fancy clothing worn by most mafia dons. He became a father to his only son, Salvatore, in 1956 and they were very close. He was a staunch Roman Catholic and raised his son in the same fashion. He reportedly did not drink heavily and remained loyal to his wife. Testa conducted his business, legitimate and otherwise, out of a restaurant in Old City Philadelphia, which he owned, and his daughter Maria managed.

In February 1981, Testa was indicted by Federal authorizes for racketeering. The case was based on an investigation called Operation Gangplank and was one of the first built on the RICO Act by the U.S. Attorney's office in Philadelphia. On March 15, 1981, less than a year after the murder of Angelo Bruno, Philip Testa was

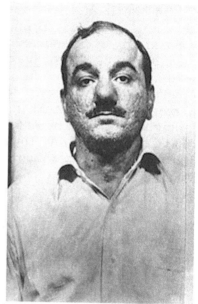

Philip "Chicken Man" Testa

killed by a bomb exploding in his home across the street from Stephen Girard Park. There were roofing nails in the bomb that apparently were to make it look like retaliation by allies of John McCullough, the roofing union leader who was killed mob style in December 1980. Testa's killing touched off a string of intra-family wars that lasted until 1995.

Salvatore "Salvie" Testa became a rising star in the mob after his father's murder. A 1974 graduate of Saint John Neumann High School, Salvie was a ruggedly handsome man who was six feet tall and 210 pounds. His parents had chosen Nicky Scarfo and his wife Domencia as his godparents. After the murder of his father, Salvie became a protegé of Nick Scarfo and was thought of as a son to Scarfo. Scarfo made him a captain (caporegime) a few months after his father's death. Newspaper accounts say that Scarfo used Salvie for over fifteen hits. He had "inherited" most of his father's business and an estate worth $800,000 that included a rundown bar in Atlantic City on a site where casino developer Donald Trump decided to build the Trump Plaza in 1984. Trump paid the young Testa $1.1 million for the right to tear it down.

Two of the hits were the men responsible for killing his father. On January 7, 1982, Chickie Narducci, the man who reportedly orchestrated the killing of Philip Testa, was shot ten times in the face, neck, and chest outside his home in south Philadelphia. On March 15, 1982, exactly one year after the bombing, Rocco Marinucci, the man

Salvatore Testa with a couple escorts.

who reportedly detonated the bomb, was found dead in a parking lot on Federal Street in Philadelphia. He had bullet wounds to the neck, chest, and head and his mouth was stuffed with three large, unexploded cherry bombs.

In April 1984, Salvie Testa was described as the "fastest rising star" in the Philadelphia mob in a front-page article of the Wall ST Journal. This made Nicky Scarfo jealous and worried that Testa was becoming too powerful, especially with his own group of young turks. According to newspaper accounts, on September 14, 1984, Scarfo ordered Testa's best friend, Joey Pungitore, to lure Testa into an ambush in the back room of the "Too Sweet" candy store on East Passyunk Avenue in Philadelphia. Scarfo had requested that his godson be strangled to death, but his

Here lies "Chicken Man" Testa and his son Salvie. Notice the grave goods left on the tomb.

killers considered this too risky given Salvie's size and strength. His hog-tied body was found at the side of a dirt road in Glouster Township, New Jersey. He was wrapped in a carpet with a rope around his neck. He had been shot twice in the back of the head. He was 28 years old.

In May of 1988, Scarfo and eight associates were acquitted on all charges in the murder of Testa. A book about the Philadelphia mob was published in 2003. It's titled *Blood and Honor: Inside the Scarfo Mob – The Mafia's Most Violet Family* by George Anastasia.

If You Go:

Holy Cross Cemetery is a large and well maintained cemetery with many interesting graves (see page 49 for the story of Dr. Henry Holmes). One such grave is that of Louis Van Zelst who was the Bat Boy and mascot for the Philadelphia Athletics from 1910 to 1914. Due to a childhood accident, his growth was stunted, and he had a hunchback. He loved sports and wandered over to Shibe Park one day in 1909 and asked Connie Mack if he could be a Bat Boy. Mack took an instant liking to Van Zelst and agreed. In the early part of the century, hunchbacks were considered to be good luck, and players would rub the hump for luck. He became a favorite of the A's players and fans, and the next year, 1910, Mack hired him for all home games and had a uniform made for him. As luck would have it, the A's won their first world championship that year, repeated in 1911 and 1913, and won the American League Pennant in 1914. He was taken on at least one road trip per year beginning in 1911 and to spring training in 1912. He had a sunny disposition and was an accomplished mimic who did a hysterical imitation of Eddie Plank in the batter's box. In the five years he was with the A's,

Here lies the Philadelphia Athletics first mascot, players used to rub his hunchback for good luck.

they won four pennants and three World Series. In the winter of 1915, he was diagnosed with Bright's disease and died in March. Connie Mack and the team were crestfallen, and the A's next pennant didn't come until 1929.

There are four Congressional Medal of Honor recipients buried at Holy Cross. William Shipman, George Crawford Platt, and William Densmore all received their Medals of Honor for bravery in the Civil War. Philip Gaughan received his Medal of Honor for his courageous action in the Spanish-American War.

Frank Hardart of the famous Horn and Hardart restaurants is also buried in Holy Cross. In 1902, they opened the first American automat in Philadelphia. Hot entrees, cold sandwiches, bowls of soup, and slices of pie awaited behind the small glass doors, which opened when the right number of nickels were inserted. He died in 1918.

Also there are two Hall of Fame Boxers and the youngest US Open Golf Champion of all time. The boxers are light Heavyweight Champion Thomas Loughran who is regarded as one of the most skilled fighters of all time and died in 1982 and Joseph (Philadelphia Jack) Hagen who was also the World Light Heavyweight Champion from 1905-1912. Hagen died in 1942. The golfer John McDermott was the first US born golfer to win the US Open and the youngest ever at 19 years 10 months in 1911.

"The Empress of the Blues"
BESSIE SMITH

County: Delaware
Town: Sharon Hill
Cemetery: Mount Lawn
Address: 84th Street and Hook Road

Bob Dylan and the Band recorded an album in 1967 titled "The Basement Tapes." The record wouldn't be released until 1975. One of the tracks is a song composed by Band members Robbie Robertson and Rick Danko on which Dylan provides the lead vocal. When he gets to the chorus he sings:

"I'm just going down the road to see Bessie
Oh, see her soon
Going down the road to see Bessie Smith
When I get there I wonder what she'll do."

The song is called Bessie Smith, and it pays homage to a woman that many consider to be the greatest blues singer of all time. Smith is buried in Sharon Hill, Pennsylvania not far from Philadelphia.

According to the 1900 census, Bessie Smith was born in Chattanooga, Tennessee in July 1892. When the 1910 census was recorded, her birth date changed to April 15, 1894. The latter date is the one she observed throughout her life. By the time Smith was nine, both of her parents had died and as a result, she was raised by an older sister. She was raised in poverty and in an attempt to bring some money into the household, Smith and one of her brothers formed a duo and began performing on the streets of Chattanooga. She would sing and dance to the music her brother supplied on his guitar.

In 1912 she auditioned for a job in a travelling show known as the Stokes troupe. She was hired as a dancer because the show already had a woman singer named Ma Rainey. Many believe that Ma Rainey helped Smith as she grew to become a stage performer. By 1913 she had developed her own act, and by 1920 she was well known throughout the south.

Bessie Smith

In 1920 a singer by the name of Mamie Smith (no relation) recorded and released a song titled "Crazy Blues." It
turned out to be a hit and prompted the recording industry
to search for other female blues singers. In 1923, Smith
signed a recording contract with Columbia records. By that
time, she had made Philadelphia her home and met and
married Jack Gee a security guard. By all accounts, the
marriage was rocky from the start with both partners having

affairs. Gee couldn't come to terms with Smith's bisexuality, and when she learned that he was having an affair with another singer she ended the relationship in 1929. Smith would eventually enter into a common-law marriage with Richard Morgan who happened to be Lionel Hampton's uncle. Their relationship would endure until the day she died.

While her personal life wasn't going well, Smith's professional career could hardly have been improved upon. Her first record called "Downhearted Blues" was a major hit. She became the highest paid black performer in the 1920's as she headed her own show that featured as many as forty other entertainers. While touring, she lived and travelled in her own private railroad car. Columbia records called her the "Queen of the Blues," but newspapers gave her the upgraded title "Empress."

Smith was known for her powerful voice that was excellent for recording. She recorded more than 150 songs for Columbia backed by some of the greatest musicians at the time including Joe Smith, Fletcher Henderson and a young fella by the name of Louis Armstrong. Her career was cut short by the Great Depression and the advent of talking movies. The first event almost ended the entire recording industry, and "talkies" pretty much ended vaudeville shows.

In 1929, Smith appeared in the film "St. Louis Blues." She sings the title song in the movie accompanied by Fletcher Henderson's band, a choir and a string section. The combination produced a sound very different from anything found on her recordings.

In the early thirties Smith continued to tour and perform. In 1933, John Hammond had her record for Okeh records. She was paid $37.50 for each recording. Music had entered the "swing era" and she was backed by notable swing era musicians including pianist Buck Washington, tenor saxophonist Chu Berry and guitarist Bobby Johnson. This recording session, which took place on November 24th, would be her last. Billie Holiday, who cited Smith as a major influence, would make her first record three days later with these same musicians.

On September 26, 1937, Smith was travelling in a car, driven by Richard Morgan, on Route 61 between Memphis, Tennessee, and Clarksdale, Mississippi. Morgan failed to properly judge the speed of a truck that was ahead of him.

He attempted to avoid hitting the truck by passing it on the left but was not successful as he hit the rear of the truck with the passenger side of his vehicle. Smith, sitting in the passenger seat, was badly hurt; Morgan had no injuries.

A Memphis surgeon by the name of Dr. Hugh Smith and his fishing partner, Henry Broughton, came upon the accident scene and stopped to offer assistance. Dr. Smith examined the injured singer and concluded that she had lost about a half pint of blood and that her right arm was almost completely severed at the elbow. Broughton and Dr. Smith moved Smith to the side of the road where he dressed the arm injury while Broughton went to a nearby home to summon an ambulance.

By the time Broughton returned to the scene, Smith was in shock. As time passed, with no ambulance arriving, Dr. Smith decided to take Smith to a hospital in his car. He had just finished clearing out his back seat when he heard a car approaching at a high rate of speed. The fast moving car hit the Doctor's vehicle sending it into Smith's car completely demolishing it. The oncoming car went into a ditch on the right side of the road barely missing Broughton and Bessie Smith.

The ambulance finally arrived, and Smith was taken to Clarksdale's G.T. Thomas Afro-American Hospital. Her right arm was amputated, but she remained in a coma. She died later that morning having never regained consciousness. After her death John Hammond circulated a rumor that she had died after being refused entrance to a whites only hospital. This was not the case for as Dr. Smith noted no ambulance driver in the south at that time "would even have thought of putting a colored person off in a hospital for white folks."

Smith's body was placed in the O.V. Catto Elks Lodge to handle the crowd who came to wish her farewell. It is estimated that 10,000 people filed past her coffin. She was laid to rest in Mount Lawn Cemetery on October 4, 1937. Though money was raised for a tombstone to mark her grave, her estranged husband Jack Gee pocketed the money, and Smith's grave remained unmarked until August 7, 1970. On that day a tombstone partially paid for by Janis Joplin was erected. Joplin also recorded a song called

"Stone for Bessie Smith" on her album "Mythical Kings and Iguanas."

Three of Bessie Smith's recordings have been inducted into the Grammy Hall of Fame. The songs "Downhearted Blues," "St. Louis Blues" and "Empty Bed Blues" were recognized for their historical significance. "Downhearted Blues" is also in the Rock and Roll Hall of Fame having been selected as one of the 500 songs that shaped that genre of music. Smith herself was inducted into the Rock and Roll Hall of Fame in 1989. She is also a member of the Blues Hall of Fame and the Big Band and Jazz Hall of Fame.

A number of great female vocalists have acknowledged that Smith influenced them. These include Billie Holiday, Sarah Vaughn, Aretha Franklin and Janis Joplin who said of Smith, "She showed me the air and taught me how to fill it."

Of course her influence has not been confined to female singers. As noted in the beginning of this chapter, Bob Dylan and the Band have also paid tribute to the great blues singer in the song "Bessie Smith." As Dylan sings in the songs last verse;

"When she sees me will she know what I've been through?
Will old times start to feeling like new?
When I get there will our love still feel so true?
Yet all I have, I'll be bringing it to you
Oh Bessie, sing them old time blues."

This tombstone partially paid for by Janis Joplin marks Bessie Smith's final resting place.

If You Go:

Mount Lawn Cemetery is the final resting place of another entertainer, Lawrence Brown Sr. who was a vocalist with Harold Melvin and the Blue Notes. In the 1970's this popular group had hits with a number of songs including, "The Love I Lost," "If You Don't Know Me By Now" and "Wake Up Everybody." Brown performed until a few months prior to his death in 2008.

Hank "The Bankman" Gathers is also buried in this cemetery. Gathers was a college basketball star who became the second player in the history of the game to lead the nation in both scoring and rebounding. He died during a game on March 4, 1990. The cause of his death was heart failure.

Another basketball player, Guy Rodgers, was also laid to rest at Mount Lawn. Rodgers had a 12 year career as a guard in the National Basketball Association. During that time he played for San Francisco Warriors, the Chicago Bulls, the Cincinnati Royals and the Milwaukee Bucks. Rodgers passed away in 2001.

Not far from Mount Lawn is the town of Essington, Pennsylvania. We stopped for refreshments at Coaches Bar and Grill located at 350 Jansen Avenue. The food was excellent and reasonably priced. There is a large outdoor patio and numerous televisions for your viewing pleasure. The wait staff was friendly, courteous and efficient. If you are in the area, we recommend a visit.

"Mad Anthony"

ANTHONY WAYNE

County: Delaware
Town: Wayne
Cemetery: Old St. David's Church
Address: 763 South Valley Forge Road

Anthony Wayne was a United States Army general in the American Revolutionary War and a statesman who is buried in two places. Had he not died suddenly at the age of 51, he might have given John Adams or Thomas Jefferson a real challenge for the Presidency in 1796 and 1800.

Wayne was born on New Years Day 1745 in Chester County, Pennsylvania, and attended a private school in Philadelphia operated by his uncle. He eventually became an excellent surveyor and in 1765 was sent to Nova Scotia as a financial agent and surveyor in the service of a real estate company on the recommendation of Benjamin Franklin. He returned to the United States in 1767, married, and continued in his profession as well as serving in several local offices. In 1774, his father Isaac died and Anthony inherited his father's prosperous tannery business. Also that year, he was chosen as one of the provincial representatives to consider the relations between the colonies and Great Britain, and was a member of the Pennsylvania convention that was held in Philadelphia to discuss this matter.

Wayne served in the Pennsylvania legislature in 1775. He was fond of military affairs. He began studying works on the art of war, and at the onset of the Revolutionary War raised a militia. In 1776, Wayne became colonel of the 4th Pennsylvania regiment. He and his regiment were part of the Continental Army's failed invasion of Canada. He attacked the British at the Battle of Three Rivers and although wounded and defeated, withdrew his troops creditably and then was ordered to assume command at Fort Ticonderoga.

In February 1777, Wayne was commissioned a brigadier general. Prior to the war, Wayne had no military experience and other more experienced officers resented

Anthony Wayne

his quick advancement. He became known for his bravado and ill-advised attacks. He earned the nickname "Mad" Anthony Wayne because of his impulsive actions on the battlefield. Wayne was known for his fiery temper and would rather attack the enemy than avoid them.

Later in 1777, he assisted George Washington in the failed defense of the nation's capitol, Philadelphia. He commanded troops at Brandywine, Germantown and Paoli. The

General Anthony Wayne, after portrait by Charles Willson Peale. The General's
portrait was painted c. 1783 with him in full Revolutionary War uniform.

British surprise attack at Paoli on September 20, 1777,
was a dark moment for Wayne. He lost a lot of men, and
some of his officers thought he handled it poorly. Wayne's
temper took hold, and he demanded first an official inquiry
and then a full court martial. The court martial unanimously exonerated Wayne and acquitted him "with the
highest honor." Washington heartily approved.

Washington relied heavily on Wayne throughout the war.
Before making strategic decisions, it was Washington's habit

to have his top generals write out their suggestions. He could always count on Wayne to propose aggressive and well thought-out plans.

During the winter of 1777-78, Wayne did much to supply the American camp at Valley Forge. In March, he made a successful raid into British lines, capturing hor-ses, cattle and other needed supplies. In June of 1778, he led the American attack at the Battle of Monmouth. It was the first time Americans held their own in toe-to-toe battle with the British troops.

The highlight of Wayne's Revolutionary War service was his victory at Stony Point, New York on July 16, 1779. Washington had asked Wayne to form and command an elite "American Light Corps" (the equivalent of to-day's Special Forces). Wayne led his troops in a carefully planned, nighttime, surprise attack against a heavily fortified stronghold on top of a steep Hudson River palisade. The assault was successful and Wayne's troops captured the fort and its occupants. Before dawn, Wayne sent Washington a message that read: "The fort and garrison with Colonel Johnston are ours. Our officers and men behaved like men who are determined to be free."

The assault at Stony Point was widely recognized as one of the most brilliant maneuvers of the war. Congress unanimously passed resolutions praising Wayne and awarded him a gold medal commemorative. The Continental Army had experienced few successes. This victory, led personally by General Wayne, substantially improved the soldiers' morale.

In 1780, Wayne helped put down a mutiny of 1,300 Pennsylvania men who had not received payment from the government. He did so by serving as the men's advocate before the Confederation Congress, where he arranged an agreement to the advantage of the government and the satisfaction of the men.

In the summer of 1781 just before the Battle of Yorktown, Wayne saved a Continental Army force led by the Marquis de Lafayette from a trap set by the commander of the British Army, Lieutenant General Lord Cornwallis, near Williamsburg, Virginia. Wayne's small contingent of 800 Pennsylvanians was the vanguard of the continental forces. They were crossing over a swamp by a narrow causeway when they were ambushed by over 4,000 British. Instead of retreating, Wayne charged. The unexpected maneuver so surprised the enemy that they fell back confused allowing the rest of Lafayette's command to avoid the trap.

After the British surrender at Yorktown on October 19, 1781, Wayne went further south and severed the British alliance with Native American tribes in Georgia. He negotiated peace treaties with both the Creek and Cherokee, for which Georgia rewarded him with the gift of a large rice plantation. In October 1783 he was promoted to major general and retired from the Continental Army.

Wayne returned to Pennsylvania and resumed his civilian life. In 1784, he was elected to the general assembly from Chester County and served in the convention that ratified the Constitution of the United States. He then moved to Georgia and was elected to the Second United States Congress in 1791. He lost that seat during a debate over his residency qualifications and declined to run for reelection.

President Washington showed his high regard for Wayne once again in 1792 when he recalled him from civilian life and appointed Wayne as the commanding general of the newly-formed "Legion of the United States." At the end of the Revolutionary War, Great Britain agreed that the Mississippi River would be the Western boundary of the United States and that the Great Lakes would be the northern border. Presumably this meant British troops would withdraw from these areas into Canada. In fact, they did not. They encouraged and supplied a Western Indian Confederacy led by Blue Jacket of the Shawnees and Little Turtle of the Miamis. The Indians had achieved major victories over U.S. forces in 1790 under command of General Josiah Harmar and in 1791 under command of General Arthur St. Clair. More than 700 Americans died in the fighting.

Wayne recruited troops from the Pittsburgh area and established a basic training facility at Legionville to prepare the men of the "Legion of the United States" for battle. Located in Beaver County, Legionville was the first facility ever established to provide basic training for U.S. Army recruits.

In August 1794, Wayne mounted an assault on the Indian confederacy at the Battle of Fallen Timbers near Toledo,

The blockhouse where Wayne died and he was originally buried.

Ohio. It was a decisive victory for the U.S. forces and ended for all time the power of the British on American soil.

Wayne then negotiated the Treaty of Greenville between the Indian tribes and the United States. The treaty was signed in August 1795 and gave most of what is now Ohio to the United States. He returned home to a hero's welcome in the Philadelphia area.

In June 1796, Wayne was back in the frontier overseeing the surrender of British forts to the U.S. In a visit to Fort Presque Isle in Erie, Pennsylvania, he suffered a serious gout attack. There were no physicians at the fort and calls went out to Pittsburgh and the Army hospitals. Unfortunately, help arrived too late, and Anthony Wayne died on December 15, 1796.

A year earlier at Fort Presque Isle, to assist in defending against attacks from Native Americans, 200 Federal troops from Wayne's army under the direction of Captain John Grubb built a blockhouse on a bluff there known as Garrison Hill. Wayne had requested that upon his death he be buried there. When he died, his body was placed in a plain oak coffin, his initials and date of death were driven

The original grave site of "Mad" Anthony Wayne.

into the wood using round-headed brass tacks, and his request was honored: he was buried at the foot of the blockhouse's flagstaff on Garrison Hill.

Twelve years later, Wayne's son, Isaac, rode to Erie in a small, two-wheeled carriage called a "sulky." He came (at the urging of his sister Peggy) to bring his father's remains back to be buried in the family plot at St. David's Church about 400 miles away outside of Philadelphia. Young Wayne enlisted the help of Dr. J.G. Wallace, who had been with Mad Anthony at the Battle of Fallen Timbers and at his side when he died.

When Wallace opened Wayne's coffin, he found little decay except in the lower portion of one leg. This caused a dilemma, as Isaac did not have enough space to transport the entire body. He expected to put bones in boxes on his sulky. Dr. Wallace used a custom common to American Indians to solve the dilemma. He dismembered the body and boiled it in a large iron kettle until the flesh dropped off. He cleaned the bones and packed them into Isaac's boxes. The task was so distasteful that Dr. Wallace threw the remaining tissue and his instruments into the coffin and closed the grave. Isaac Wayne made the long journey across Pennsylvania with his father's bones in the back of his sulky. The bones were interred at Old St. David's Church Cemetery with funeral rites celebrated on July 4, 1809. A huge crowd attended.

Memorial marks one of the gravesites that hold the remains of a hero of the American Revolution Mad Anthony Wayne.

General Anthony Wayne is well-memorialized. He has a long list of cities, towns and municipalities named after him, including 15 states that have a Wayne County. In Pennsylvania, there is a Wayne County as well as a Waynesboro and a Waynesburg. He has schools, bridges, a university (Wayne State University in Detroit), a brewing company (Mad Anthony Brewing Co. in Fort Wayne, Indiana), an ale (Mad Anthony Ale, a product of Erie Brewing Co.), a hotel (General Wayne Inn in Merion, PA), parks, hospitals and even a barber shop named in his honor. There is a large statue in Fort Wayne, Indiana, as well as a gilded bronze equestrian statue at the Philadelphia Museum of Art and one at Valley Forge. In 1929, the U.S. Post Office issued a stamp honoring Wayne and commemorating the 150th anniversary of the Battle of Fallen Timbers.

If You Go:

Anthony Wayne's strange interment has given rise to a popular ghost story. It was a long, tough trip from Erie to Wayne over 380 miles of unpaved roads of what is now Route 322. The story goes that Isaac had many prob-lems along the way and that the trunk kept falling off and breaking open, losing bones along the way. Some claim that on each New Year's Day (Wayne's birthday), his ghost rises from his grave in Wayne and rides across the state searching for his missing bones. The kettle used to boil Wayne's body and the dis-section instruments used by Dr. Wallace are on display at the Erie County History Center on State Street in Erie.

Very nearby is Erie Cemetery, which contains the graves of a number of interesting people, including famous Civil War General Strong Vincent, who was a hero at the Battle of Gettysburg where he died; Harry Burleigh, the internationally known African-American baritone and composer who composed such spirituals as "Swing Low Sweet Chariot" and "Nobody Knows the Trouble I've Seen;" Andrew Forbeck, a Congressional Medal of Honor recipient from the Philippine Insurrection; and Samuel Jethroe, who was the oldest man to win baseball's Rookie of the Year award in 1950 at the age of 32.

About 15 miles outside of Erie is the small town of Girard, which is home to the Battles Bank Gallery. Battles was a bank until the late 1980's but its owner, Charlotte Elizabeth Battles, brought much attention to Girard when she defied President Roosevelt's order to close in 1933. She sent a note to FDR saying "Mr. President, we're minding our business, you do the same. Since I do not presume to tell you how to run the country, please do not presume to tell me how to run my bank." Ms. Battles, who died in 1952, is buried in Girard Cemetery.

The Girard Borough Building contains a statue of a dog that is an interesting grave story. For over 100 years the statue of a dog named "Shep" had stood vigilantly over the grave of his master, H.C. Davis, who died in 1881. Shep died of poisoning in 1884 and was buried in the same plot. Mrs. Davis commissioned the statue in 1889 using a photograph to sculpt a life-sized figure of Shep sitting in a captain's chair. The statue was placed to mark the family plot

This is the caldron of death where Wayne's son boiled the body down to the bare bones.

in 1890. On September 30, 1993, the statue of Shep suddenly disappeared, the victim of an apparent theft. The town was stunned and angered. A reward fund was organized and flyers bearing a picture of the statue were distributed nationwide. Despite these efforts, local police went years without a lead in the case.

   In 1997, Girard police received a phone call from an antique dealer in New Haven, Connecticut. The dealer had recently purchased a statue matching the description on the flyer. The police invest-igated and found the statue had traveled through antique dealers in Pennsylvania, Ohio, New York, Maine and Connecticut. The police never solved the case as the first buyer of the statue had passed away in 1995. The dealer graciously agreed to return the statue to

Girard and many in town were delighted. Once back in his hometown, Shep was donated by the descendants of the dog's owner to the Borough of Girard. Today, Shep remains on display in the lobby of the Girard Borough Municipal Building.

There are also interesting people buried at Old St. David's Church Cemetery (sometimes referred to today as St. David's Episcopal Church or simply "Old Saint David's") in the town of Wayne. Two of note are William Wallace Atterbury and Richard Norris Williams.

Known as the "Railroad General" in World War I, Atterbury was operating vice-president of the Pennsylvania Railroad at the outbreak of the war and reorganized the European railroad network to create rapid movement of allied troops and equipment that contributed greatly to victory. He was awarded medals by the United States, France, England, Serbia and Romania. He appeared on the cover of Time Magazine in February 1933.

R. Norris Williams (as he was generally known) was a champion tennis player, a Titanic survivor, and the great-great-grandson of Benjamin Franklin. He won two U.S. Open singles championships in 1914 and 1916. He also was on the victorious American Davis Cup teams in 1925 and 1926, and at the 1924 Olympics in Paris he won a gold medal in mixed doubles. All of this came after surviving the Titanic disaster, where his father with whom he was traveling died. His story is amazing and the subject of another chapter in this book. Williams was inducted into the International Tennis Hall of Fame in 1957.

"The Horse"

ALAN AMECHE

County: Montgomery
Town: West Conshohocken
Cemetery: Calvary Cemetery
Address: Gulph Road and Matsonford Road

He was a Heisman Trophy winner. He played in the National Football League for six years. In 1955 he was the league's rookie of the year. Four times he was selected to play in the Pro Bowl. He scored the winning touchdown in the 1958 NFL Championship game which has been called "The Greatest Game Ever Played." His name was Alan Ameche.

Ameche was born on June 1, 1933. He was raised in Kenosha, Wisconsin where he attended Kenosha's Bradford High School. It was here he began his football career. In 1950 his team went undefeated scoring more touchdowns than their opposition scored points. Ameche scored 108 points that year and was an all-state fullback. His athletic achievements were not limited to the gridiron. He set city records in track (running the 100 and relays) and in throwing the shot put. In Wisconsin the fact that Ameche was very strong was well known. In 1949, he decided to box in the Golden Gloves competition. When news of his entry spread his opponents withdrew and he was declared champion by default.

After graduation Ameche decided to attend the University of Wisconsin. His first game was a JV game versus Iowa on September 28, 1951. While he didn't start the game he made a definite impression on the coaches by scoring two touchdowns. The next day the freshman running back suited up with the varsity squad to face Marquette. In week 4, he carried the pigskin for 148 yards against Purdue. He would start almost every Wisconsin game for the next 4 years.

Somewhere along the line, Ameche acquired a nickname, he was dubbed "The Horse." There are conflicting stories relative to how he earned the name. Wisconsin assistant coach George Lanphear claimed he came up with

Alan Ameche

the name because Ameche worked like a horse in practice.
Others claimed it came from his strength and others still
that it was because of his distinctive high-stepping gait.
The name fit because Ameche, who was known to be a very
polite young man, was a major force on the football field. In
the 1951 season Ameche became the first freshman to lead
the Big 10 in rushing as he gained 774 yards on 147 carries. When one includes non-conference games, he rushed
for 824 yards: a Wisconsin record.

Wisconsin was expected to be a power in 1952. They did not disappoint finishing tied with Purdue for the conference title. Ameche again led the Big 10 in rushing and for the first of three consecutive years he was named to the First-Team All Big Ten squad. The '52 Wisconsin team was picked to play USC in the Rose Bowl. It was the first post-season appearance for the Badgers. The game turned into a defensive battle, and USC scored in the final minutes to secure a 7-0 win. Despite losing, Ameche carried the ball 28 times for 133 yards. Ameche had quite a year off the field as well since he got married to his high school sweetheart. As a matter of fact, he would have two children while he was still at Wisconsin.

In 1953 the double platoon system was abolished in college football. Now in addition to running the football Ameche would line up as a linebacker on defense. He would play both positions for the next two years successfully. By the end of his senior year he was the all-time rushing leader with 3,212 yards. In addition he had scored 25 touchdowns and rushed for more than 100 yards on numerous occasions. He received numerous awards, he was a consensus All-American and an Academic All-American. He was the initial winner of the Walter Camp Memorial Trophy and last but certainly not least the 1954 Heisman Trophy winner. Fans in his hometown threw his family a party after his graduation. There were multiple gifts that included a horse and 3,212 one dollar bills one for each yard he had gained at Wisconsin.

In the 1955 NFL draft Ameche was selected in the first round by the Baltimore Colts. For some reason, the Colts coach Weeb Ewbank took an immediate dislike to Ameche. The great Gino Marchetti remembers vividly the first time he saw Ameche. He was coming from a team meeting walking with coach Ewbank and Ameche was in front of them. Ewbank turned to Marchetti and said, "There is our big draft pick. He was babied in college. He was spoiled at Wisconsin. They didn't baby you in college, did they Gino?"

Ewbank and Ameche never got along, and it baffled the rest of the Colts. Ameche's teammates saw a hard worker who put up great numbers in actual games. Marchetti remarked, "Alan worked hard, he played hard, he was a good blocker. He did everything that was asked of him, but

Weeb would never give the guy a break." There are those that believe Ameche's habit of barely making it on time for meetings, practices and pre-game meals is what bothered Ewbank.

Ameche made an immediate impression the first time he touched the ball in an NFL game; he ran 79 yards for a touchdown against the Chicago Bears. He ran for a total of 194 yards that day on 16 carries. In his first season, he led the NFL in rushing and was named Rookie of the Year. He was the only rookie picked to play in the Pro Bowl. It would mark the first of four consecutive Pro Bowl appearances for Ameche. For the rest of his injury shortened career, Ameche played on winning Colt teams that were led by the great Johnny Unitas.

On December 28, 1958, the Colts faced the New York Giants in the NFL Championship game which was held at Yankee Stadium. To many it remains the greatest NFL game ever played. The game was watched by 45 million people on television, a number unheard of at the time for a football game. The two teams had met during the regular season with the Giants winning by a score of 24-21, but Johnny Unitas was hurt and didn't play in that game.

The game opened with Baltimore fielding the kickoff. On the first series Sam Huff forced a fumble while sacking Unitas and the Giants recovered at the Colts' 37 yard line. One play later Gino Marchetti returned the favor by forcing a fumble that the Colts recovered. Baltimore squandered the opportunity when a Unitas pass was picked off. The Giants drew first blood when Pat Summerall kicked a 36 yard field goal.

In the second quarter the Colts responded when Ameche scored on a two yard run. New York was forced to punt on their next drive but caught a big break when the Colt punt returner fumbled and the Giants recovered on the Colts' 10 yard line. However a couple of plays later Giant back Frank Gifford fumbled and the Colts recovered the football at their own 14. Unitas led the Colts on a 15 play drive that culminated with a 15 yard touchdown pass to Raymond Berry. The score gave Baltimore a 14-3 halftime lead.

Things were going well for the Colts in the third quarter as they drove to the New York one yard line. The momentum turned when the Giants stopped Ameche twice and took over the ball on downs. On the subsequent series Giant quarterback Charlie Conerly connected with Kyle Rote on an 86 yard pass play. Rote had been tackled from behind at the Colt 25 yard line where he fumbled but New York's Alex Webster picked up the ball and carried it to the one yard line. The Giants scored to make it 14-10. The Giants took the lead in the 4th quarter on a 15 yard pass to Gifford.

With a little over two minutes left in the game Baltimore got the ball on their own 14 yard line. Unitas then directed one of the most famous drives in history running a superb two minute drill before anyone knew what that was. With 7 seconds left in the game he had moved the Colts to the Giants 13 yard line where a 20 yard field goal knotted the score at 17 resulting in the first sudden death overtime in NFL history.

The Giants won the toss and took the ball but went three and out. Baltimore got the ball back on their own 20. They would go 80 yards in 13 plays. On third and 8 from their own 33 Unitas connected with Ameche for the necessary yardage. A few plays later Ameche carried the ball 22 yards to the Giant 20 yard line. Unitas then connected with Berry for a twelve yard gain. On first down Ameche gained one yard, but this was followed by a six yard Unitas completion. On third down the Colts went to Ameche again and he scored the game's winning touchdown. The Colts had prevailed 23-17 and Ameche had scored twice. 30,000 fans were waiting for the Colts when they returned to the Baltimore airport. It was a sign that professional football had arrived in America.

Ameche's career was cut short due to an injury to his Achilles' tendon. He played six seasons and made it to the pro bowl four times. In those six years he played on two championship teams, rushed for 4,045 yards, had 191 receptions for 733 yards and he scored 40 touchdowns. After Ameche retired Raymond Berry said the Colts never had an effective running game and were forced to rely far too much on Unitas. Without a running threat the Colt's opponents took their pass rush to another level.

Ameche was very successful in retirement. In 1957, he and three other teammates, including Gino Marchetti, opened Gino's Restaurant in Baltimore. The hamburger

This tombstone marks the final resting place of Heisman Trophy winner and NFL great Alan (the Horse) Ameche.

joint became a chain that, at its peak, had over 300 locations. When the partners sold it to the Marriott
Corporation, Ameche became a multimillionaire.

Ameche continued to be recognized after his retirement.
In 1975, he was inducted into the College Football Hall of
Fame. Previously he had been named to Wisconsin's All-
Time team and was declared the All-Time greatest player.
He didn't forget his alma mater as he presented his Heis-
man trophy to the University of Wisconsin as a gift. The
trophy is on display in the lobby of Camp Randall Stadium.
In 1991, Ameche was one of 35 charter members inducted
into the University of Wisconsin Athletic Hall of Fame. On
September 9, 2000, Wisconsin retired his number 35 and
his name was added to the stadium's facade.

On August 8, 1988, Ameche died after suffering a heart
attack. Years after his death, his wife remarried another
Heisman trophy winner, Glen Davis, who won the award in
1946. One of Ameche's children Cathy Ameche married
Michael Cappelletti brother of the 1973 Heisman winner
John Cappelletti.

If You Go:

Calvary Cemetery is a Mecca for sports fans. In addition to
Ameche it is the final resting place for former NFL commissioner Bert Bell (see page 108).

You can also find Francis James Bagnell at Calvary. He was an All-American football player at the University of Pennsylvania. He won the Maxwell Trophy and finished second in the voting for the Heisman. He is a member of the College Football Hall of Fame.

Henry Charles (Shag) Crawford was buried at Calvary in 2007. Crawford was a catcher in the minor leagues and when his playing career was over he became an umpire. He would umpire over 3,000 games between 1956 and 1975. Well respected in the game, he worked three World Series and two national League Championship Series.

Finally the much respected NFL referee Stanley Javie can also be found at Calvary. Javie worked for the NFL from 1951 to 1980 and he was selected to referee four Super Bowls. Calvary is a good sized cemetery so we suggest a visit to the office to get directions to the graves.

If you visit Calvary you are not far from the final resting place of baseball great Richie Ashburn (see page 94). In addition you are close to Philadelphia where you can find loads of fine establishments that offer refreshments.

"His Whiteness"
DON RICHARD "RICHIE" ASHBURN

County: Montgomery
Town: Gladwyne
Cemetery: Gladwyne United Methodist Church
Address: 316 Righters Mill Road

The 1950's has long been considered part of the "Golden Age of Baseball." There is little doubt that the glamour position during that decade was centerfield. Three centerfielders, all of whom played for teams who made their home in New York City, dominated the attention of baseball fans around the country. Mickey Mantle, Willie Mays and Duke Snider were all prolific sluggers and of course baseball fans love the long ball. Songs have been written about the trio, and to this day their fans still argue over who was better. While all this was going on, another centerfielder was plying his trade in a city just down the road. By the end of the 50's, no major leaguer had banged out more base hits during that decade than this Philadelphia Phillie. His name was Richie Ashburn.

The future Hall of Famer was born on a farm in Tilden, Nebraska on March 19, 1927. His father operated the largest general store in the area. Among his childhood friends was a young man by the name of Johnny Carson who would go on to make quite a name for himself as an entertainer. Ashburn was drawn to the national pastime and played for the American Legion as well as Tilden High School. In 1944 he was selected to represent Nebraska in the prestigious Esquire all-star game held in New York City. It was there his talents began to draw the attention of major league scouts.

The Philadelphia Phillies signed Ashburn in 1945. He made that team's major league roster in 1948 when he was 21. In his rookie year he showcased the abilities that would mark his career hitting .333 with an on base percentage of .410 and stealing 32 bases in 117 games. There were many who felt that Ashburn deserved rookie of the year honors, but the award went to Alvin Dark.

Richard Ashburn

The 1950 Phillies team was nicknamed the "Whiz Kids" based on the fact that the average age of the team was 26.4 years. This young team played consistent baseball throughout the season, and by September 20th they found themselves in first place with a 7 1/2 game lead over Boston and a 9 game lead over Brooklyn. It was at this point in the season that injuries began to take their toll, and the losses mounted. On the last day of the season the Phils held a 1 game lead over the team they would play to finish the year, the Brooklyn Dodgers.

The Phillies started their pitching ace, Robin Roberts, in the season finale, and the Dodgers sent Don Newcombe to the mound. Both men pitched extremely well, and after 8 innings the score was tied at 1-1. In the last of the 9th Roberts walked Cal Abrams, and he moved to second on a single by Pee Wee Reese. Duke Snider hit a hard single to center that was fielded by Ashburn. Abrams attempted to score, but a perfect throw from Ashburn nailed him at the plate. Roberts then retired the side, and the game went into extra innings. The Phillies opened the top of the 10th with consecutive singles, putting men on first and second with Ashburn coming to the plate. He laid down a sacrifice bunt that advanced the runners to second and third. Dick Sisler followed with a three run homer that provided the margin of victory as the Phillies won their first pennant since 1915.

The "Whiz Kids" faced the heavily favored New York Yankees in the World Series. Three of the four games were decided by 1 run, but the Phillies lost all three contests. The Yankees completed the sweep by winning game 4 by a score of 5-2. Philadelphia only managed three earned runs in the series, one of which was driven in by Ashburn. While many thought this would be the first of many post game appearances for the Phillies, it would be the first and last World Series for Ashburn. The Phillie centerfielder was quite candid in his opinion as to why this young team failed to repeat: "We were the last to get any black players. We were still pretty good, but they were just getting better." In light of Ashburn's opinion, it is worth remembering that the 1950 World Series was the last in baseball history to match two all-white teams.

While post season honors may have eluded Ashburn he continued to perform during the regular season. He had a fifteen year major league career that included twelve years playing for the Phillies. He was among the most consistent leadoff hitters in major league history and was a terrific centerfielder. Ashburn won the National League batting title twice first in 1955 and again in 1958. In three other years his batting average was good enough for a second place finish. He consistently hit for average, batting over . 300 nine times and retiring with a lifetime average of .308. Ashburn was also a great fielder as demonstrated by the fact that he routinely led the league in fielding percentage. In addition he had a good eye at the plate leading the league in walks four times, and he was an excellent base runner.

Ashburn was named to the National League All Star Team five times (1948, 1951, 1953, 1958 and 1962). He finished his career with more than 2,500 hits. He had a reputation for being a spray hitter meaning he could hit the ball to all parts of the diamond. This ability made it extremely difficult for opposing teams to effectively defend him when he had the bat in his hands.

Ashburn was nicknamed "Putt-Putt" by Ted Williams because he ran the bases so fast that you would think he had twin motors in his pants. Later he became known as "Whitey" due to his light blond hair. After he retired Harry Kalas (see page 264), his broadcasting partner, referred to Ashburn as "His Whiteness."

One of the great Richie Ashburn stories took place during a game played in 1957. Ashburn was at the plate when he fouled off a pitch into the stands. The ball hit Alice Roth, the wife of the Philadelphia Bulletin sports editor, square in the face. The impact not only stunned Mrs. Roth, it broke her nose. Play on the field was halted while medical personnel rushed to Mrs. Roth to provide assistance. After a quick examination, it was decided that she should be removed from the stadium using a stretcher. As Mrs. Roth was being carried out, play resumed, and Ashburn fouled off another pitch that struck the poor woman yet again. After the incident, Ashburn and Roth became friends and remained so for many years.

After the 1959 season, the Phillies traded Ashburn to the Chicago Cubs. He remained a Cub for two years before being selected by the New York Mets in the expansion draft of 1962. The original Mets who were described by their manager Casey Stengel as "amazing" may have been the worst team in the history of the major leagues. They finished the season with a record of 40-120, a dubious mark that no other team has been able to equal. While Ashburn had a good season and was named Most Valuable Met after hitting .305, the mountain of losses was too much for him to take. He retired at the end of the season and later re-marked, "I just didn't think I could go through another year like that."

Upon his retirement Ashburn soon became a radio and television commentator for the Phillies. He also wrote sports columns for the Philadelphia Bulletin and later for the Daily News. Eventually he was paired up with Harry Kalas to form the Phillies broadcasting team. The two became best friends as well as Philadelphia sports icons. Ashburn and Kalas called Phillies games for 27 years. Ashburn was known for his sense of humor as a broadcaster. He once told a story about a habit he had of keeping a bat that he was hitting well with in bed with him so he was sure to have it for the next game. He ended the story by saying, "I slept with a lot of old bats in my day." He also liked to talk about how he felt about pitchers. "After fifteen years of facing them, you don't really get over them. They're devious. They're the only players in the game allowed to cheat. They throw illegal pitches and they sneak foreign substances on the ball. They can inflict pain whenever they wish and, they're the only ones on the diamond who have high ground."

Years after he retired, Ashburn openly complained about being snubbed by the Baseball Writers Association in their voting to elect new members to the Baseball Hall of Fame. The three famous New York centerfielders, Willie, Mickey and the Duke, were all quickly enshrined in the hall. Ashburn was thought to be left out because he was a singles hitter unlike the sluggers from New York. That didn't stop Ashburn supporters from placing bumper stick-ers on their cars that read "Richie Ashburn: Why the Hall Not?" The efforts of Ashburn and his fans paid off as he was finally elected to the Hall of fame in 1995.

On September 9, 1997, Ashburn finished broadcasting a Phillies – Mets game in New York City. He died of a heart attack later that night in his hotel room. There was a pub-lic viewing held in Fairmont Park that drew thousands of his admirers. The baseball fields in the park are named for him as is the centerfield entertainment area at Citizen's Bank Park; that area is known as Ashburn's Alley. His uni-form number (1) was retired by the Phillies in 1979.

This tombstone marks the final resting place of baseball great Richie Ashburn who claimed that he slept with a lot of old bats during his baseball career.

Richie Ashburn is buried in a modest grave in the Gladwyne Methodist Church Cemetery in Montgomery County. In 2005 a book titled *Richie Ashburn Remembered* was published. The book's foreword was penned by Harry Kalas.

If You Go:
Richie Ashburn's grave is in the Philadelphia area. Therefore there are many other sites you may wish to visit that we cover in this volume. After visiting Ashburn, you might want to take in the beautiful grave site of his partner Harry Kalas.

We were both hungry and thirsty after our visit to Ashburn's grave, so we stopped at the Stella Blue and the Star Bar in West Conshohocken. It proved to be a good choice. The bartender was friendly, and the food and drinks hit the spot. The bar has a sleek contemporary décor and an interesting and varied menu and drinks list. It looks like it would be a great spot in the evening, but we were there in the afternoon and had more to do. Hopefully we can make it back there for happy hour on one of our trips.

"What Did He Know, and When Did He Know It?"

LAFAYETTE C. BAKER

County: Montgomery
Town: Huntingdon Valley
Cemetery: Forest Hills Memorial Park
Address: 101 Byberry Road

Lafayette Curry Baker was a Union investigator and spy, serving under Presidents Abraham Lincoln and Andrew Johnson. Baker was born in Stafford, Genesee County, New York on October 13, 1826. Though he later claimed to be a descendant of one of Ethan Allen's Green Mountain Boys, who had named him after the Marquise de Lafayette of American Revolution fame, no such lineage actually existed.

In 1839, his father, a poor farmer, moved the family to Michigan, where Baker spent the rest of his childhood. By 1848, Baker was a mechanic in Philadelphia and then New York. In 1853, he moved to Gold Rush-era California, pursuing the same occupation. By 1856, he had made a name for himself with the Vigilance Committee in San Francisco. During this period he was involved in several lynchings, acting as a bouncer at a local saloon, and informant to the local constabulary.

At the outbreak of the Civil War, Baker convinced General Winfield Scott he could spy on the Confederate military in Virginia. Scott agreed to the proposal and Baker's life as a spy began. His initial plan was to pose as a photographer, under the alias Samuel Munson, who would photograph the leaders of the Confederate Army. However, on July 11, 1861, Baker was arrested by the Union Army at Alexandria, Virginia, as a Confederate spy. He was in danger of being executed until General Scott intervened on his behalf.

Baker eventually reached the Confederacy, but he was quickly arrested by a Confederate patrol. According to Baker, he was interviewed by President Jefferson Davis, Vice President Alexander Stephens and General Pierre T. Beauregard, the latter granting his release after he provided details about Union positions. Baker then began carrying a

Lafayette Curry Baker

photograph of Beauregard with him, which he used to help him enter Confederate Army military camps. In Fredericksburg, Baker was once again arrested as a Union Army spy. Convinced that he was about to be executed, Baker managed to use a small knife that he had hidden in his shoe to free two loose bars in his cell, slipped through the opening, and made his escape. He then returned to Washington.

At least, that was the story Baker later wrote.

The truth was much less spectacular. Baker was, indeed, captured and taken before Jefferson Davis. However, Davis did not give him a pass as a photographer. He did at least take a few minutes to listen to Baker's inept lies and then . . . promptly declared him a spy and ordered that he be held for trial. Baker did manage to escape from the Richmond jail, after which he wandered for weeks through Virginia, living in shacks and in the woods, and steal-ing food where he could find

General Winfield Scott

it as he desperately tried to get to the Union lines. He was picked up in Fredericksburg as a vagrant and later held as a spy, but he again escaped, this time with the help of a lo-cal prostitute with whom he had been staying. Finally, he managed to return to General Scott's headquarters. The tales of Baker photographing Confederate officers was non-sense. He had lost his camera before being picked up by the first Confederate patrol. The information regarding Confederate forces he later relayed to Scott had been ob-tained by Baker from a Union officer he had met in the Richmond prison. All of the information was outdated by the time Baker passed it on to Scott.

Baker took advantage of Scott's old age and lack of knowledge about espionage. Scott was so impressed he not only granted a commission to the conniving Baker, but he retold Baker's saga to several members of Lincoln's cabi-net. Secretary of War Edwin M. Stanton was most interest-ed in the tale and quickly recruited Baker to be the replacement for Allan Pinkerton, head of the Union Intelli-gence Service. Baker was given the job as head of the Na-tional Detective Police (NDP), an undercover, anti-subversive, spy organization.

Baker had some minor successes that did not amount to much. He was suspected of corruption. Apparently, he would intimidate people who were themselves making profits from illegal business activities. He would arrest and jail those who refused to share their illegal gains with him. Baker was eventually caught tapping telegraph lines between Nashville and the office of Edwin M. Stanton. For this, he was demoted and sent to New York, where he was assigned to Assistant Secretary of War, Charles Dana.

Secretary of War Edwin Stanton

Upon Abraham Lincoln's assassination on April 14, 1865, Baker was summoned by Stanton to Washington by telegraph: "Come here immediately and see if you can find the murderer of the President." Baker arrived on April 16 and sent out his agents to pick up what information they could about the people involved in the assassination. Within two days Baker had arrested Mary Surratt, Lewis Powell (a/k/a, "Paine"), George Atzerodt and Edman Spangler. He also had the names of the fellow conspirators: John Wilkes Booth and David Herold.

After the assassination, Stanton had taken over the government, declaring martial law. He issued a $100,000 reward for the capture of John Wilkes Booth, dead or alive. Much later, Baker admitted, before Lincoln had been shot, neither he nor Stanton had any knowledge regarding any supposed conspiracy. Yet within two days, Baker was able to round up all of the conspirators? Somehow, Baker knew exactly where to find George Atzerodt (who failed to kill Vice President Andrew Johnson), Lewis Powell/Paine (who was targeting Seward), and Edward Spangler, the carpenter at Ford's Theater who had made a portable barrier for Booth so that he could successfully bar the inside of the door to Lincoln's box. Baker also knew that Spangler had drilled a hole in the door leading to Lincoln's box for Booth to spy on the President. Lastly, Baker somehow quickly deduced the exact escape route taken by John Wilkes Booth and David Herold.

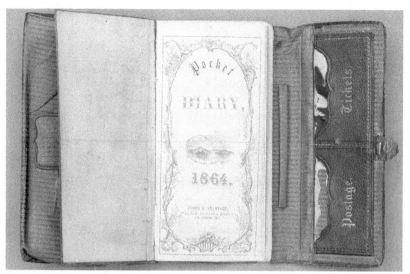

The diary of John Wilkes Booth

When Baker's agents discovered Booth had crossed the Potomac near Mathias Point on April 22, he sent Lieutenant Edward P. Doherty and 25 men from the 16th New York Cavalry to capture them. On April 26, Doherty and his men caught up with John Wilkes Booth and David Herold on a farm owned by Richard Garrett. Doherty ordered the men to surrender. Herold came out of the barn but Booth refused and so the barn was set on fire. While this was happening one of the soldiers, Sergeant Boston Corbett, found a large crack in the barn and was able to shoot Booth in the back. His body was dragged from the barn and, after being searched, the soldiers recovered his leather bound diary. The bullet had punctured his spinal cord and he died in great agony two hours later. Booth's diary was handed to Baker who later passed it on to Stanton. Baker was rewarded for his success by a promotion to brigadier general and receipt of a substantial portion of the $100,000 reward.

In January 1867, Baker published his book "History of the Secret Service" where he described his role in the capture of the conspirators. He also revealed that a diary had been taken from John Wilkes Booth when he had been shot. This information about Booth's diary resulted in Baker being called before a Congressional committee investigating the assassination. Stanton and the War Department were forced to hand over Booth's diary. When shown the diary by the committee, Baker claimed that someone had "cut out eighteen leaves." When called before the committee, Stanton denied being the person responsible for removing the pages. Speculation grew that the missing pages included the names of people who had been involved in the conspiracy.

Baker maintained his power for some time under Stanton's rule, even after President Johnson fired Stanton (who refused to leave his headquarters). In this incredible political battle for power, Stanton refused to leave his headquarters and threatened Johnson. Johnson was incensed at this insubordination. Baker intervened, blackmailing Johnson with the release of scandalous information unless Johnson made peace with Stanton.

President Johnson replied by accusing Baker of spying on the White House. He fired Baker. Subsequently, both Stanton and Baker worked hard to have Johnson impeached. Baker testified at the impeachment hearings in 1868, but the scandalous documents he claimed to have could not be produced. As a result, the impeachment failed.

After his appearance before the Congressional committee, Baker became convinced someone in the government intended to murder him. He was found dead at his home in Philadelphia on July 3, 1868. Officially, Lafayette Baker died of meningitis. Some have suggested, however, that he was silenced by the War Department.

In recent years, using an atomic absorption spectrophotometer to analyze several hairs from Baker's head, Ray A. Neff, a professor at Indiana State University, determined Baker was killed by arsenic poisoning rather than meningitis. Baker had been unwittingly consuming the poison for months, mixed into imported beer provided by his wife's brother, Wally Pollack. "The Lincoln Conspiracy," by Balsiger and Sellier, cites a diary Baker's wife kept which chronicled several dates Pollack brought Baker beer; they correspond to the gradually elevated levels of toxin in the Baker hair samples Neff studied. Wally worked for the War Department, though whether he acted on orders or alone has yet to be determined. Nevertheless, Neff's studies, along with the information chronicled in Baker's diary,

*Behind this marker are the Mutual Family Cemetery graves
at Forest Hills Memorial Park*

serve to bolster a cogent and provocative alternate history
of the Lincoln assassination, one distinct from the chronol-
ogy most commonly promulgated by mainstream U.S. historians. Baker had also left cryptic notes that pointed to a
high-level conspiracy to murder Lincoln—one going far beyond that involving John Wilkes Booth.

Some years later, President Lincoln's only surviving
son, Robert, was visited by a family friend in his home.
Robert was in the process of burning papers in the fire-
place. The friend tried to prevent the destruction of these
historic documents, written in President Lincoln's own
hand. Robert Lincoln was firm and continued tossing
sheaves of paper into the fire, saying, "I must—some of
these letters prove that there was a traitor in my father's
cabinet."

Originally buried in the Mutual Family Cemetery,
Baker's remains (and all others in this cemetery) were
moved en masse to Forest Hills Memorial Park in Huntingdon Valley, Pennsylvania. All of the graves from the
Mutual Family Cemetery are unmarked, but according to
local cemetery historians, the locations of these re-intern-
ments are "behind the Hanover-Kensington M.E. Church
Memorial."

If You Go:
About 15 miles southwest of Forest Hills Memorial Park is
St. James-the-Less Episcopal Churchyard, located at West

Clearfield Street & Hunting Park Avenue, in the Allegheny West section of North Philadelphia. Brigadier General William Reading Montgomery is buried there. See also, the *"If You Go"* section of Chapter 15 (Oliver Knowles).

Also nearby is St. Dominic Church Cemetery, located at 8504 Frankford Avenue in Torresdale, Pennsylvania (about 11 miles east of St. James-the-Less Episcopal Churchyard). The remains of Major General Thomas Kilby Smith are buried there.

"Modern Football's Founding Father"
DE BONNEVILLE "BERT" BELL

County: Montgomery
Town: West Conshohocken
Cemetery: Calvary
Address: Gulph Road and Matsonford Road

In 1958, Bert Bell had one of his regular doctor appointments. His physician looked at him from behind his desk and advised Bell to avoid going to any more football games. Bell told his doctor that he'd much rather die at a football game than at home in bed. Although the Philadelphia Eagles held complimentary box seats for Bell and any guests he might have, he preferred buying his own tickets and sitting with the other fans. On October 11, 1959, he was doing just that, sitting in the end zone watching the Eagles play the visiting Pittsburgh Steelers. In the fourth quarter, he suffered a heart attack and died later that day. He was sixty-four at the time.

Bert Bell was born in Philadelphia on February 25, 1895. Bert's father, John C. Bell, was a successful attorney who would eventually serve as Philadelphia's District Attorney and later as Attorney General of Pennsylvania. Bert's mother could trace her ancestors in America to prior to the American Revolution. His parents could only be described as very wealthy. He had one older brother John C. Bell Jr. who would make quite a name for himself as well.

Bell's father went to the University of Pennsylvania where he played the position of end on the football team. When Bert was six years old, his father took him to his first football game at Penn, and the young boy fell in love with the game. As he grew older he attended various schools until he was ready for high school when he enrolled in the Haverford School. He was a tremendous sports star at Haverford, and in his senior year he captained the school's football, basketball and baseball teams. While baseball was his best sport, football was still his favorite. It was at this time that Bert's father was named a trustee for life at Penn. While serving in this position, he helped form the NCAA. When asked about Bert's college

Bert Bell circa 1925.

plans, his father was clear and to the point, he said, "Bert will go to Penn or he will go to hell."

It should come with little surprise that Bert Bell entered Penn in the fall of 1914. That year he became the starting quarterback for the freshman team. The following year, Coach George Brooke selected Bell to be the starting varsity quarterback, which was quite an accomplishment for a sophomore. He also played as a defender, punter and punt returner. By mid-season Coach Brooke decided to use a two quarterback system which did not have the desired results. The coach then resigned his position before the eighth game of the year, and Penn ended the season with a 3-5-2 record.

Later in life, Bell would tell a story about a train ride he took around this time. Following a Penn game, Bell boarded a train and found a seat next to an older man. The man looked at Bell and asked if he'd seen the game today. Bell nodded yes. That set his fellow passenger off, "Isn't Bell the lousiest thing you ever saw?" He began to answer, but the passenger was far from finished. He described Bell as a safety that couldn't catch a punt and a punter who kicked the ball backwards over his own head. He went on to say that the only reason Bell was on the team was because of his dad's money and influence. The man was still railing on young Bell's performance when the train pulled into the passenger's station. The man got up to leave, held out his hand, and provided Bell with his name. The man then asked for Bert's name. Taking the man's hand and shaking it, the young quarterback responded, "Bert Bell."

Bell's mother died in September 1916 while he was on his way to say his final goodbyes to her. This didn't cause him to miss the start of the Penn Football season playing for new coach Bob Folwell. Once again his performance was inconsistent, and Folwell turned to a two quarterback system. The team's record improved to 7-2-1 and after both Harvard and Yale turned down an invitations to the 1917 Rose Bowl, Penn was offered the chance and accepted. Penn's opponent in the game was the Oregon Ducks. While Penn piled up slightly more yardage than Oregon and Bell had the largest gain from scrimmage measuring 20 yards, he threw a key interception in the fourth quarter that led to a 14-0 Oregon win.

In 1917 Bell had his best year leading Penn to a 9-2 record. In December of that year, after the war to end all wars had drawn in the United States, he was inducted into the United States Army. After a few months of training, he was sent to France. Bell performed well in the war, and he volunteered for more than one dangerous mission. He ended up being promoted to sergeant, and at the war's end, he returned to the United States in March of 1919. That year he was named captain of the Penn football team, but his inconsistent play continued to plague him, and his team finished with a 6-2-1 record. His college career was over, and he was considered to have been an average player. His performance in the classroom was less than average; he failed to apply himself and as a result he left Penn without a degree.

Bell decided to stay in football and became an assistant coach at Penn. By all reports he was highly regarded as an assistant and received a number of head coaching offers. He turned these down believing that a head coach's job took up too much time. Prior to the 1929 season Bell resigned from his position at Penn, and his father got him a job managing the Ritz Carleton Hotel. He also became a stock broker during this period and managed to lose about $50,000 when the market crashed. His father came to his aid and took care of his losses.

Late in 1929 he accepted a position as assistant coach at Temple University in Philadelphia. He served as the backfield coach from 1930 through 1932. In 1933 Temple hired Pop Warner as head football coach, and he let Bell go. Bell enjoyed his life as an assistant using his free time to socialize and gamble. He loved the Saratoga Race Course and visited there every year. While at Saratoga he enjoyed hanging out with the Vanderbuilts, Tim Mara, the Whitneys and Art Rooney.

George Preston Marshall urged Bell to purchase a National Football League (NFL) franchise in 1932. In Bell's view the college game was far more popular so he dismissed the idea. By 1933, for some reason, he had changed his mind and decided he would buy a team. The NFL was interested in having a team in Pennsylvania, but the league informed Bell that the problem was the Pennsylvania Blue Laws that prohibited games being played on Sunday. Bell convinced Art Rooney to apply for an NFL franchise while he went to work on Pennsylvania's Governor Gifford Pinchot (for more information on Pinchot, see *Keystone Tombstones – Anthracite Region*, p. 80). Convincing Pinchot to change the laws would be no easy task. The Governor favored prohibition and was disappointed when the ban against liquor sales was repealed. Pinchot viewed the Blue laws as yet another roadblock making it more difficult for the public to purchase liquor. Bell's efforts resulted in the Governor consenting to a bill that would allow local communities to determine the extent of the blue laws in their own municipalities through referendums. The Pennsylvania General Assembly passed the bill in April of 1933, and the Governor signed it into law.

Bell now needed monetary backing to buy a team. He went to his father who refused because he disapproved of his son's choice to make football a career. Bell moved on without his father, borrowing the money from Frances Upton, a Broadway actress and devout Roman Catholic whom he would eventually secretly marry. The couple would have three children together two boys and a girl. Bell would also convert to Catholicism in the last year of his life. The conversion was a result of the consistent urging of his wife as well as his long friendship with another Catholic by the name of Art Rooney. Bell partnered with Lud Wray a fellow college assistant coach and others to purchase the Frankford Yellow Jackets. Bell and his partners renamed the team the Philadelphia Eagles and paid the NFL a $2,500 entrance fee.

The voters in Philadelphia passed a referendum easing the Blue Laws. Wray became the Eagles head coach, and Bell became the club's president. As president, he negotiated a deal with the Baker Bowl, an 18,500 seat stadium, to serve as the Eagles home field. In their initial season in the league, the Eagles finished 3-5-1. In 1934 they improved slightly to 4-7, but 1935 saw their record drop to 2-9. Because the Eagles could not compete with the rest of the league, ticket sales fell and between 1933 and 1935, the franchise had lost approximately $85,000. Bell grew frustrated because the best players were signing with the teams that had the most money. In his view the only way the league could achieve parity would be for all the teams to have an equal shot at signing new players.

On May 18, 1935, a league meeting was held where Bell proposed that the League institute a draft system in order to level the competitive playing field and ensure that all teams would remain financially viable. The league adopted Bell's proposal without objection. The following year the first NFL draft was held. Of course it continues to this day.

One has to wonder what Bell would think of his creation and the fan magnet it has become. ESPN covers the draft every year, and it gets excellent television ratings.

In 1936 the Eagles were sold through a public auction, and Bell became sole owner. Because of the team's financial situation Bell let Wray go, and he assumed coaching duties himself. In addition he moved the Eagles home field to Municipal Stadium which could house over 100,000 fans. In the 1936 season that Bell coached, the Eagles finished 1-11 which represented their poorest showing ever. The following year was not much better as the team came in with a record of 2-8-1. In 1938 Bell had his best year, finishing 5-6 and the franchise made a $7,000 profit. However the Eagles could not maintain this momentum, and in 1939 they finished 1-9-1. They followed that with a 1-10 record.

In November of 1940 Bell got in touch with Pittsburgh Steeler owner Art Rooney and informed him that Alexis Thompson had approached him about buying the Eagles. Rooney, who had consistently lost money with the Steeler franchise, now saw a way out. He convinced the Steelers' Board of Directors to offer Bell a 20% commission for negotiating the sale of the Steelers to Thompson. Bell's efforts proved successful and Rooney sold his team for about $165,000. As soon as the sale went through Rooney purchased 50% of the Eagles. It was decided that Rooney would be the General manager, and Bell would continue as coach.

Next came a series of events that Pennsylvania sports historians refer to as the "Pennsylvania Polka." In April of 1941 it was announced that the Eagles would be moving to Pittsburgh and play under the name of the Steelers and at the same time Thompson would move his team to Philadelphia and they would be called the Eagles. The Steelers lost their first two games of the 1941 season, and Rooney convinced Bell to resign as coach. His career record was 10-46-2, and for coaches with at least five years at the helm, nobody had done worse.

As World War II drew more and more men into the Armed Forces, there were fewer players available to play football. Some owners wanted to shut down the league until the war ended, but Bell was against that proposal, noting that major League baseball was continuing to operate. In 1943 it got so bad that the Steelers and the Eagles were forced to combine roosters and create a team known as the Steagles. Bell continued to suffer financially during his partnership with Rooney, and Rooney eventually bought him out and took complete control of the Steelers.

The fact that he was no longer an owner put Bell in a position to get the job where his influence on NFL football would be felt for years to come. In 1941 Elmer Layden (one of the legendary Four Horsemen of Notre Dame) was named Commissioner of the NFL. Many NFL owners felt they had been left out of the decision to hire Layden. More than a few of the owners believed that Arch Ward, the sports editor of the Chicago Tribune, was the man who got Layden the job. NFL owners were naturally upset when in September of 1944 Ward organized a group of investors to create a new league, the All-American Football Conference (AAFC) to compete against the NFL. In addition Ward had drawn the interest of a number of potential investors for the new league that included John Keeshin a trucking executive from Chicago, oilmen James Breuil and Ray Ryan, former heavyweight boxing champion Gene Tunney and Lou Gehrig's widow Eleanor. A league was indeed formed and Jim Crowley (yet another of the Four Horseman. See *Keystone Tombstones – Anthracite Region*, p. 15) was named Commissioner.

Some NFL owners felt that Layden had a conflict of interest with dealing properly relative to the AAFC since in their view Ward had been his benefactor. In addition some of the owners didn't believe that Layden took the new league seriously as a threat nor did he appear concerned with the rise in players' salaries due to the competition between the leagues. As a result Layden was fired on January 11, 1946 and Bell was chosen to replace him.

It didn't take long before Bell faced his first crisis. Dan Reeves, the owner of the Cleveland Browns asked for permission to move his team to Los Angeles. The other owners denied his request. Reeves threatened to disband his team, and Bell was forced to step in. The new Commissioner negotiated a settlement that resulted in the creation of the Los Angeles Rams.

Gambling had been a concern of the NFL ever since the league was established. Early in Bell's tenure, he was forced to face the issue. The day before the 1946 Championship game, two New York Giant players, Frank Filchock and Merle Hapes, were accused of having been offered bribes by a man named Alvin Paris in exchange for fixing the game. The Mayor of New York at the time was William O'Dwyer, and he informed the owner of the Giants and Bell of the evidence that had been gathered against the two players. The players were brought to the Mayor's residence where O'Dwyer interviewed them separately. Hapes admitted he had been offered money to fix the game, and Filchock denied the charge. The authorities quickly arrested Paris who confessed to the charges against him. Bell suspended Hapes, but he allowed Filchock to play in the championship. When Paris went to jail and Filchock was put under oath at Paris's trial, Filchock admitted he had been offered a bribe.

After this incident, Commissioner Bell moved against gamblers. He worked with state legislatures throughout the country urging them to pass legislation to make it illegal to fix games. His brother John by this time was the Lieutenant Governor of Pennsylvania (he would later serve as a Justice and then become the Chief Justice of the Pennsylvania Supreme Court), and he promised to lobby the Pennsylvania General Assembly to enact strict gambling laws. Bell himself wrote an antigambling resolution that he was successful in having added to the league constitution. This resolution gave the league Commissioner the authority to permanently ban players for betting on a game or failing to inform league officials if they knew of any game being possibly fixed. Bell immediately used this power to ban Hapes and Filchock from the league. In July of 1947, Bell mandated that each team had to publish an injury report 48 hours before each game. The report was to include information on what players would not or may not play. The purpose of this move was to deny gamblers inside information. To this day the NFL still requires teams to publish injury reports prior to every game.

The next problem that Commissioner Bell found on his plate was the threat of a new league: the AAFC. Ever since the establishment of the league was announced, it had had an adverse effect on the pocketbooks of NFL franchise owners. Both leagues were in a battle for the best talent, and as a result NFL payrolls had increased by 250%. In addition, the AAFC outdrew the NFL in terms of attendance in both

1947 and 1948. However nobody was making money; for three years in a row, neither league made a profit. Bell convinced a majority of the owners to allow him to open negotiations with the AAFC. On December 9, 1949, Bell emerged victorious; he reached a settlement with the AAFC that removed the competition and at the same time merged three former AAFC teams into the NFL. Under the agreement Bell would remain as Commissioner and the Cleveland Browns, the San Francisco 49ers and the Baltimore Colts would join the NFL. NFL owners were so pleased with the settlement that they extended Bell's contract by 5 years.

As the number of television sets in American homes began to increase in the late 1940's and then skyrocket in the 1950's, the rights to televise the games and the NFL's blackout policy became a major issue. Bell felt, and he informed the owners of his opinion, that televising home games locally hurt the sale of tickets to the game. As a result, the NFL blacked out home games to local television stations, with the exception of the Los Angeles Rams, for the entire season in 1950. In response, the United States Justice Department opened an investigation of the league to determine if there had been a violation of the Sherman Antitrust Act. By the end of the season, the Rams, who broadcast all of their home games, saw their home attendance plummet by 50%. Prior to the start of the 1951 season, Bell put the blackout rule back into effect. It was the Commissioner's view that if you gave the game to fans for free on TV, you couldn't expect them to come to the stadium. This position led to the Justice Department filing suit against the NFL. The case was scheduled for trial in January 1952.

The Rams decided to black out their home games for the 1951 season and attendance increased back to its 1949 levels. After the 1951 season, Bell obtained the authority to set the television policy for every NFL team. He worked out a deal with the DuMont Television Network which awarded that network the right to do a national broadcast of one NFL game a week. Bell took the revenue from the deal and divided it equally among all the NFL teams. This worked out to about $50,000 per team. That November, a judge ruled in the Justice Department case. The ruling found that Bell could not institute a policy that blacked out all NFL games. However the judge also found that each NFL team was free to determine its own policy relative to blackouts. Bell was more than pleased with the decision.

Setting up the NFL schedule had been an issue with NFL owners since the day the league was established. In the thirties, the NFL President set up the schedule. The president at the time held the philosophy that any schedule should favor the large city teams. Eventually the owners took back the responsibility of setting the schedule, and this led to numerous disagreements as each owner fought for a schedule that would most benefit their team. Finally in 1948 the owners gave Bell the authority to schedule. Bell decided that early in the season weak teams would play weak teams and the strong teams would also play each other. Bell felt that attendance would be helped if the differences in team standings could be minimized as long as possible.

Bell and the NFL found themselves back in the courts in the 1950's. This case involved a former player for the Detroit Lions named Bill Radovich. Radovich was one of the NFL players who left the league to play in the AAFC. The NFL passed a rule that banned any of these players from working for the NFL for a five year period. After playing in the AAFC for two years, Radovich was offered a job with the San Francisco Clippers, a Pacific Coast League team that was affiliated with the NFL. The NFL warned the Clippers that there would be sanctions if they hired Radovich, and as a result the Clippers withdrew their job offer. Radovich responded by filing suit against the NFL seeking damages. The case gradually worked its way through the judicial system. Bell's brother, John, who by now was the Chief Justice of the Pennsylvania Supreme Court, told his brother that the NFL case was a losing one. Bell's brother's judgment proved correct and in 1957 the United States Supreme Court ruled in favor of Radovich. The loss of the individual case was not what Bell found alarming about the decision. What concerned him was that the Supreme Court had ruled that the NFL was subject to antitrust laws.

Congress immediately set hearings to study the effect of the ruling. Bell argued through the media that the NFL was a sport and not a business and therefore not subject to antitrust laws. Representatives of the NFL Players Association (NFLPA, the players union) appeared before Congress and took the position that both the NFL draft and the reserve clause were anti-labor and needed to be eliminated. Seeing that Congress was going to become involved in the running of the NFL, Bell formally recognized the Players Association and the crisis passed.

While all this was going on, professional football continued to gain a larger share of the American audience. The 1958 NFL Championship was much anticipated though no one knew at the time that it would mark a surge in the NFL's popularity that would take the league to the top of the sports market in the United States. The Championship was scheduled to be played in historic Yankee Stadium on December 28, 1958. It's ironic that the game that provided the foundation for football to pass baseball as America's favorite sport was played in the House that Ruth built.

The two teams who would face each other were the Baltimore Colts and the New York Giants. To give you an idea of how star studded this game was, seventeen individuals (including coaches) involved in the contest are current members of the Pro Football hall of Fame. The Giants fielded Sam Huff and Frank Gifford and had a defensive coordinator by the name of Tom Landry and an offensive coordinator named Vince Lombardi. Baltimore was led by a quarterback named Johnny Unitas, a defensive lineman Gino Marchetti and a running back\wide receiver named Lenny Moore. Bell somehow sensed the importance of the contest, and he lifted the NFL blackout rules; the game would be televised nationally.

The game lived up to its billing. The Giants were ahead 17-14 late in the fourth quarter when they punted the ball to the Baltimore 14 yard line. Unitas then led one of the most famous drives in NFL history. He threw two incomplete passes before connecting with Moore for an 11 yard gain. After missing with another pass he connected with Raymond Berry three straight times putting the ball on the Giant 13 yard line with just seven seconds left in the game. The Colts kicked a 20 yard field goal and the game was sent into a sudden death overtime. The Giants won the toss and took the ball first in the overtime but they were unable to get a first down so they punted. Unitas once

Here lies the man who may be responsible for making
professional football America's national pastime.

again led the Colts down the field on a 13 play 80 yard drive that ended when Alan Ameche scored on a third down run from the one yard line to give the Colts the Championship by a score of 23-17. This would be the last NFL Championship Bell would ever witness, and he viewed it as the culmination of a life's work. By the conclusion of the game the Commissioner was in tears.

As mentioned previously, Bell died the following year. His funeral was held in Saint Margaret Roman Catholic Church on October 14, 1959. Dignitaries, friends and admirers attended the funeral mass. The owners of the NFL teams and the President of the Green Bay Packers served as honorary pall bearers. Bell was laid to rest at Calvary Cemetery in West Conshohocken, Pennsylvania.

After Bell's death the great sportswriter, Red Smith, noted that, "He was watching the Eagles, the team he had created with his own sweat and tears and money, playing his other team, the Steelers, which he operated with Art Rooney during the war. They were playing on Franklin Field, where forty years earlier a little Penn quarterback had played the game that was to become his life. It was almost as though he were allowed to choose the time and place."

If You Go:

Calvary Cemetery is a Mecca for sports fans. Alan Dante "The Horse" Ameche (p. 87) was laid to rest there in 1988. Ameche won the 1954 Heisman trophy as a running back at Wisconsin. He was drafted in the first round by the Baltimore Colts, and on his first NFL play he went 79 yards for a touchdown. He was the 1955 NFL Rookie of the Year. Ameche is best remembered for scoring the winning touchdown in overtime to give the Colts the Championship in the 1958 final played in Yankee stadium. Yes, Ameche scored the touchdown that left Bert Bell in tears. How ironic is it that they are buried in the same cemetery?

You can also find Francis James Bagnell at Calvary. He was an All-American football player at the University of Pennsylvania. He won the Maxwell Trophy and finished second in the voting for the Heisman. He is a member of the College Football Hall of Fame.

Henry Charles ("Shag") Crawford was buried at Calvary in 2007. Crawford was a catcher in the minor leagues, and when his playing career ended he became an umpire. He would umpire over 3,000 games between 1956 and 1975. Well respected in the game, he worked three World Series and two National League Championship Series.

Finally the much respected NFL referee Stanley Javie can also be found at Calvary. Javie worked for the NFL from 1951 to 1980 and he was selected to referee four Super Bowls. Calvary is a good size cemetery, so the authors suggest a visit to the cemetery office where you can get directions to the sites .

If you visit Calvary you are not far from the final resting place of baseball great Richie Ashburn (see page 94). In addition you are very close to Philadelphia where you can visit the graves of the people covered in this volume as well as those that can be found in *Keystone Tombstones Volume One*.

"Cooke's Books"

JAY COOKE

County: Montgomery
Town: Elkins Park
Cemetery: St. Paul's Episcopal Church
Address: Old York and Ashbourne Roads

Jay Cooke was the leading financier of the Union war effort during the Civil War. He was also a key investor in the postwar development of railroads in the northwestern United States.

Cooke was born in Sandusky, Ohio on August 10, 1821. The family estate, a limestone dwelling overlooking Sandusky Bay and Lake Erie, was named "Ogontz" in honor of an Indian chief who once lived nearby. The area was a paradise of teeming deer, waterfowl and fish. While growing up there, Jay developed his lifelong passion for hunting and fishing.

Jay's father, Eleutheros Cooke, a lawyer and Whig congressman, and his mother, Martha Caswell, were well-educated and very active politically. Jay's early education was mainly from home schooling. At age 14, he began work at a Sandusky dry goods store where he became the head clerk while the owner taught him business and financial procedures. At only 16, he moved to St. Louis and was employed with Seymour & Bool, where he earned an unheard of sum of $600 a year. He lost that job due to the Panic of 1837 and returned to Ohio. In 1838, he moved to Philadelphia, Pennsylvania, where he accepted a position with a packet company. This company failed soon thereafter, and Cooke became a bookkeeper in a local hotel. Next, at age 18, he landed a clerk position with the banking firm E.W. Clark & Company which, five years later, led to a full partnership. The company earned its investors a lot of money through its investments in railroads and loans to the federal government to fund the Mexican War. The company collapsed during the Panic of 1857, but Cooke emerged from the economic hard times a very wealthy man.

On January 1, 1861, just months before the start of the Civil War, Cooke opened the private banking house of Jay

Jay Cooke during the Civil War

Cooke & Company in Philadelphia. As the war began, the state of Pennsylvania borrowed $3 million from the firm to fund its war efforts. Cooke also worked with Treasury Secretary Salmon P. Chase to secure loans from the leading bankers in the north. Cooke and his brother, a newspaper editor, had helped Chase get his job by lobbying for him.

7³⁄₁₀ NEW 7³⁄₁₀
U. S. LOAN
Fundable in **5-20** Bonds
IN THREE YEARS.
FOR SALE HERE.

Union bond advertisement

Cooke's firm was so successful in distributing Treasury notes that Chase engaged him as a special agent to sell the $500 million in bonds which the Treasury had previously tried and failed to sell. Promised a sales commission of 0.5 percent of the revenue from the first $10 million, and 0.375 percent of subsequent bonds, Cooke financed a nationwide sales campaign, appointing about 2,500 sub-agents who traveled through every northern and western state and territory, as well as the southern states as they came under control of the Union Army. Meanwhile, Cooke secured the support of most northern newspapers, purchasing ads through advertising agencies, and often working directly with editors on lengthy articles about the virtues of buying government bonds. These efforts heralded a particular type of patriotism based on classical liberalist notions of self-interest. His editorials, articles, handbills, circulars, and signs most often appealed to Americans' desire to turn a profit, while simultaneously aiding the war effort. Cooke quickly sold the $500 million in bonds plus $11 million more. Congress immediately sanctioned the excess.

Although Cooke's bond campaigns were widely praised as a patriotic contribution to the Union cause, his huge personal financial gains did not go unnoticed. Notorious for stalling the deposit of bond proceeds into federal coffers, he was accused of corruption, and on December 22, 1862, Massachusetts Representative Charles R. Train proposed a Congressional investigation of the Treasury—though the investigation never materialized.

In the early months of 1865, the government faced pressing financial needs. After the national banks saw disappointing bond sales, the government again turned to Cooke. He sent his agents into remote villages and hamlets, and even into isolated mining camps in the West, and persuaded rural newspapers to praise the bonds. Between February and July 1865, he disposed of $830 million in notes. This allowed the Union soldiers to be supplied and paid during the final months of the war. During this effort, Cooke pioneered the use of price stabilization, a practice whereby bankers stabilize the price of a new issue. It is still in use by investment bankers in IPOs and other security issuances.

During these years, Cooke built a multi-room limestone dwelling (dubbed "Cooke Castle"), constructed in 1864-65 and still standing, on the small island of Gibraltar in the Lake Erie harbor of Put-in-Bay, Ohio. The island, which has the highest land elevation in the Put-In-Bay area, was the lookout point for Commander Oliver Perry in the fight against the British during the War of 1812 (on September 10, 1813, Perry and his men defeated a fleet of British vessels during the famous Battle of Lake Erie).

Cooke also constructed a palatial residence in Cheltenham Township, Pennsylvania dubbed Ogontz after his boyhood home in Sandusky. This influenced the naming of many area Philadelphia landmarks, including Ogontz Avenue. Two decades later, the estate and dwelling became the exclusive Ogontz School for Girls and the surrounding area became the city of Ogontz, Pennsylvania.

By the end of the war Cooke had three banking houses (each with a separate group of partners) in Philadelphia, New York and Washington. In 1870, a similar bank was set up in London, and the next year all were brought together as a single partnership. Cooke expanded into many fields. He had been friendly to the National Banking Act of 1863 and obtained charters for national banks in Washington and New York; the national banks were the prime source of Cooke's strength.

To these banks and to small investors at home and abroad Cooke—now an investment banker—sold participation in state and railroad loans; the largest loans went to the great land-grant Northern Pacific Railroad, which was chartered to run from Duluth, Minnesota, to Tacoma, Washington. In this connection, Cooke introduced two new ideas into banking: the establishment of banking syndicates as underwriters to handle particular issues; and the active participation by bankers in the affairs of the companies they were helping finance. Thus, Cooke became the banker and fiscal agent of the Northern Pacific in 1869, and he made short-term loans to the railroad out of his

Painting of Jay Cooke as an old man

Jay Cooke's crypt

own house's resources—what would prove to be a fatal step.

In 1870, Cooke was responsible for the proposal to refund the Civil War loans. Congress authorized the sale of $1.5 billion worth of lower rate Treasury securities in exchange for wartime issues. Meanwhile, Cooke's troubles with the Northern Pacific Railroad were mounting. In addition to making loans to the railroad, he underwrote mortgage bonds which sold very slowly. The firm continued to make advances to the railroad out of the demand liabilities of its customers—a risky business. When the economy weakened in early 1873, investment markets dried up. Cooke's banks and his associated houses could not meet the demands of their depositors. On September 18, 1873, the New York office of Jay Cooke and Company shut its doors, as did the banks with which it was associated. This started the Panic of 1873, which in turn resulting in the complete collapse of the Cooke financial empire and the end of Cooke's influence in the money markets. His personal fortune was wiped out.

Later, in the 1870's, he invested a small sum in a silver mine which turned out to be a bonanza. Cooke was able to sell his holdings for $1 million, thus assuring a comfortable old age.

Cooke and his family spent every summer at Cooke Castle until his death. Today, Gibraltar Island and the Castle belong to Ohio State University and is a lake laboratory for the purpose of teaching, learning and research.

The Castle is a Federal Historical Site and is currently being refurbished.

A devout Episcopalian, Cooke regularly gave 10 percent of his income for religious and charitable purposes. He donated funds to the Philadelphia Divinity School and for the building of Episcopal churches, including St. Paul's Episcopal Church in Elkins Park, Pennsylvania (near his Philadelphia "Ogontz" residence) and another on South Bass Island (across the bay from his "Cooke Castle" summer home). After he had been forced to give up his Ogontz estate in bankruptcy, he later repurchased it and converted it into a school for girls.

Cooke died in the Ogontz (now Elkins Park) section of Cheltenham Township, Pennsylvania, on February 16, 1905. He is buried there at St. Paul's Episcopal, in a mausoleum that he designed.

A number of geographic features are named in Cooke's honor, including:

- *Jay Cooke State Park*, a large state park located near Duluth, Minnesota.
- The village of *Cooke City, Montana.*
- *Cooke Township* in Cumberland County, Pennsylvania.
- *Jay Cooke Elementary School* in Philadelphia, Pennsylvania.
- *Cooke Road* in Cheltenham Township, Pennsylvania.
- *Jay, Pitt, and Cooke Streets* in the Lakeside neighborhood of Duluth, Minnesota.
- A statue of *Jay Cooke* by Henry Shrady is located in Jay Cooke Plaza near the intersection of 9th Avenue East and Superior Street in Duluth, Minnesota.

If You Go:

Also buried at St. Paul's is Brigadier General Ario Pardee Jr. He commanded the 28th Pennsylvania Infantry at Antietam. He was brigadier commander at Gettysburg and on Sherman's March to the Sea. For his special gallantry at the Battle of Peach Tree Creek during the Atlanta Campaign, he was brevetted brigadier general.

"The Communicator"

DAVE GARROWAY

County: Montgomery
Town: Bala Cynwyd
Cemetery: West Laurel Hill
Address: 215 Belmont Avenue

Dave Garroway was a broadcast pioneer. He was the original host of the morning television program "Today" on NBC television. The first show to combine news and entertainment, "Today" was considered a brash experiment when it premiered in 1952.

David Cunningham Garroway was born in Schenectady, New York on July 13, 1913. His family moved many times before eventually settling in St. Louis, Missouri, when Dave was 14. He attended University City High School and Washington University in St. Louis, where he earned a degree in psychology.

After graduation in 1935, Garroway tried his hand as a lab assistant at Harvard, and then as a salesman (selling books initially, and then later piston rings—neither successfully). He decided to take a stab at broadcasting after he made it through the highly competitive interview process to land a position as a page at NBC. The page program gave young people a temporary job at Radio City in New York and later the NBC Studios in Hollywood. NBC's pages would work in various departments at the network, being groomed for a career with NBC. In addition, the pages acted as ushers and tour guides. Only 60-80 pages were selected from thousands of applicants each year, one of whom in 1938 was Dave Garroway.

Garroway got off to a rather mediocre start by graduating 23rd of 24 in his class at the NBC announcer school in 1939. Nevertheless, he landed a job at influential Pittsburgh radio station KDKA and built a reputation as the station's "Roving Announcer." He roamed the region filing a number of memorable reports from both above and below the Earth's surface (aboard a hot-air balloon and from deep within a coal mine, respectively) as well as underwater (aboard a U.S. Navy submarine in the Ohio River). This

Dave Garroway, "Peace"

experience brought out Garroway's ability to find a compelling story in any situation. He soon became the station's special events director.

After two years at KDKA, Garroway left Pittsburgh for a job in Chicago. However, his career in broadcasting was interrupted in 1941 by the outbreak of World War II. He enlisted in the Navy and was stationed in Honolulu. When he was off duty, he hosted a radio show, playing jazz and reminiscing about Chicago.

After the war, he returned to Chicago and worked as a disc jockey at WMAQ (AM). He hosted a variety of programs and promoted the Chicago jazz scene. One of his innovations was to convince his studio audience to show approval for a song by snapping their fingers instead of clapping, just like the "hepcats" did in the coffee shops. He was voted the nation's best disc jockey in the Billboard polls in 1948, 1949 and 1951.

Garroway broke into television when he hosted the experimental musical variety show "Garroway at Large," which was telecast live from Chicago. The show ran from 1949 to 1954 on NBC. He abandoned the usual conventions for a more casual approach and personal, informal style. In 1951, he came to the attention of legendary NBC president Pat Weaver, who recruited Garroway to host a new morning news-and-entertainment experiment called the "Today" show. The show debuted on January 14, 1952 and the critics initially panned it, but Garroway's laid-back style attracted a large audience that enjoyed his easygoing presence early in the morning.

On "Today," Garroway—who wore bowties and horn-rimmed glasses—was officially called "a communicator," and his former colleagues say the term was especially apt. His signature sign-off at the end of each broadcast was an up-raised hand (palm out) saying "Peace." Barbara Walters, who Garroway hired to be a writer on "Today," said of Garroway, "I have never seen anyone in this business who could communicate the way he could. He could look at the camera and make you feel that he was talking only with you."

Garroway's co-host was a cute chimpanzee named J. Fred Muggs, and Garroway took the show to Paris and Rome, to car shows and expos, to plays and movies, and even on board an Air Force B-52 for a practice bombing run.

Garroway was a hard worker. At the same time he did "Today," he hosted a Friday night variety series called "The Dave Garroway Show," which ran from 1953 to June 1954. In 1955, he began hosting NBC's Sunday afternoon live documentary, "Wide Wide World," which ran until 1958. The premiere episode—featuring entertainment from the U.S., Canada and Mexico—was the first international North American telecast in the history of the medium. He also hosted a radio show, "Dial Dave Garroway," that went on the air as soon as the "Today" show wrapped up each morning, and for those who couldn't get enough of him there was a board game called "Dave Garroway's Today Game," which debuted in 1960.

Despite his easygoing camera presence, Garroway frequently battled depression. After his second wife, Pamela Wilde, committed suicide via drug overdose in April 1961, his condition worsened. A month later he resigned and on June 16, 1961, he hosted his last "Today."

After leaving the show, Garroway tried his hand at educational television (a series called "Exploring the Universe"), a return to radio, and even started a magazine. He studied acting (landing a role in an episode of the western series "Alias Smith and Jones" in 1972), narrated a compilation of songs performed by the Boston Pops Orchestra, and wrote a book (*Fun on Wheels*) to amuse children on road trips. He appeared sporadically on various television programs but never again achieved the success

Here is the grave of the broadcast pioneer Dave Garroway.

or recognition he enjoyed on "Today." He appeared on "Today" anniversary shows in the 60's and 70's; his final appearance was on the 30th anniversary show on January 14, 1982.

He had many interests and hobbies, such as restoring classic cars, astronomy, music and auto racing. He appeared in television commercials for the first Corvette in 1953 and the Ford Falcon in 1964. His interest in astronomy led him to his third wife, Sarah Lee Lippincott, an astronomer whom he married in 1980.

In 1982, Dave Garroway had open heart surgery. Various postoperative complications soon followed. On July 21, 1982, he was found dead of a self-inflicted gunshot wound at his home in Swarthmore, Pennsylvania. He was 69 years old.

The Hollywood Walk of Fame honored Dave Garroway with a star at 6264 Hollywood Boulevard for his contributions to television, and another, separate star at 6355 Hollywood Boulevard for his contributions to radio. Because of his dedication to the cause of mental health, his third wife, Sarah, helped establish the Dave Garroway Laboratory for the Study of Depression at the University of Pennsylvania. He is buried in West Laurel Hill Cemetery in Bala Cynwyd.

If You Go:
West Laurel Hill is a beautiful, large cemetery, containing the graves of many famous and interesting people, several of whom are identified in of this volume (see Teddy Pendergrass, p. 157). Some others are:

William Breyer (1828-1882), the founder of Breyer's Ice Cream;

Hobart "Hobey" Baker (1892-1918), the Hall-of-Fame hockey player and World War I hero;

Robert Cooper Grier (1794-1870), a United States Supreme Court Justice, Grier was plucked from relative obscurity in August 1846 and nominated for appointment to the nation's highest bench by President James K. Polk, but not until *after* one of Polk's first nominees (fellow Pennsylvanian and future President of the United States, James Buchanan) refused the appointment; and

Herman Haupt (1817-1904), a very important Civil War general (see page 150).

"Hancock the Superb"
WINFIELD SCOTT HANCOCK

County: Montgomery
Town: Norristown
Cemetery: Montgomery
Address: 1 Hartranft Avenue

Winfield Scott Hancock was an American hero named after an American hero and given an appropriate and well-earned nickname, "Hancock the Superb." He was a career U.S. Army Officer, a hero in the Civil War, a commanding general at the Battle of Gettysburg, and the Democratic nominee for president in 1880.

Winfield Scott Hancock was born in Montgomery County, Pennsylvania on Valentine's Day in 1824. He was named after General Winfield Scott, a hero in the War of 1812. Hancock was born with an identical twin brother named Hilary Booker Hancock. Hancock was educated at Norristown Academy at first but transferred to public schools in the late 1830's. In 1840, he was nominated to West Point by Congressman Joseph Fornance. He graduated in 1844 ranked eighteenth of twenty-five. He was commissioned a second lieutenant and assigned to the infantry.

When the Mexican War broke out in 1846, he was initially assigned to recruiting in Kentucky. He worked hard to get assigned to the front, but he was so successful as a recruiter, they were reluctant to let him go. He finally did get assigned to the front in July of 1847 in a regiment that made up part of the army led by General Winfield Scott. He was promoted to 1st Lieutenant for "gallant and meritorious conduct" at the Battle of Churubasco where he was wounded in the knee and developed a fever. The fever kept him from participating in the final breakthrough at Mexico City much to his regret. He remained in Mexico until the peace treaty was signed in 1848.

After the Mexican War he served in the West, in Florida, and elsewhere. It was while serving in St. Louis that he met Almira (Allie) Russell whom he married in 1850. The couple had two children, Russell (1850-1884) and

Winfield Scott Hancock

Ada (1857-1875). In 1855, he was promoted to Captain and in November 1858, he was stationed in Southern California and joined by Almira and the children. There, Hancock became friends with several officers from the South and became especially close to Lewis Armistead of Virginia. At the outbreak of the Civil War, Armistead and other Southerners were leaving to join the Confederate Army, while Hancock was remaining in the U.S Army.

On June 15, 1861, Hancock and Almira hosted a party for their friends who were scattering because of the war. The party has become legend and is recounted in Michael Shaara's "The Killer Angels" and in the movie "Gettysburg." Armistead, who was widowed twice, had grown very close to the Hancock's and shed tears when it became time to end the party and depart. He gave some personal effects to Almira for safe keeping and promised he would not take arms against his friend "Winnie." Almira said later that at the Battle of

This monument marks the spot on the Gettysburg where Hancock was wounded. The bullet that was removed from Hancock is preserved by the Montgomery County Historical Society.

Gettysburg, Hancock's men killed three of the six Confederates who attended that party.

Hancock headed east to assume quartermaster duties for a rapidly growing army but on September 23, 1861 was promoted to brigadier general and given command of an infantry brigade in the Amy of the Potomac. He took part in the Peninsula Campaign and at the Battle of Williamsburg on May 5, 1862 he handled his troop so well that General George McClellan reported "Hancock was Superb." The epithet seemed to stick to him afterwards and "Hancock the Superb" was born.

He played a significant role at the Battle of Antietam and shortly afterwards was promoted to Major General of Volunteers in November 1862. He led his division in the disastrous attack on Marye's Heights in the Battle of Fredericksburg the following month, where he was wounded in the abdomen. He was wounded again at the Battle of

This is the Friend to Friend monument in the Gettysburg National Cemetery. The monument portrays the final moments in the life of Confederate General Lewis Armistead who died at Gettysburg and was close friends with General Hancock.

Chancellorsville covering General Hooker's withdrawal. On that day, General Darius Couch asked to be transferred out of the Army of the Potomac in protest of the actions of General Hooker. As a result, Hancock assumed command of 11 corps, which he would lead until shortly before the war's end (General Couch had a long distinguished military career and has the remains of a fortification built to defend Harrisburg named after him in Lemoyne, PA).

Hancock's most famous service was at the Battle of Gettysburg during July 1-3 1863. On the first day, after his friend Maj. Gen. John Reynolds (see *Keystone Tombstones – Susquehanna Valley Region*, p. 134) was killed, Gen. George Meade (see page 281), the new commander of the Army of the Potomac, sent Hancock ahead to take command and to decide whether to continue to fight there or to fall back. He decided to stay, rallied his troops, and held Cemetery Ridge until the arrival of the main body of the Federal Army. During the second day's battle, he commanded the left center and, after General Sickles had been

This monument on the Gettysburg battlefield marks the spot where Confederate General Lewis Armistead fell mortally wounded.

wounded, the whole left wing. On the third day, he commanded the left center and thus bore the brunt of Pickett's Charge. Hancock was shot in the groin while rallying and commanding his troops on horseback. Although severely wounded, he refused to be evacuated to the rear until the battle was resolved. During the battle, his old friend General Lewis Armistead was mortally wounded. As he lay wounded and dying, he asked to see Hancock. When told that Hancock could not come to see him because he had been wounded himself, Armistead asked that Hancock be told that he was sorry. Armistead died two days later while Hancock took six months to recover enough to return to command. There is a monument on the Gettysburg battlefield commemorating their friendship and another marking the spot where Armistead fell. Hancock was considered by many to have made the most impact by a general at Gettysburg. His courage in the face of fire and leadership played a huge role in the Union victory.

Hancock suffered from the effects of his Gettysburg wound for the rest of the war. After recuperating in Norristown, he returned in March to the front and led his old

corps under General Ulysses S. Grant in the 1864 Overland
Campaign but was never quite his old self. He performed
well at the Battle of the Wilderness, which began in May,
and continued to fight at Yellow Tavern, North Anna, Old
Church, Cold Harbor, Trevilian Station, and finally the siege
of Petersburg. In June, his Gettysburg wound reopened but
he soon resumed command, sometimes travelling by ambulance. After his corps participated in the assaults at Deep
Bottom, Hancock was promoted to Brigadier General in the
Regular Army, effective August 12, 1864.

In Grant's campaign against Lee, Hancock and his
famed 11 Corps were repeatedly called upon to plunge into
the very worst of the fighting, and the casualties were terrible. The losses and lingering effects of his Gettysburg
wound caused Hancock to give up field command in November 1864. He left the 11 Corps after a year in which it
had suffered over 40,000 casualties but had achieved significant military victories. He was again promoted in March
1865 to Brevet Major General in the Regular Army.

After the assassination of Abraham Lincoln in April,
Hancock was placed in charge of Washington D.C. and it
was under his command that John Wilkes Booth's accom-
plices were tried and executed. Hancock was reluctant to
execute some of the less-culpable conspirators, especially
Mary Surratt. He hoped Surratt would receive a pardon

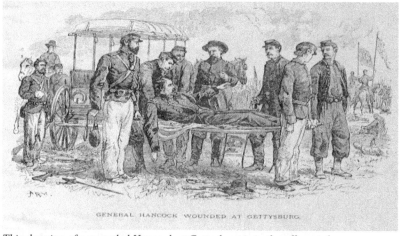

GENERAL HANCOCK WOUNDED AT GETTYSBURG

*This drawing of a wounded Hancock at Gettysburg is in the office at the
Montgomery Cemetery.*

from President Johnson. He was so hopeful that he posted messengers from the Arsenal, where the hangings took place, to the White House, ready to relay the news of a pardon to him, but no pardon was forthcoming. Afterwards, he wrote that "every soldier was bound to act as I did under similar circumstances."

Hancock remained in the postwar army, and in 1866 Grant had him promoted to Major General in the Regular Army, and he served at that rank for the rest of his life. He served briefly in the west and then was named military governor of Louisiana during reconstruction. His policies there angered Republicans and Grant but made him popular among Democrats. When Grant won the presidency in 1868, Hancock found himself transferred to the Department of Dakota, which covered Minnesota, Montana, and the Dakotas. It was during this tour that Hancock contributed to the creation of Yellowstone National Park and had a summit (Mt. Hancock) at the southern boundary named in his honor.

With the death of General George Meade in 1872, Hancock became the senior major general in the U.S. Army and was assigned to take Meade's place as commander of the Division of the Atlantic at Governor's Island in New York Harbor.

Hancock had been considered as a presidential nominee by the Democrats as early as 1864. In 1880, he was finally chosen at the convention in Cincinnati along with William Hayden English of Indiana as his running mate. They ran against James Garfield and Chester Arthur in an election that was very close in the popular vote, but not so close in the electoral. Garfield won by less than 10,000 votes, but won the electoral vote 214 to 155. Garfield was assassinated in September 1881.

Hancock finished his life as Commander of the Division of the Atlantic and died at Governor's Island from an infected Carbuncle complicated by diabetes on February 9, 1886.After a funeral in New York City, General Hancock's remains were taken to his boyhood home of Norristown, PA and placed with his daughter Ada in a mausoleum that he had designed.

Winfield Scott Hancock is memorialized three times at Gettysburg: once in a statue on Cemetery Hill, once on a statue as part of the Pennsylvania Memorial, and as a

Here is the grave of one of the greatest Union Civil War Generals.

sculpture on the New York State Monument. There are statues in Washington DC at Pennsylvania Avenue and 7th street N.W. and in Fairmont Park in Philadelphia and a bronze bust in Hancock Square, New York City. His portrait adorns U.S. currency on the $2 Silver Certificate series of 1886 and is quite valuable today.

Hancock was portrayed by actor Brian Mallon in two films about the Civil War: *Gettysburg* (1993) and *Gods and Generals* (2003). He is portrayed very favorably in both films. There are numerous books about Hancock, the most notable is *Winfield Scott Hancock: A Soldier's Life* written by David M. Jordan and published in 1998.

If You Go:
There are a few other interesting graves in Montgomery Cemetery. The most notable is the grave of John Frederick Hartranft (see page 142).

Also buried in Montgomery Cemetery with Hancock is Brigadier General Samuel Kosciuszko Zook (see page 182) who fought with him at Gettysburg and was fatally wounded on the second day of the battle.

Here are the Joes at Brother Paul's at 3300 Ridge Pike, Eagleville, PA, refreshing themselves after visiting Montgomery Cemetery. They hope to get back to visit the brothers in the future.

You may also want to visit the grave of Brigadier General Adam Jacoby Slemmer, who steadfastly refused to surrender Fort Pickens in Pensacola Harbor to the Alabama and Florida authorities during the early days of secession. He had moved his forces from Fort Barrancas to Fort Pickens, which was more easily defended. Fort Pickens remained under Federal control for the duration of the war and ensured Union control of the Gulf of Mexico. Slemmer was assigned to General Don Carlos Buell's command later in the year and took part in the Corinth Campaign and the relief of Nashville. He was wounded in the Battle of Stones River, Tennessee, receiving a wound that incapacitated him for the rest of the war. He died on October 7, 1868 at the age of forty, from typhoid fever that he had contracted during the war. At the time of his death he was in command of Fort Laramie, Wyoming.

"Old Johnny"
JOHN FREDERICK HARTRANFT

County: Montgomery
Town: Norristown
Cemetery: Montgomery Cemetery
Address: 1 Hartranft Avenue

John Frederick Hartranft was a union Major General and recipient of the Congressional Medal of Honor. He also served as Pennsylvania's Auditor General and then two terms as Governor from 1873 to 1879.

Hartranft was born in Fagleysville which is a village in New Hanover Township in Montgomery County Pennsylvania on December 16, 1830. He received a degree in civil engineering from Union College in Schenectady, New York in 1853 and worked for two railroads in eastern Pennsylvania before returning to Norristown to work with his father's real estate and stagecoach businesses.

In the spring of 1861 his militia outfit became a 90-day volunteer regiment and were sent to Washington D.C. On the eve of the First Battle of Bull Run, the regiment turned its back on the enemy and marched home just as the firing began. Their 90-day enlistment period was over and despite pleas for them to stay from General Irvin McDowell, they left. Hartranft was humiliated by his men's decision and he stayed to fight on July 21, 1861. This act earned him the Medal of Honor.

After Bull Run, he raised the 51st Pennsylvanian Infantry, a three year regiment, and became its colonel. They first served on the North Carolina coast in the Burnside Expedition and then at the Battle of Roanoke Island and New Bern. In 1862 they fought in the Second Battle of Bull Run and at South Mountain. On September 17, 1862 at Antietan, Hartranft led the 51st in its famous charge across Burnside's Bridge, suffering 120 casualties. They braved a storm of rifle and cannon fire to cross the bridge and threaten the Confederate right flank. They also participated in the Battle of Fredericksburg before being transferred to the Western Theater where Hartranft saw action at the battles of Vicksburg, Campbells Station and Knoxville. He fought at

John F. Hartranft

the Wilderness and at Spotsylvania after which he was promoted to brigadier general. After continuing to lead his forces against Richmond and Petersburg, he helped repulse General Robert E. Lee's last offensive at the Battle of Fort Stedman on March 25, 1865. His role at Fort Stedman led to him being brevetted major general by U.S. Grant.

The end of the war did not end the violence and death in Hartranft's life. President Andrew Johnson appointed

John Hartranft

him the provost marshal during the trial of those accused
in the Lincoln assassination. The accused were being held
in the Arsenal Penitentiary in Washington D.C. and he was
responsible for the defense of the Arsenal as well as the su-
pervision of every aspect of the prisoner's daily lives. He
would make sure they were fed and cleaned and that no
one would communicate with them unless authorized by
Secretary of War Stanton.

   He also saw to it that the inmates were never allowed to
occupy adjacent cells so as to prevent tapping out mes-
sages through the walls. The guard detail was changed on

Hartranft reads the Orders of Execution

a daily basis to make sure that no single guard would guard the same prisoner more than once. On July 7, 1865 General Hartranft completed his duties by seeing to it that the sentence of Death for four of the prisoners was carried out. Hartranft led Mary Suratt, Lewis Paine, David Herold and George Atzerodt to the gallows in what is now called Fort Lesley McNair. They had received the news of their sentence only 24 hours earlier. One by one the conspirators were assisted up the thirteen steps of the scaffold by the execution party and seated. All four sat quietly while Hartranft publicly read the Orders of Execution, a five page hand-written document stating the charges against each of the four prisoners and the sentences of death that they received. Prayers followed and then the prisoners were told to stand and were positioned on the traps that would be knocked out from under them. Their arms and legs were bound, nooses were fitted around the necks and canvas hoods placed over their heads. From the scaffold Powell said "Mrs. Surratt is innocent. She doesn't deserve to die with the rest of us." Surratt would be the first women ever executed by the Federal Government. The signal was given by Hartranft and the condemned fell. Surratt and Atzerodt appeared to die quickly. Herold and Powell struggled for nearly five minutes, strangling to death.

"Destruction of the Union Depot" by M.B. Leiser, shows burning of Union Depot, Pittsburgh, PA during Great railroad strike of 1877 from pgs. 624, 625 of "Harper's Weekly, Journal of Civilization," Vol XXL, No. 1076, New York, Saturday, August 11, 1877.

Shortly after, Hartranft decided to end his military career. "Old Johnny" as his troops called him resigned from the army and decided to enter politics. He switched from the Democratic to the Republican party and gained the support of Republican state boss Simon Cameron (see *Keystone Tombstones – Susquehanna Valley Region,* p. 85) who recognized the voter appeal of his war record. He ran successfully for state auditor General in 1866 and again in 1869.

In 1872 he was Cameron's personal choice to succeed another Civil War hero John Geary (*see Keystone Tombstones – Susquehanna Valley Region,* p. 91) as governor and he won and served two terms until 1879. In contrast to Governor Geary, Hartranft had no objection to the expanding influence of the Pennsylvania Railroad and other industrial interests.

During his administration the revision of the Commonwealth's Constitution was completed and ratified as the Constitution of 1873. He played an important role in celebrating our nation's centennial in 1876 that was centered in Philadelphia's Fairmount Park. At the Republican National Convention in June 1876 he was a contender for the presidential nomination that eventually went to Rutherford

B. Hayes of Ohio. Hartranft's second term was marred by economic depression, unemploy-ment, strikes and civil unrest. He permitted the execution of twenty one coal miners convicted of various crimes in the coal region in North East Pennsylvania. Called the Molly Maguires, these men were leaders of labor unrest in the coal region. Ten of them were hanged in one day in Pottsville and Mauch Chunk on June 21, 1877 (see page 246) The "King of the Mollies," Jack Kehoe, was also executed on December 18, 1878 after another extremely controversial prosecution in which coal company employees conducted the investig-ation, arrested Kehoe and then prosecuted him. Hartranft reportedly hesitated to implement the sentence explaining that he thought Kehoe should be punished but not hanged. Yet he waited until after the fall election and then signed a death warrant with one month left in his term. In July 1877 a series of riots broke out triggered by wage cuts for railroad workers. The worst riots were in Pittsburgh and Hartranft sent state militia and National Guard troops to maintain order. When outraged protest-ers cornered troops in a Pennsylvania Railroad round-house the soldiers opened fire, killing

Hartranft's obelisk

Hartranft's grave

twenty and wounding many more. In response, furious workers destroyed tracks, roundhouses, engines and other railroad property. Protests spread to Altoona and Reading where National Guard troops killed another ten people. As the violence spread to Philadelphia, Hartranft asked for (and received) federal troops from President Hayes, making him the first governor in U.S. history to request federal troops to put down a labor uprising.

In 1877, when 78-year-old Simon Cameron resigned his Senate seat, Hartranft appointed Donald Cameron—the Senator's son—to replace him. After leaving office, Hartranft returned to his home in Montgomery County and accepted the position of Postmaster. He later was appointed Collector of the Philadelphia Port.

John Hartranft died in Norristown on October 17, 1889. He is buried in a large grave marked by a large obelisk in Montgomery Cemetery, near Norristown. The Pennsylvania National Guard provided the obelisk for his grave. Ten years after his death, a heroic bronze, mounted statue of him was dedicated on the grounds of the Pennsylvania State Capitol in Harrisburg.

Marble monuments at Petersburg and Vicksburg honor his Civil War service. Elementary schools in Norristown and Philadelphia are named after the governor, as is a residence hall at Penn State University. There are streets named after him in South Philadelphia and in the Brookline section of Pittsburgh, and three avenues in Montgomery County are named in his honor. His Medal of Honor is commemorated by a stone bearing his name in Soldiers' and Sailors' Grove behind the State Capitol Building in Harrisburg.

General Winfield Scott Hancock

If You Go:

There are a number of interesting Civil War graves in Montgomery Cemetery. There are Generals Winfield Scott Hancock (see page 133) and Samuel Kosciuszko Zook (p. 182). Also buried there is General Matthew McClennan who led his troops in battles in the Richmond Campaign and Edwin Schall who served as Lt. Colonel of the 51st Pennsylvania and was killed at the Battle of Cold Harbor in June 1864.

Congressional Medal of Honor recipient Hillary Beyer is buried in a neighboring cemetery, and Brother Paul's is a great place to eat nearby.

"That Man Haupt ..."

HERMAN HAUPT

County: Montgomery
Town: Bala Cynwyd
Cemetery: West Laurel Hill
Address: 227 Belmont Avenue

"That man Haupt has built a bridge four hundred feet long and one hundred feet high, across Potomac Creek, on which loaded trains are passing every hour, and upon my word, gentlemen, there is nothing in it but cornstalks and beanpoles."
—*Abraham Lincoln, discussing Haupt's timely repairs to the Potomac Creek Bridge after the Battle of Fredericksburg, May 28, 1862.*

Herman Haupt was born in Philadephia, Pennsylvania on March 26, 1817. He was the son of Jacob Haupt, a merchant by trade, and Anna Margaretta Wiall Haupt. His father died when Herman was only 12 years old, leaving widow Anna to support her three sons and two daughters.

A child engineering prodigy, he was appointed to the United States Military Academy at only 14, and graduated at the age of 18 with the 1835 Class (ranked 35th out of 56). Upon graduation, he was commissioned a second lieutenant in the 3rd U.S. Infantry, but resigned his commission a couple of months later to become a civil engineer. In 1838, he married Ann Cecelia Keller in Gettysburg, Pennsylvania, with whom he had seven sons and four daughters.

Prior to the Civil War, Haupt worked primarily in the railroad industry as an engineer designing bridges and tunnels. He patented a bridge construction technique known as the "Haupt Truss." For most of the 1840's, he was a professor of mathematics and engineering at Pennsylvania (now Gettysburg) College, before returning to the railroad industry.

Early in 1862, the second year of the Civil War, Secretary of War Edwin M. Stanton appointed Haupt chief of all U.S. military railroads and transportation, with the rank of colonel, serving under General Irvin McDowell, who was

Herman Haupt

responsible for the defense of Washington, D.C. Haupt repaired damaged rail lines, built bridges and improved telegraph communications.

On September 5, 1862, Haupt was promoted to brigadier general of volunteers. He refused the appointment, but was willing to serve without rank or pay. He did not enjoy the protocols of military service and wanted the freedom to continue working in private business. The offer

HAUPT TRUSS BRIDGE

C. 1854

PENNSYLVANIA RAILROAD

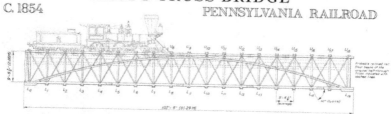

was officially rescinded one year later, in September of 1863, at which time he left the military.

However, during his year of service, he made an enormous impact on the Union war effort, being one of the few experts in the nation at that early time who understood the functioning of railroads and their value to the military. He assisted the Union Army of Virginia and the Army of the Potomac in the Northern Virginia Campaign, the Maryland Campaign, and was particularly effective in supporting the Gettysburg Campaign, conducted in an area he knew well from his youth. His hastily organized trains kept the Union Army well supplied, and he organized the returning trains to carry thousands of Union wounded to hospitals.

Haupt was known to show up at the war front or the White House at key points in the war — like at George Mc-Clellan's headquarters just after the Second Battle of Bull Run, and at Joseph Hooker's headquarters before Lee's invasion of Maryland. Haupt also visited Fredericksburg shortly after the battle there in December 1862. According to Haupt biographer James A. Ward, "That evening Haupt and Congressman John Covode called on Lincoln in Washington to present firsthand reports of the battle. Haupt's account so upset the president that the three men walked at once to Halleck's house to confer on future action."

While on his way to Gettysburg, during a stop in Harrisburg, Haupt observed to a subordinate about the coming conflict:

"We are in the most critical condition we have been in since the war commenced, and nothing but the interposition of Providence can save us. If the army is destroyed, no new force can be collected in time to make effectual resistance. Washington, Baltimore, Philadelphia and New York will fall, and the enemy can then, as masters of the situation, dictate their own terms."

Haupt was very disappointed with General Meade's unwillingness to pursue Lee's army after Gettysburg. Said Haupt on July 5, 1863, to Meade, who was sure the Confederates' retreat would be slowed by the lack of bridges:

"Do not place confidence in that. I have men in my Construction Corps who could construct bridges in forty-eight hours sufficient to pass that army, if they have no other material than such as they could gather from old buildings or from the woods, and it is not safe to assume that the enemy cannot do what we can."

After this meeting, around midnight, Haupt jumped on a locomotive and rushed to Washington. Before breakfast, he showed up at President Lincoln's office. According to historian Fletcher Pratt:

"On July 6 came Haupt in person to the White House, direct from the front, and officers with eyewitness accounts of the battle, including General Daniel Sickles, who had had a leg shot off on the second day. Haupt was no more comforting than Meade's order; he had seen the General the day before to tell him that the new railhead and telegraph had been carried through Hanover Junction to Gettysburg (which surprised Meade very much), and to plead with him to follow the enemy hard. Meade replied that his men needed rest; Haupt told him they could not be as tired as the Confederates: 'You must pursue Lee and crush him. His ammunition and stores must be exhausted, and his supply trains can be easily cut off. He is in desperate straits, like a rat in a trap, and you can whip and capture him'."

Upon hearing this report, Lincoln asked of Stanton, "What shall we do with your man, Meade, Mr. Secretary?"

"Tell him," said Stanton to Haupt, "Lee is trapped and must be taken."

Excavating for "Y" at Devereux Station, Orange & Alexandria Railroad. The locomotive, "General Haupt" is being used for work detail. Standing on the bank is USMRR Supt. for the O & A railroad, John Henry Devereux, who reported to General Haupt.

Then Stanton turned to Lincoln and added, "He can be removed as easily as he was appointed, if he makes no proper effort to end this war now, while he has Lee in a trap."

Haupt then hastened back to Gettysburg by train, expecting the orders from Washington would be obeyed. He offered his help, but Meade did nothing, thereby allowing Lee to escape. This greatly disappointed Lincoln, Stanton and Halleck, and frustrated Haupt. If Meade had acted, or if anyone had thought to place Haupt in command on Sunday, July 5, 1863, Lee would doubtless have been captured and the war ended.

Said Robert Lincoln, the President's son, about one of his visits to the White House in mid-July, 1863:

"Entering my father's room right after the battle of Gettysburg, I found him in tears with his head bowed upon his arms resting on the table at which he sat. 'Why, what is

USMRR engine General Haupt

the matter, father?' I asked. For a brief interval he remained silent, then raised his head, and the explanation of his grief was forthcoming. 'My boy,' he said, 'when I heard that the bridge at Williamsport had been swept away, I sent for General Haupt and asked him how soon he could replace the same. He replied, 'If I were uninterrupted I could build a bridge with the material there within twenty-four hours, and Mr. President, General Lee has engineers as skillful as I am.' Upon hearing this I at once wrote Meade to attack without delay, and if successful to destroy my letter, but in case of failure to preserve it for his vindication. I have just learned that at a council of war of Meade and his generals, it has been determined not to pursue Lee, and now the opportune chance of ending this bitter struggle is lost."

After his war service, Haupt returned to the railroad business. He and his wife purchased a small resort hotel at Mountain Lake in Giles County, Virginia. He invented a prize-winning drilling machine and was the first to prove the practicability of transporting oil in pipes. Haupt became wealthy from his investments in railroads, mining, and real estate, but he eventually lost most of his fortune due to political complications involving the completion of the Hoosac Tunnel in Massachusetts.

Herman Haupt died of a heart attack at age 88, on December 14, 1905, in Jersey City, New Jersey. He was stricken while traveling by train on a journey from New York to Philadelphia. He is buried in West Laurel Hill Cemetery in Bala Cynwyd, Pennsylvania. He outlived every one of his West Point classmates.

If You Go:
West Laurel Hill Cemetery is a large, beautiful cemetery filled with history and interesting stories. It is home to the graves of eight Civil War Medal of Honor recipients, including: George Stockman; Elwood Williams; Wallace Johnson; Richard Binder; Jacob Orth; Joseph Corson; Charles Betts; and Moses Veale.

Also buried at West Laurel Hill Cemetery is Francis Adams Donaldson, whose letters and correspondence during the war to his family were published in the book *Inside the Army of the Potomac: The Wartime Letters of Captain Francis Adams Donaldson.*

Haupt's grave

"Life Is a Song Worth Singing"

TEDDY PENDERGRASS

County: Montgomery
Town: Bala Cynwyd
Cemetery: West Laurel Hill
Address: 215 Belmont Avenue

Theodore DeReese Pendergrass was a major figure in the American soul and rhythm and blues genres as both a signer and a songwriter during the 1970's and 80's. He first rose to fame as the lead singer of the group "Harold Melvin and the Blue Notes" in the 70's before having a successful solo career. Even after he was severely injured in an auto accident, he fought through arduous physical rehabilitation to be able to continue to sing and continue his magnificent career.

Teddy Pendergrass was born in Philadelphia's Thomas Jefferson Hospital on March 26, 1950. His parents Ida and Jesse Pendergrass were both children of South Carolina sharecroppers. Ida's multiple miscarriages before Teddy was born prompted her to name him Theodore, which means "God's Gift."

Jesse Pendergrass left the family when Teddy was a small child and according to newspaper accounts, Teddy did not see his biological father again until 1961, one year before Jesse was murdered by a neighborhood friend over a gambling debt.

Teddy's early years were filled with love and affection from his mother and several aunts. He grew up in Philadelphia and sang often at church. When he was 10 years old, he was ordained as a youth minister. His singing in the McIntyre Elementary School choir and The All-City Stetson Junior High School choir was where he discovered his ability and discovered his taste for singing in front of large audiences.

He attended Thomas Edison High School, and when he was 15 years old his mother gave him a set of drums, which he taught himself how to play. He dropped out of high school in 11th grade to pursue a career as a musician. He worked with a number of R&B and doo-wop

Teddy Pendergrass album cover

groups and in 1968 took a job as the drummer for a group called "The Cadillacs." The Cadillacs, along with Harold Melvin and the Blue Notes, were the best known R&B bands in Philadelphia. In 1970, the two groups merged and several of the Cadillacs (including Pendergrass) joined the Blue Notes. Soon after, Harold Melvin asked Teddy to become the lead singer and from there the Blue Notes took off.

They landed a recording deal with Philadelphia International Records, and their first single—"I Miss You"—became an instant hit on the Pop and R&B charts. The song was written for the Dells, but they passed on it. The group's follow-up single was intended for fellow Philadelphian Patti LaBelle, but her group "LaBelle" could not get their schedule together, and it went to Harold Melvin and the Blue Notes. The song—"If You Don't Know Me By Now"— brought the group to the mainstream. It reached No. 3 on the Pop charts and No. 1 on the Soul chart.

A series of hits followed, such as: "Wake Up Everybody;" "Bad Luck;" "To Be True;" and "The Love I Lost." Meanwhile, however, trouble was developing behind the scenes between Pendergrass and Melvin. In 1976, they parted company. For a while, there were two groups called the Blue Notes, one led by Pendergrass and the other by Melvin.

The confusion ended in 1977 when Pendergrass official- ly went solo with the release of his first album, "Teddy Pen- dergrass." It sold more than a million copies and generated several No. 1 hits. The concerts that supported the album were a smash and showed him as a powerful force as a solo artist. More success followed. Between 1977 and 1981, Pendergrass had five consecutive platinum albums and a number of national awards such as the Billboard New Artist Award (1977), two Grammy nominations, and an American Music Award.

Pendergrass' manager noticed at his sold-out solo per- formances that a huge portion of his audiences were wom- en. That led to a series of "women-only" concerts. At some of these concerts, audience members were given chocolate teddy bear-shaped lollipops to lick. Around that time, co- median Eddie Murphy made several humorous observa- tions about Pendergrass in his landmark HBO special "Delirious." He began by describing Pendergrass as a "dude with a masculine voice," whose singing style and lyrics such as "You got, you got, YOU GOT WHAT I NEED!!" would lead to women throwing their panties on stage.

By early 1982, Pendergrass was the leading R&B male artist of his day. But on March 18th of that year, Pender- grass was involved in an auto accident in Philadelphia. He lost control of his car, hit a guardrail, crossed the opposite traffic lane and hit two trees. He and his passenger, a friend, Tenika Watson, were trapped in the wreckage for 45 min- utes. Watson was unhurt, but Pendergrass suffered a spinal cord injury, leaving him paralyzed from the chest down.

In 1984, he decided to restart his career from a wheel- chair after arduous physical and psychotherapy as well as

This beautiful monument marks the final resting place of the great soul and blues singer Teddy Pendergrass (plus a bonus reflection of Joe Farrell).

several surgeries. His contract with Philadelphia International had run out, and he struggled to find a recording deal. He got a deal with Asylum Records and released his ninth studio album "Love Language," which included a pop ballad called "Hold Me" featuring a then-unknown Whitney Houston. The album did well, peaking at No. 38 on Billboard.

In July 1985, Teddy Pendergrass made an emotional return to the concert stage for the first time since the accident at the historic Live Aid concert in Philadelphia. In front of a live audience of 100,000 and an estimated viewing audience of 1.5 billion people, Pendergrass tearfully thanked fans for all the well-wishes, support and prayers, and performed the song "Reach Out and Touch."

In 1987, Pendergrass married Karen Smith, his long-time girlfriend. They divorced in 2003. In 1988, his album entitled "Joy" brought him a Grammy nomination and two hit singles. He continued to record and release albums throughout the 80's and 90's but never regained the prestige and success he once enjoyed.

In 1998, Pendergrass published his autobiography, *Truly Blessed*, which got a good review from *The New York Times*' Eric Nash, who wrote: "The book is both a richly textured history of Pendergrass' musical roots in the creative explosion of 70's soul that shaped his gruff, sexy style, and an unflinching look at what it is like to be disabled."

In 2006, Pendergrass announced his retirement from the music business and met Joan Williams whom he married in 2008. The following year, he did appear and sing at a concert in his honor, held at the Kimmel Center in Philadelphia. The show was called "Teddy 25: A Celebration of Life, Hope and Possibilities." It marked the 25th anniversary of his accident and was a star-studded fundraiser for the Teddy Pendergrass Alliance, a non-profit organization which has raised awareness of quality-of-life issues for people with spinal cord injuries.

Pendergrass was diagnosed with colon cancer in 2009 and died of complications after surgery on January 13, 2010, in Bryn Mawr Hospital in suburban Philadelphia. He is buried in a beautiful grave in West Laurel Hill Cemetery in Bala Cynwyd, Montgomery County.

If You Go:
West Laurel Hill Cemetery is a large, beautiful cemetery containing many graves of interesting and historical people, two of whom are featured in chapters in this Volume:

Television broadcast journalist and "The Today Show" host Dave Garroway (1913-1982) – see page 128; and

Brilliant saxophonist Grover Washington, Jr. (1943-1999) – see page 172.

Two famous psychologists are also buried in West Laurel Hill:

Almost any Introduction to Psychology book will contain a reference to the work of *Frederick Winslow Taylor (1856-1915)*, who is regarded as the father of scientific management; and

Helen Bradford Thompson Woolley (1874-1947), who was a leading force in establishing child development studies in the United States.

Two famous sculptors (father and son) are also buried in West Laurel Hill:

Alexander Milne Calder (1846-1923), who is best known for the architectural sculpture of Philadelphia City Hall; and

Alexander's son, *A. Stirling Calder (1870-1945),* who is best known for the sculpture referred to as *George Washington as President, Accompanied by Wisdom*

Frederick Winslow Taylor

and Justice (which appears on the Washington Square Arch in New York City), and also for the Swann Memorial Fountain sculpture in Philadelphia, which is in the center of Logan Circle.

Other notable graves are those of:

Anna Jarvis (1864-1948), the founder of the Mother's Day holiday;

Hyman Aaron "Hy" Lit (1934-2007), the famous disc jockey and pioneer of rock-and-roll radio; and

Henry Williams (1834-1917), a rare, peacetime Medal of Honor recipient, who was given the award for his valiant repair work during a storm that saved the *USS Constitution* in 1879.

"The Single Bullet Theory Senator"
ARLEN SPECTER

County: Montgomery
Town: Huntingdon Valley
Cemetery: Shalom memorial Park
Address: 101 Byberry Road

He was a district attorney for the city of Philadelphia. As a staff member for the Warren Commission he is largely credited with the development of the controversial single bullet theory that allowed the Commission to conclude that Lee Harvey Oswald assassinated President John F. Kennedy and that he acted alone. He represented Pennsylvania in the United States Senate for 30 years. His name was Arlen Specter.

Specter was born on February 12, 1930, in Wichita, Kansas. His parents, Harry Specter and Lillie Shanin, who were Jewish, had come to the United States from Russia, and Arlen was their youngest child. Specter's father served the United States during World War 1, and after the war he worked as a fruit peddler, a tailor and as a junkyard owner.

Specter's family moved from Wichita to Russell, Kansas where Specter graduated from Russell High School in 1947. He first attended college at the University of Oklahoma before transferring to the University of Pennsylvania. His major was international relations, and he graduated in 1951. After graduation he enlisted in the United States Air Force where he served from 1951 to 1953. It was in 1953 that he married Joan Levy. He then entered Yale University where he studied law and graduated in 1956. That same year Specter was admitted to the Pennsylvania Bar. During this time, Specter's family had moved from Kansas to Philadelphia. Specter said they made the move because his sister Shirley had reached marriageable age, and there were no other Jews in Russell.

Specter then opened the law practice of "Specter and Katz" (Marvin Katz would go on to be a Federal District Court judge in Philadelphia). In 1959 Specter went to work in the Philadelphia District Attorney's office as an assistant

Arlen Specter

district attorney. He would serve in that position until 1964.

In 1964 Specter became an assistant counsel for the Warren Commission which had been established to investigate the assassination of President Kennedy. The investigation was divided into six different areas and Specter was assigned to area 1 which was "The Basic Facts of the Assassination." This area would determine the number and source of the shots. Francis Adams and Specter were placed in charge of this area. When Adams resigned in March of 1964, Specter went on to be the primary manager of this critical area. By the time Specter was finished with this job, he would have done something for which he will always be remembered, namely, the development of the single bullet theory.

Soon after it was created, the Warren Commission received a report from the FBI that indicated three shots had been fired at the Kennedy motorcade. The report went on to state that Kennedy had been hit in the back by the first shot, that Texas Governor John Connally seated in front of the president was struck by the second bullet and that the third shot hit President Kennedy in the head killing him. The FBI also concluded that the three shots originated from the 6Th floor window of a building known as the Texas School Book Depository and that they had been fired by an employee there named Lee Harvey Oswald.

That was all well and good until it was discovered that a spectator in Dealey Plaza on that fateful day by the name of James Tague had been stuck by a piece of cement that came from a nearby curb after it had been hit by a bullet. Since a film of the assassination known as the Zapruder film existed, the FBI was able to determine the maximum amount of time in which the three shots could have been fired from Oswald's rifle. When the Tague shot was discovered, it was obvious that Oswald could not have fired four shots in the time allowed. Therefore to admit the existence of a fourth shot meant there had to be another shooter besides Oswald present that day in Dallas.

This is where Specter came to the rescue. He was the key figure in developing the theory that the first shot entered Kennedy in the back exited his throat and then struck Connally causing all of his wounds. So now the finding was that the first bullet wounded both Kennedy and Connally, that the second missed and hit the curb wounding Tague and the third killed Kennedy. This explanation has become known in history as the single bullet theory. Despite the fact that at least two members of the Commission never accepted the theory it was adopted and presented as what had occurred in their report to President Johnson.

When the Commission's report was made public it didn't take critics long to attack the single bullet theory. They were aided by the fact that the bullet had been found on a stretcher in Parkland hospital. They pointed out that the bullet had been fired from a high powered rifle and that if it hit the two men it caused seven wounds including shattering a rib and a wrist bone, yet it was discovered in nearly pristine condition. The critics dubbed it the "magic bullet."

Arguments over Specter's theory continue to the present day over fifty years since the assassination. New books come out on a consistent basis taking one side or the other. Specter's name will forever be associated with the theory. Specter even made it into the Oliver Stone movie "JFK." In a courtroom scene Kevin Costner, playing New Orleans District Attorney Jim Garrison, delivers a speech where he says,

"So a single bullet remained to account for all seven wounds in Kennedy and Connally. But rather than admit to a conspiracy or investigate further, the Commissioners chose to endorse the theory put forth by an ambitious junior counselor, Arlen Specter. One of the grossest lies ever forced on the American people, we've come to know it as the 'magic bullet' theory."

With his work for the Commission completed Specter, who was a registered Democrat, ran for Philadelphia District Attorney as a Republican in 1965. He beat James Crumlish, the man he used to work for and who during the campaign referred to him as "Benedict Arlen.' He would serve as Philadelphia District Attorney until 1975 when he resumed his law practice.

In 1976 Specter entered the Republican primary, along with five other candidates, in an attempt to secure the nomination to run for the United States Senate. He finished second losing to John Heinz who went on to win the general election. In 1978 he ran for the office of Governor of Pennsylvania but was defeated in the Republican primary by Dick Thornburgh. In 1980 Specter ran yet again for a seat in the United States Senate, and this time he was successful. He took office in 1981. It was a seat he would hold for thirty years.

As a Senator he took an active interest in foreign affairs and met with many foreign leaders. He was a strong supporter of appropriations used to fight the global AIDS epidemic. He also backed free trade agreements between the United States and under-developed countries. He also worked with local leaders from his state to help them secure federal aid and grants. During his time in office Specter brought more financial resources to Pennsylvania than any other politician. Still, as a Senator, he is probably best remembered for the work he did on the Senate Judiciary Committee which he chaired from 2005 to 2007.

As a member of the Judiciary Committee, Specter participated in the confirmation hearings of 14 Supreme Court nominees. His actions with regard to two of these nominees stand out. Of course, we're talking about Robert Bork and Clarence Thomas.

On July 1, 1987, President Ronald Reagan nominated Robert Bork to fill a vacancy on the Supreme Court. Within 45 minutes of the nomination Senator Ted Kennedy took the Senate floor and declared,

"Robert Bork's America is a land in which women would be forced into back-alley abortions, blacks would sit at segregated lunch counters, rogue police could break down citizens doors in midnight raids, schoolchildren could not be taught about evolution, writers and artists could be censored at the whim of the government and the doors of the federal courts would be shut on the fingers of millions of citizens."

It was clear that there was going to be a real fight over this nomination. Specter became one of the leaders in the fight against the Senate confirmation of Bork. On October 6, 1987, the Judiciary Committee voted 9 to 5 to send Bork's nomination to the Senate floor with an unfavorable recommendation. Specter was the only Republican on the committee voting with the majority. On October 23, 1987, the Senate rejected Bork's nomination by a vote of 58 to 42. Conservative Republicans would never forgive Specter for his position relative to Bork's nomination.

After his defeat, Bork claimed that Specter came into the hearings with his mind made up. Specter denied the charge saying he spent two weeks reading all of Bork's speeches and his opinions. As a matter of fact Specter said, "I knew more about his record than he did."

On July 1, 1991, President George Bush nominated Clarence Thomas to fill a vacancy on the Supreme Court. His confirmation hearings before the Judiciary Committee were televised and captured the attention of the nation. A woman, named Anita Hill, testified that when she worked for Thomas at the Department of Education he repeatedly talked about sex and pornographic films. Specter was Hill's harshest questioner and many felt that his approach inflamed racial and gender divisions. Thomas was eventually confirmed by a vote of 52 to 48 with Specter voting yes. Specter would later say that his aggressive questioning almost cost him his Senate seat in the election of 1992.

In that election a political novice a woman by the name of Lynn Yeakel entered the Democrat primary seeking the party's nomination to run against Specter. She was given little chance. She ignored her primary opponents and decided to run against Specter from the start. She said that Specter's questioning of Anita Hill showed an absolute disrespect for women. Her strategy worked, and she came from nowhere to win the primary. In the general election, which was bitterly contested, Specter won by just over two percentage points.

In June of 1993, Specter faced the first of several serious health problems he would battle late in his life. He had a brain tumor removed at the University of Pennsylvania Hospital in Philadelphia. On that same day, Pennsylvania's Governor Bob Casey (see *Keystone Tombstones – Anthracite Region*, p. 23) underwent a double-organ transplant receiving a new heart and liver at the University of Pittsburgh Medical Center. Specter had tumors removed again in 1996, and then in 1998 he underwent open heart surgery.

As evidenced by his vote not to confirm Robert Bork, Specter was not afraid to go against the wishes of the Republican Party. In 1998 and 1999, Specter criticized his party for impeaching President Bill Clinton. When his turn came to vote on impeaching the President, Specter cited Scots law and rendered a verdict of not proven. The Senate recorded his vote as not guilty. He voted in favor of the Iraq war and was a strong supporter of embryonic stem cell research.

Despite his years of service Specter, as the Republican Party became more conservative, was viewed as a RINO meaning a Republican in name only. In 2004, a conservative Pennsylvania Congressman named Pat Toomey challenged Specter in the Republican primary. Toomey had strong conservative support and financial backing. Specter won the primary by just 1.6 percent.

After that election, Specter once again angered conservative Republicans when he said,

"When you talk about judges who would change the right of a woman to choose, overturn Roe v. Wade, I think confirmation is unlikely. The president is well aware of what happened, when a number of his nominees were sent up, with the filibuster...And I would expect the president to be mindful of the considerations I am mentioning."

Conservative groups interpreted this as a warning and some even a threat to President Bush.

Specter even got involved in a Super Bowl controversy. During the 2007-2008 NFL season, Specter wrote to the league's commissioner Roger Goodell. Specter was interested in the destruction of the New England Patriots Spygate tapes, and he questioned whether the tapes were tied to

Arlen Specter reproducing the assumed alignment of the single-bullet theory.

This is the grave of the man who championed the single bullet theory while a member of the Warren Commission.

the Patriots Super Bowl victory over the Philadelphia Eagles. Goodell responded that the tapes had been destroyed because they confirmed what he already knew. Specter then made a public statement calling for the NFL to initiate a Mitchell type investigation. Specter stated, "I have been careful not to call for a Congressional hearing because I believe the NFL should step forward and embrace an independent inquiry and Congress is extraordinarily busy on other matters. If the NFL continues to leave a vacuum, Congress may be tempted to fill it."

In March of 2009, one year before he would again seek reelection, the political columnist John Baer suggested that it was time for Specter to "come home" to the Democratic Party. Specter stated that he had no intention of doing so. Pat Toomey was likely to challenge him in the

Republican primary again, and polls showed him beating Specter easily. Specter, seeing the writing on the wall, announced he was switching parties in April of 2009. The switch provided Democrats with a sixty seat filibuster proof majority in the Senate.

Becoming a Democrat did not save Specter from a primary challenge in 2010. A Congressman from suburban Philadelphia named Joe Sestak decided to run against Specter. Few gave Sestak any chance of beating Specter, but he ran an aggressive and tireless campaign. When the votes were counted, Sestak won the primary taking 53.9 percent of the vote. Sestak went on to lose the general election to Toomey.

After leaving the Senate, Specter became an adjunct professor at the University of Pennsylvania Law School. He taught a course on the relationship between Congress and the Supreme Court. The "National Jurist" named him as one of the 23 professors to take before you die.

In 2005, Specter announced that he had been diagnosed with an advanced form of Hodgkin's lymphoma, a type of cancer. In 2012 he was hospitalized, and it was announced that he was battling cancer. After he was released from the hospital, he returned home where he died on October 14, 2012. He was 82 years old. President Obama ordered United States flags to be lowered to half staff upon hearing of Specter's death.

If You Go:
The authors highly recommend a stop at Miller's Ale House located at 2300 Easton Road in Willow Grove. Miller's features a wide variety of draft beers and a menu that appeals to all tastes. In addition the servers are friendly and eager to meet your every need.

"The Smooth Jazzman"

Grover Washington Jr.

County: Montgomery
Town: Bala Cynwyd
Cemetery: West Laurel Hill
Address: 215 Belmont Avenue

He grew up surrounded by music. He would become one of the most popular soul and jazz saxophonist of all time. He would write much of his own material and later be recognized as an arranger and a producer. He is widely considered to be one of the founders of the smooth jazz genre. While some jazz critics found his music to be simplistic, he became one of the most commercially successful saxophonists in history. His name was Grover Washington Jr.

Washington was born in Buffalo, New York on December 12, 1943. His father played the saxophone and was a collector of jazz records. His mother was in the church choir. He grew up listening to his father's records. When he was ten years old his dad gave him a saxophone. He would practice on his own and by the time he was twelve he was playing in clubs.

As he grew older Washington played with a group from the Midwest who went by the clever name The Four Clefts. His next band was called the Mark III Trio. He was then drafted into the U. S. Army. It was in the army that he met a drummer from New York by the name of Billy Cobham. Cobham was an established New York musician and he introduced Washington to other musicians from the big apple. After he was discharged Washington exhibited his talents in New York before heading to Philadelphia in 1967 where he became closely identified with that city. Leon Spencer released two albums in the early 70's and Washington appeared on both.

Then Washington caught a break when another sax musician was unable to make a recording date. Washington stepped in and played impressively. This led to Washington's first solo album "Inner City Blues." The record showcased his talent with the soprano, alto, tenor and baritone saxophones. He was becoming known as an up and coming jazz artist.

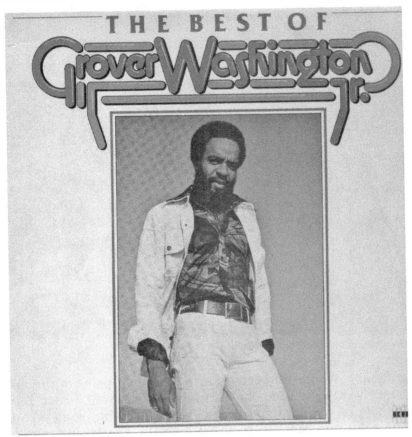

A Grover Washington Jr. album cover

In the early 70's he released three albums that made him a force in the world of jazz and soul music. In 1974 he released his fourth album "Mister Magic" and it became a major commercial success. The record made it to number 10 on the Billboard charts and the title track made it to number 16 on the R&B singles chart. His next album "Feels So Good" also made it to number 10 on Billboard.

In the late 70's Washington signed with Elektra Records which was part of the Warner Music Group. In 1980 he released "Winelight" the record that many believe to represent his best effort. Washington loved basketball and he was a big fan of the Philadelphia 76ers which led to him dedicating the second track on the record "Let It Flow" to Julius Erving. He also occasionally played the national

Grave site of the noted smooth jazz man.

anthem prior to the 76ers games. The high point of the album "Winelight" was his work with the soul artist Bill Withers on the song "Just The Two of Us." That song was a major hit and reached number 2 on the charts and won a Grammy in 1982 for Best R&B Song, it was also a Song of the Year nominee. The album which went platinum won the Grammy for Best Jazz Fusion Performance. "Winelight" was also nominated for record of the year.

In the 1980's Washington moved toward the jazz mainstream. Among the artists he worked with was Herbie Hancock. He also released the first album of music from the "Cosby Show." During a 1989 interview Washington said, "There's a record player playing in here all the time." At the time he was pointing at his head. "I'm listening to everything. The screech of brakes. Three or four people walking and you can hear their heels clicking. Railroad tracks."

In 1996, he played at President Clinton's 50th birthday celebration at Radio City Music Hall. Clinton later said, "Grover Washington was as versatile as any jazz musician in America moving with ease and fluency from vintage jazz to funk, and from gospel to blues to pop." Washington once said, "I want to be able to visit any genre and converse there with my horn." Noting that quote Clinton added, "Grover Washington did exactly that, and beautifully."

On December 17, 1999, Washington performed four songs for the "Saturday Early Show" on CBS. While waiting in the green room he collapsed and was rushed to a local New York hospital where he died that evening. It was determined that he had suffered a massive heart attack. He was laid to rest in West Laurel Hill Cemetery. He was 56 years old.

If You Go:

See the "If You Go" section of Teddy Pendergrass on page 157.

"The Father of Professional Baseball"
HARRY WRIGHT

County: Montgomery
Town: Bala Cynwyd
Cemetery: West Laurel Hill
Address: 227 Belmont Avenue

William Henry ("Harry") Wright was one of the most important names in 19th century baseball. Although a good player in his day, when he was elected to the Baseball Hall of Fame in 1953 it was largely for his contributions as a baseball pioneer and innovator. He assembled, managed and played center field for baseball's first fully-professional team, the 1869 Cincinnati Red Stockings. Throughout his career, he would introduce many innovations, including the introduction of spring training, doubleheaders, pre-game batting practice, the double steal, fielders backing up one another, and the "shift" (moving the defensive positioning of players on the field to meet hitters' tendencies). His most important contribution, however, was his introduction of professionalism to the game. Wright was the first to make baseball into a business by paying his players up to seven times the pay of the average working man.

Wright was born in 1835 in Sheffield, England. He was the eldest of five children and the son of a professional cricket player. His family came to America in 1836 based on the promise of a spot on the St. George Dragonslayers cricket team for his father, Samuel Wright Sr., and a job as groundskeeper at the St. George's Cricket Club in New York.

Harry dropped out of school at 14 to apprentice as a jeweler at Tiffany's and the next year joined the Dragonslayers, on which his father was the star and idol of cricket circles. Before the Civil War, baseball competed for public interest with cricket and regional variants of baseball, notably "town ball" in Philadelphia and the "Massachusetts Game" played in New England. As late as 1855, the New York press was devoting more space to coverage of cricket than to baseball. In 1857, sixteen New York-area clubs formed the National Association of Base Ball Players

1874 photo of Harry Wright.

(NABBP), the first organization to govern the sport and to establish a championship.

Although Wright was receiving money for his cricket performances, when he discovered baseball, he quickly adapted to it and grew to love it. He joined the New York Knickerbockers Base Ball Club. In 1858, he participated in the first games of baseball to charge admission. He played for the All-Stars of New York against the All-Stars of Brooklyn at the Fashion Race Course in Corona (Queens Co.), New York.

The Civil War so decimated the Knickerbockers that Wright switched to the New York Gothams in 1864. In 1865, he gave up baseball and decided to start over as an instructor at the Union Cricket Club in Cincinnati. When the war ended and baseball boomed, he was approached to join the Cincinnati baseball club and started a mass exodus of cricket players to baseball. He became a pitcher for the Red Stockings in 1867 on a strong team that lost only to the Washington Nationals (for whom his brother, George, played shortstop).

In 1869, the NABBP permitted professionalism, and the Red Stockings decided they would field an openly all-professional team. Wright was designated as scout and general manager. He signed his brother George – who at the time was considered by many to be the best player in baseball – to a contract that paid $1,400 for nine months, the highest on the team. He instituted such methods as hand signals, calling balls in the air, having one fielder back up another, platooning, and the hit-and-run.

The success of Wright's management was apparent, and the Red Stockings dominated. They toured the continent and went undefeated. In fact, in 1869 and 1870, the team won 130 consecutive games before losing a violently disputed extra-inning contest to the Brooklyn Atlantics. The winning was not enough, however, to overcome the toll that touring took on the Red Stockings' home fan base. Cincinnati dropped professional baseball, and the NABBP passed from the scene.

Harry moved on to help form the National Association, the first professional league. Taking the reins of the Boston entry, which at the time also used the moniker "Red Stockings," his team lost the 1871 pennant to Philadelphia but then proceeded to sweep four straight pennants before the league folded in 1875 due to competitive imbalance, player drunkenness and rumors of fixed games.

In 1876, the Boston club joined the new National League. They became the "Red Caps" in deference to the resurrected Cincinnati Red Stockings. Although Harry was nearly done as a player, he succeeded in managing Boston to two more pennants in 1877 and 1878.

This impressive tombstone honors the "Father of Baseball" Harry Wright.

He moved on to Providence in 1882 to manage the Providence Grays. It was there he instituted the concept of a farm system. Wright thought it would be beneficial to assemble a club of amateurs to play on the Providence grounds while the first team was on the road. He figured to use the second team as a breeding ground for talent that could be used as replacements in case of injury or poor play.

In 1884, Wright was hired to manage the Philadelphia Quakers, who had finished 17-81 the previous year. He improved the team but never won a pennant in the 10 years he managed there. In 1886, they went 71-43. While managing the Quakers, Wright instituted what we now know as "spring training." It was then referred to as a "southern trip." He figured such a warm-up would give his team an advantage over other teams once the actual regular season began. By 1890, every club went south in the spring.

During Wright's tenure in Philadelphia, he often clashed with management. After the 1893 season, they chose not to renew Wright's contract—a move loudly protested by the Philadelphia press and fans.

In 23 seasons of managing in the National Association and National League, Wright's teams won six league championships and finished second three times.

Wright died on October 3, 1895, after contracting a serious illness in his lungs. He had been diagnosed on September 21 and went to Atlantic City, a favorite vacation spot, in the hopes of relieving the problem by inhaling salty air. He died in Atlantic City the day after an operation on his lungs. He is buried in West Laurel Hill Cemetery in Bala Cynwyd.

To honor his memory, the National League held a "Harry Wright Day" on May 13, 1896, from which all proceeds went towards building a memorial upon his gravesite.

Harry Wright was inducted into the Baseball Hall of Fame in 1953. His brother George is also a member of the Hall of Fame, having been enshrined in 1937.

If You Go:
West Laurel Hill Cemetery is a large, beautiful cemetery filled with history and interesting stories. Two other notable sports figures buried there are:

Benjamin Shibe (1838-1922), who was co-owner of the Philadelphia Athletics with Connie Mack (see page 273); and

Hobart "Hobey" Baker (1892-1918), who was a Hall-of-Fame hockey player and World War I hero. The NCAA established the "Hobey Baker Award" in 1981, which is awarded annually to the top player in college hockey.

Ben Shibe

"The Mennonite Master of Profanity"
SAMUEL K. ZOOK

County: Montgomery
Town: Norristown
Cemetery: Montgomery
Address: 1 Hartranft Avenue

From his obelisk monument at the Wheatfield on the Gettysburg Battlefield:

> *To the memory of*
> *Samuel*
> *Kosciusko Zook.*
> *Brevet Major*
> *General U.S. Vols.*
> *Who fell mortally*
> *wounded at or near*
> *this spot. while*
> *gallantly leading*
> *his brigade in battle*
> *July 2nd 1863.*
> *Erected by Gen. Zook*
> *Post. No 11 G.A.R.*
> *of Norristown, Pa.*
> *July 25th, 1882.*

General Samuel Kosciuszko Zook (born Samuel Kurtz Zook) (March 27, 1821 – July 3, 1863) was born and raised in Tredyffrin Township, Chester County, Pennsylvania, not far from George Washington's Valley Forge encampment. On his father's side, he was descended from Mennonites, specifically the Anabaptist order started by Menno Simmons in Switzerland. As a boy, Zook played soldier on the earthworks where the Revolutionary War soldiers roamed. His grandfather Zook was a major during the American Revolution. As a young man, he decided to take Kosciuszko as his middle name, in honor of the Revolutionary War general from Poland who assisted the Americans. Of course, all of this martial activity among the Zooks is contrary to the pacifist practices of the Mennonites. Clearly the Zooks had not been pacifists for several generations.

Samuel K. Zook

In the years prior to the Civil War, Zook was a pioneer in the information technology of his day – the telegraph. As Kenneth Silverman writes in his book *Lightning Man: The Accursed Life of Samuel B. Morse*:

"On the New Orleans route, O'Reilly intended to use what he advertised as 'A NEW AND IMPROVED TELE-GRAPH (and NOT Morse's plan).' Not Morse's, or

House's either. While publicly beating the drum for House's telegraph, he had always privately thought it 'not simple enough.' For his potentially lucrative line to New Orleans, he chose an instrument called the Columbian telegraph, designed by two young telegraphers in his Cincinnati office, Samuel K. Zook and E. F. Barnes. Admirers of the Columbian alleged that it differed from Morse's system in two ways. Its registers used permanent magnets instead of electromagnets; and it had a novel galvanometer-like relay that supposedly protected transmission during thunderstorms...."

Morse thought this was an infringement of his patent and the two sides battled for years in the marketplace. When the patent suit was heard in September 1848, the judge ruled for Morse. O'Reilly was not deterred and continued his battles for several more years before eventually relenting. Zook, meanwhile, moved to New York City and became the superintendent of the Washington and New York Telegraph Company. While in New York, he had risen to lieutenant colonel in the 6th New York Governor's Guard by the time of the Civil War.

During the summer of 1861, while with the 6th New York Militia, Zook served as the military governor of Annapolis. When this 90-day regiment was mustered out (thanks to connections made in Annapolis), he raised a new regiment — the 57th New York, to which he was colonel.

Zook's first action was in 1862, serving in Major General Edwin V. Sumner's division of the Army of the Potomac, during the Seven Days Battles. While scouting enemy positions at the Battle of Gaines's Mill, Zook noticed a Confederate deception regarding troop numbers. Zook reported this discovery up to General George McClellan, but was ignored and an opportunity was lost.

Zook missed the battle of Antietam while on medical leave, but returned in time for Fredericksburg. There, he served in the division of Major General Winfield S. Hancock (see page 133). Zook's brigade arrived early at the battle. Zook recognized the Union could gain significant advantage if he could cross the Rappahannock River immediately. However, the new commander of the Army of the Potomac, Ambrose Burnside, preferred to wait until more troops arrived and pontoon bridges could be put in place. Wrote Zook of this missed opportunity:

"If we had had the pontoons promised when we arrived here we could have the hills on the other side of the river without cost over 50 men — now it will cost at least 10,000 if not more."

While he waited, Zook served as military governor of Falmouth, Virginia. During the ensuing battle, Zook's brigade led the first assault on Marye's Heights, achieving one of the farthest advances of the battle. Zook had his horse shot out from under him as the Confederates repulsed the attack. Hancock was very pleased with Zook's bravery on the field. In March 1863, Zook was promoted to brigadier general. Zook wrote about the Fredericksburg battle:

"I walked over the field, close under the enemy's picket line, last night about 3 o'clock. The ground was strewn thickly with corpses of the heroes who perished there on Saturday. I never realized before what war was. I never before felt so horribly since I was born. To see men dashed to pieces by shot & torn into shreds by

Zook's obelisk

shells during the heat and crash of battle is bad enough, God knows, but to walk alone amongst slaughtered brave in the 'still small hours' of the night would make the bravest man living 'blue'. God grant I may never have to repeat my last night's experience."
—Samuel K. Zook, letter to E. I. Wade, December 16, 1862

Zook had a reputation for being a disciplinarian and a master of profanity, despite his Mennonite background. While on the road to Chancellorsville, he was one half of a famous battle of profanity with General Hancock. Wrote an enlisted man about the incident:

> "It was the greatest cursing match I ever listened to; Zook took advantage of Hancock, by waiting until the latter got out of breath, and then he opened his pipe organ, and the air was very blue."

Zook fought at Chancellorsville and then missed some time due to rheumatism. He returned to the field in time for Gettysburg, where he served under Brigadier General John C. Caldwell. On the second day, at the Wheatfield, while reinforcing Stony Hill, which was under attacked by Longstreet, Zook was shot three times in the shoulder, chest and abdomen. He was moved to the Hoke house on the Baltimore Pike, in the care of Dr. William Potter, a friend of the general. Wrote Potter about Zook's wounds:

> "fatally shot, a shell having torn open his left shoulder and chest, exposing the heart-beats to observation."

Zook succumbed to his wounds the next day. He was posthumously awarded the rank of major general.

Samuel K. Zook is buried near his good friend and cursing partner General Winfield S. Hancock at Montgomery Cemetery, near Norristown, Pennsylvania.

If You Go:

See the "If You Go" sections of Winfield Hancock (p. 133) and John Hartranft (p. 142).

PHILADELPHIA COUNTY

"Golf's Forgotten Legend"
WILLIAM (WILLIE) LAW ANDERSON

County: Philadelphia
Town: Philadelphia
Cemetery: Ivy Hill
Address: 1201 Easton Road

Only four golfers have won four United States Open championships. Three of the four, Bobby Jones, Ben Hogan, and Jack Nicklaus are well known to golf fans everywhere. Such is not the case for the first man to do it. Not only did William (Willie) Law Anderson win four Opens, he did something the other three never accomplished, Anderson won three in a row.

Anderson was born on October 21, 1879, in Scotland. He became a licensed caddie at the age of eleven. In addition, he apprenticed as a golf club maker under Alex Aitken. Aitken's clubs, by the year 1896, were being exported to the United States and he had also produced a set of clubs for the British Prime Minister. Anderson would later use the skills he learned from Aitken in designing some of his own clubs

In 1896, Anderson, his father, and his brother Tom arrived in the United States. The following year, Anderson entered the United States Open for the first time. He was tied for the lead with Joe Lloyd when they reached the final hole. Lloyd's approach shot stopped eight feet from the pin. He sank the putt for a birdie three, beating Anderson by one stroke.

By now Anderson was making his living as a golf professional. He worked at ten different clubs over a fourteen year period. During this time he also competed in tournaments and exhibitions. His first big tournament win came in 1899 at the Southern California Open. He won the by one stroke, beating Alex Smith, a man who would finish second to him twice in United States Open play.

In 1901, the Open was played near Boston, Massachusetts at the Myopia Hunt Golf Club. After 72 holes Anderson and Smith, were tied at 331. The tournament ended on a Friday, but the first 18 hole playoff in Open history did not take place until Monday. Saturday and Sunday were

Willie Anderson with his arm around Alex Smith.

club member days, so the course was unavailable. That Monday, Anderson won his first Open, beating Smith once again by a single stroke.

In 1902, Anderson entered the Western Open. At the time winning the Western was comparable to winning the Masters today. Anderson won the tournament by recording a 299 over the 72 holes. In one round he shot a 69. The win made Anderson the first player to hold two major American golf titles. In addition, with his score of 299, he became the first golfer to score under 300 in a 72 hole tournament held in America. That same year he again competed in the United States Open where he finished fifth.

The 1903 Open was held at Baltusrol in New Jersey. Anderson had worked at this club as its first professional in 1898. After 36 holes, Anderson had a six stroke lead. The margin evaporated nine holes later when he carded an 8. At the conclusion of the 72 hole tournament he found himself in a tie with Davie Brown. The playoff took place in a driving rain and Anderson prevailed by two strokes. His Open streak began.

In 1904, Anderson became the first two time winner of the Western Open. He won the tournament by beating Alex Smith by four strokes. The win earned him $200.

A week later, he was once again playing in the United States Open. This one was played at the Glen View Course in Chicago. In 1904, there would be no playoff. Anderson set a scoring record by posting a 303. He won easily by five strokes. He was now a three time Open champion and he had won two in a row.

The following year the Open started out poorly for Anderson. In the first round, he shot an 81 and he followed that with an 80. After 36 holes, he was five strokes off the lead and a third straight Open title looked out of reach. In round three, Anderson started strong. After the fourth hole, he was two under for the day. He continued to narrow the margin between himself and the leaders until he took the lead. By the 70th hole, he found himself four shots in front. He held on to win by two. He was now a four time Open champion, and he had won three in a row.

Anderson would never win another Open title, though he would be quite competitive. After his fourth win he finished third once, fourth twice, fifth twice, eleventh twice, and fifteenth once. His days of winning tournaments were not behind him. He won the Western Open in both 1908 and 1909, thus becoming the first four time winner of that event.

By this time Anderson's health had begun to deteriorate. He was unable to defend his Western Open title in 1910. Anderson played in his last tournament in July of 1910 at the Deal Golf and Country Club in New Jersey. While his game was clearly not what it once was, he finished just out of the money in 12th place.

Anderson continued playing exhibitions where he made most of his money. In October of 1910, he traveled to Pittsburgh to play a series of matches with other pros and amateurs. The final match he played was lost on the last hole. He returned to his home in Philadelphia on October the 24th. The next day he died. He was 31 years old.

How good was he? His contemporaries had no problem comparing him to Bobby Jones and Walter Hagen. He was known for his accuracy, whatever club was in his hand. In addition, pressure did not bother him. He was viewed by his competitors as a formidable foe that would make you crack before he would. One would have to conclude he was among the greatest golfers of his time and perhaps the greatest in America in the early 1900's.

The cause of his death remains a controversy. It was reported that he died from arteriosclerosis, a fatal hardening of the arteries. One newspaper said it was a brain tumor. The official report named the cause of death as epilepsy. One golf historian reported that Anderson had drank himself to death.

Anderson was inducted into the golf Hall of Fame in 1975. The great Gene Sarazen accepted the honor on his behalf. He had finally joined his special fraternity.

Anderson is buried in the Ivy Hill Cemetery in Philadelphia. His tombstone, which is unique, was erected by the Eastern Professional Golfers Association. In the opinion of the authors it is worth seeing. In fact, if you visit you might want to leave a golf ball or tee at the grave.

If You Go:
Others buried in Ivy Hill Cemetery include Franklin Gowen and Bill Tilden. Gowen was famous for leading the prosecution, some would say persecution, of the Molly Maguires in the 1870s (see page 246). Tilden was a tennis great who dominated that sport in the 1920s and 30s (see page 324). Both Harold Melvin of Harold Melvin and the Blue Notes and Marion Williams the famed gospel singer are also buried at Ivy Hill, but they are in unmarked graves. You can still visit their gravesites as the folks working in the cemetery office will be glad to provide you with their locations. In addition if you are at Ivy Hill, you are about a mile away from Holy Sepulcher Cemetery. Frank Rizzo and Connie Mack are buried there. Rizzo was a colorful and controversial Mayor of Philadelphia (see page 319). Mack was a legendary major league baseball manager (see page 273).

"The Great Profile"
JOHN BARRYMORE

County: Philadelphia
Town: Philadelphia
Cemetery: Mount Vernon
Address: Intersection of Ridge and Lehigh Avenue

He was born into an acting family. He first made a name for himself on stage starting with light comedy and then appearing in dramas. He was especially praised for his work in Shakespearean plays. From the stage he moved to the silver screen where he met with immediate and great success. He was envied for his good looks which earned him the moniker "the Great Profile." His name was John Barrymore.

Barrymore was born on February 15, 1882, in Philadelphia. His father, Herbert Arthur Chamberlayne Blythe, was a British actor who performed under the name Maurice Barrymore. His mother, Georgie Drew Barrymore, was an actress as well. Barrymore had a brother Lionel and a sister Ethel. His maternal grandmother was Louisa Lane Drew who was also an actress and theatre manager. Drew was instrumental in directing all three siblings into acting. Growing up in such a theatrical family resulted in Barrymore meeting some of the leading actors of the day including Edwin Booth.

While he was still in his teens he dated the showgirl Evelyn Nesbitt (see Harry Thaw in *Keystone Tombstones – Pittsburgh Region*, p. 85). There were rumors that Nesbitt had become pregnant and that Barrymore arranged for her to have an abortion. In 1906, Nesbitt's husband Harry Thaw shot one of her former lovers, the noted architect Stanford White, to death on the rooftop of Madison Square Garden. Questions were prepared to ask Barrymore at the trial the purpose of which was to attack Nesbitt's character. The trial however was settled by an insanity plea and Barrymore was never called to the stand.

Initially Barrymore attempted to avoid following in his parents footsteps by trying to make a living as a reporter and a cartoonist. He went to art school and worked for several New York newspapers before he made the decision to

John Barrymore

become an actor. He made his stage debut in 1903 at the Cleveland Theatre in Chicago. He then moved on to Broadway where he performed for two years before heading to England to appear in a play called "The Dictator."

In 1906 Barrymore was staying in a hotel in San Francisco when the earthquake hit. He was starring in a production of "The Dictator" and was set to go to Australia to tour in that play. Barrymore had no desire to make that trip so he went into hiding spending the next few days at the house of a friend where he went on a drinking binge.

While he was drinking he came up with an idea as to how he could use the earthquake for his own benefit. He posed as a reporter and simply made up scenes he claimed to have witnessed. Years later in a letter to his sister he admitted he had done so. When the information became public it did Barrymore no harm as by that time he was widely known and admired for his talent.

In 1910, Barrymore married an actress named Katherine Corri Harris. It was the first of his four marriages, and the couple divorced in 1917. By 1912, Barrymore was the American actor who ruled the American stage. It was at this highpoint in his career that he decided to make motion pictures. He began to make films at that time but he still worked on Broadway. In 1913 he made the decision to abandon the stage in order to make films full time. That same year he starred in the silent film "An American Citizen."

At first Barrymore concentrated on making light comedies. A friend of his convinced him to try his hand at drama. In 1916 he appeared in a film called "Justice" to critical acclaim. One of his co-stars was Cathleen Nesbitt who would introduce him to his second wife Blanche Oelrichs. They would marry in 1920 and divorce in 1925. The union would produce one child a daughter named Diana Blanche Barrymore. Diana would die at that age of 38 from an overdose of alcohol combined with sleeping pills. Barrymore would make a movie with Errol Flynn called "Too Much, Too Soon" based on her life.

When World War 1 saw the United States enter the fray in 1917, Barrymore, who was 35 at the time, tried to enlist in the armed forces. He failed the physical due to varicose veins. That same year he returned to Broadway to star in a play called "Peter Ibbetson" in a role his father had always wanted to play. In 1919 he starred with his brother Lionel in "The Jest." Then it was back to Shakespeare when he appeared in "Richard III" in 1920. This was followed by what many consider his greatest stage triumph, his starring role in "Hamlet" in 1922. The play ran for 101 performances, and Barrymore broke the record for consecutive appearances that had been held by Edwin Booth.

Barrymore closed out his silent film career by appearing in a number of successful films. These included "Dr.

Jekyll and Mr. Hyde" (the band Queen used scenes from this film in their music video Under Pressure), "Sherlock Holmes" and "Don Juan."

In 1928 he married the model and actress Dolores Costello. They were divorced in 1935. The union produced two children a girl born in 1930 named Dolores Ethel Mae Barrymore and a son born in 1932 named John Drew Barrymore. John is the father of the actress Drew Barrymore.

Talking pictures proved to be a big plus for Barrymore. His debut in talkies was a dramatic reading of the Duke of Gloucester's speech from "Henry VI." Clearly Barrymore's stage trained voice fit perfectly with talking pictures. In 1930 he reprised a role he had played in a silent film starring as Captain Ahab in "Moby Dick." He then made a few movies with his brother Lionel including "Arsene Lupin," "The Mad Genius" and in 1932 "Grand Hotel." In addition to the Barrymore's the latter film featured an all-star cast that included Joan Crawford and Greta Garbo. That same year the brothers starred in "Rasputin and the Princess" followed by "Dinner at Eight" in 1933.

Over the years Barrymore appeared with most of the leading ladies of the time including Myrna Loy, Katherine Hepburn and Jean Harlow. In the 1933 film "Counsellor at Law" Barrymore portrayed a Jewish attorney. The film critic Pauline Kael would later praise this performance calling it "one of the few screen roles that reveal his measure as an actor." She added that his "presence is apparent in every scene; so are his restraint, his humor and his zest."

In the 30's Barrymore's return to the stage met with much success. He actually inspired several plays including "The Royal family" and "My Dear Children." Both of these plays would become films. He also served as the inspiration for two films "Sing Baby Sing" and "The Great Profile." In 1936 he gave a critically praised performance playing Mercutio in "Romeo and Juliet." That same year he was married for the fourth and final time to Elaine Barrie an actress, the two would divorce in 1940.

In 1937 he appeared in a film with Jeanette MacDonald called "Maytime." It became the top grossing film of the year worldwide. It is still regarded as one of the best film musicals of the 1930's.

In the late 30's Barrymore began losing the ability to remember his lines. As a result when he made films they were forced to use cue cards. His films began losing money and by 1938 he was considered box office poison along with others such as Fred Astaire and Joan Crawford.

Barrymore collapsed while appearing on Rudy Vallee's Radio show in 1942. He was rushed to the hospital. He had been a smoker his whole life and also suffered from chronic alcoholism, heart problems and pneumonia. According to one of his biographers Barrymore roused and tried to say something to his brother Lionel, and Lionel asked him to repeat what he had said and Barrymore replied, "You heard me, Mike." He then met death with a smile on May 29, 1942. According to Errol Flynn's memoirs the film director Roaul Walsh took Barrymore's body and placed it in a chair in Flynn's house, left to be discovered by Flynn when he returned home from a night of drinking. Walsh said the story was true in a 1973 documentary called "The Men Who Made the Movies." The story was challenged by a friend of Barrymore's who claimed that he and his son stayed with the body at the funeral right up to the burial. Among Barrymore's pallbearers were W. C. Fields, Louis B. Mayer and David O. Selznick. He was laid to rest in Mount Vernon Cemetery in Philadelphia.

For his work in films Barrymore was awarded a star on the Hollywood Walk of Fame. Unlike his sister Ethel and his brother Lionel he never won an Academy Award. However all three siblings have been inducted into the American Theatre Hall of Fame.

Barrymore was a good friend and drinking Buddy of W. C. Fields. In the 1976 film, "W. C. Fields and Me," Barrymore was portrayed by Jack Cassidy. He is also mentioned in the song "I May Be Wrong (But I think You're Wonderful)" which was recorded by a number of artists including Doris Day.

If You Go:

What can we say except that attempting to visit this grave site proved to be a first for us. I suppose we can begin by telling you that you need to call the cemetery at least 24 hours before you visit to make an appointment. This is necessary because the grounds are locked and someone needs to meet you there in order for you to gain entrance. When we called we spoke to a man who identified himself as the owner of the property. We informed him of who we wanted to visit and he asked us if we were relatives. We told him no and explained the reason for our visit. He responded by telling us that we would need to pay a fee to photograph the grave. He said that according to his attorney the site was his "intellectual property." We chose not to pay so this marks the first grave included in this series that we were unable to visit. We hope our readers have better luck and we continue to wonder what Drew Barrymore might think of the stand taken by the owner with regard to our attempt to visit her grandfather's grave.

"The Dahlgren Affair"

ULRIC DAHLGREN

County: Philadelphia
Town: Philadelphia
Cemetery: Laurel Hill
Address: 3822 Ridge Avenue

Ulric Dahlgren was born on April 3, 1842, in Bucks County, Pennsylvania. His father was Rear-Admiral John Adolf Dahlgren. Dahlgren's father influenced much of his short life. After completing school in 1858, he decided to go into civil engineering as he had already received training in this field from his father. In 1860, obeying the wishes of his father, he began work in a Philadelphia law office. After President Lincoln took office, Dahlgren was determined to serve his country and was assigned to a naval expedition that was to aid in the defense of Alexandria, Virginia. In 1862, he joined a light artillery company in Philadelphia. In that same year Dahlgren, who was only 20 years old, was put in charge of a battery of navy howitzers at Harper's Ferry.

Dahlgren quickly earned the reputation of being an effective and heroic officer. At Fredericksburg on November 9, 1862, he led 60 men into the city while facing an enemy force that numbered between 500 and 600. He held the city for three hours and captured 31 Confederate soldiers. He also participated in the battles of Chancellorsville (April 30–May 6, 1863) and Beverly Ford (June 9, 1863). On July 4, while in charge of 100 men, Dahlgren attacked Confederate cavalry and captured Greencastle, Pennsylvania. On July 6, in another attack, Dahlgren was wounded and his foot was amputated. Shortly thereafter he was promoted to the rank of colonel.

Dahlgren returned to active duty on February 18, 1864, serving under General Hugh Judson Kilpatrick. On February 28, Kilpatrick led 3,600 Union cavalry troopers south toward Richmond, with a plan to raid the city and free Union prisoners being held there. The next day, on February 29, Kilpatrick sent Dahlgren at the head of 460 men off to the west. The plan called for Dahlgren to attack Richmond from the south while Kilpatrick led an attack from the north.

Ulric Dahlgren

The plan was doomed to failure from the outset. Dahlgren found that the James River had swelled due to winter rains and he was unable to cross. He continued toward Richmond but he was on the wrong side of the river. Next he ran into Confederates and was forced to turn north. Kilpatrick reached Richmond but was turned back. Meanwhile in a cold hard rain, Dahlgren and about 100 of his men were separated from the rest of his command. On the night of March 2, Dahlgren and his men were ambushed by rebel troops and he was killed.

Ulric Dahlgren was killed in a raid on Richmond, while carrying orders to assassinate Confederate President Jefferson Davis.

A young boy searched Dahlgren's body and found two documents that historians would call the "Dahlgren Papers." The papers indicated that Dahlgren had been ordered to destroy the city of Richmond and to kill Confederate President Jefferson Davis and his cabinet members. The Dahlgren Papers were published in the Richmond newspapers, and there were those in the South who wanted to put Dahlgren's captured men on trial, convict them, and then execute them. Robert E. Lee's opposition may have saved the prisoners. However, Lee did have photographs of the Dahlgren Papers taken. He sent the photographs to General George Meade, along with a letter asking whether the United States government had approved these orders. Meade responded that the government had issued no such order. Privately however, Meade had his doubts. He confided to his wife that "I regret to say that Kilpatrick's reputation, and collateral evidence in my possession, rather go against this theory."

Northern newspapers and Dahlgren's father claimed that the papers were forgeries. Whatever the real story is, the Dahlgren Papers provided the southern leaders with a reason to approve plans for southern sympathizers in the North to join in the rebellion. They even encouraged a plan to bomb the White House. John Wilkes Booth was reportedly

Tombstone of Ulric Dahlgren.

part of that plan, and some believe that when it failed he may have decided to take matters into his own hands.

Seven months after Lee surrendered at Appomattox, Secretary of War Edwin Stanton took custody of the Dahlgren Papers. One historian later conducted an extensive search for the papers and finally concluded that Stanton had destroyed them.

Dahlgren was originally buried in Richmond but after the war his remains were sent north. His body lay in state in Washington's City Hall and in Independence Hall in Philadelphia. General George Meade attended the funeral, and Dahlgren was buried with distinguished honors in Laurel Hill Cemetery in Philadelphia.

If You Go:

See the "If You Go" sections of George Meade (p. 281), Samuel Crawford (p. 213), Oliver Knowles (p. 268), and "General Controversy," p. 237.

"Four Founders"

JOSEPH HEWES
FRANCIS HOPKINSON
GEORGE ROSS
BENJAMIN RUSH

County: Philadelphia
Town: Philadelphia
Cemetery: Christ Church Burial Ground
Address: 5th and Arch Streets

They were all American Patriots who risked all for their country. They were all signers of the Declaration of Independence. They all contributed to the American victory during the Revolution. Joseph Hewes amassed a fortune in the shipping business in Wilmington, North Carolina. Francis Hopkinson was from New Jersey and made a name for himself as a lawyer, judge, composer, poet and satirist. George Ross served as a colonel in the Continental Army and as judge of the Admiralty Court of Pennsylvania. Benjamin Rush was a physician who is known as the father of American psychiatry. In addition he was a professor of chemistry and a social reformer. What they all had in common was a firm belief that America required independence.

Joseph Hewes was born in Princeton, New Jersey, on January 23, 1730. His parents were Quakers, a religion Hewes would eventually renounce. Hewes attended Princeton University, but there is no evidence that he ever graduated. As a young man he became an apprentice of a very successful merchant. His work as an apprentice earned him the respect of others and a strong reputation. At the age of thirty he moved to North Carolina where the people grew to like and respect him as a result of his honesty in conducting business. In 1763, after living in North Carolina for just three years, he was elected to the state legislature. During this time he amassed a fortune in the shipping business.

By 1773, a majority of the people living in North Carolina favored independence. Hewes was elected to represent

Joseph Hewes

the colony as a representative to the Continental Congress
in 1774. Unlike the people of his state, Hewes did not favor
independence; he was convinced that reconciliation with
England was possible. Hewes attempted to bring representatives from other states around to his view with little success. As a result he threw himself into his work. He worked
on numerous committees and ironically most that he
served on favored independence.

By 1776, Hewes had already sacrificed quite a bit for his country. For two years Congress had been pushing for a system of nonimportation in order to hurt the English economy, but the idea had gone nowhere. Hewes worked with some of his counterparts and together they formed a nonimportation association. Belonging to such an organization was costly for Hewes as a huge chunk of his business involved English imports.

By the summer of 1776, it was obvious the Congress was going to declare independence. On July 1,1776,as John Adams argued for independence Hewes said, "It is done! I will abide by it." Hewes signed the Declaration of Independece.

Hewes put his ships at the new country's disposal to use as they saw fit. Hewes had a friend by the name of John Paul Jones. Through Hewes, Jones obtained a navy commander's assignment. Jones would become the United State's first navel hero. Hewes would serve as Secretary of the Navel Affairs Committee until 1779 and as a result he could be considered the "Father of the U. S. Navy." Hewes returned to North Carlina to settle business and private affairs.

He returned to Philadelphia in 1779, where he fell ill on October 29,1779. He died on November 10th and was laid to rest at the Christ Church Burial Ground. Before his death, he described himself as a sad and lonely man. The woman he loved died a few days before their wedding, and he never married. As a result there were no children to inherit his money and estates.

Francis Hopkinson was born in Philadelphia on October 2, 1737. He was a member of the first class of the College of Philadelphia (now the University of Pennsylvania) when he was 14. He graduated in 1757, and received a master's degree in 1760.That same year he began the study of law with Benjamin Chew and in 1761, he was admitted to the bar. Hopkinson's first significant position was secretary to the Pennsylvania Indian Commission in 1761, where he assisted in developing a treaty with the Delaware and Iroquois Indian tribes.

Hopkinson was an author and songwriter. He wrote political satires in the form of poems and pamphlets. When

Francis Hopkinson

he was 17 he began studying the harpsichord. He is said to be the first American composer to write a composition and put it on paper with his 1759 work "My Days Have Been So Wondrous Free." Hopkinson also played the organ at Christ Church in Philadelphia. In the 1780's he modified a harmonica which was to be played with a keyboard and invented an instrument called the Bellarmonic. In 1778 he published eight songs for his friend George Washington

Hopkinson made his living in the dry goods business. He was married in 1768, and he and his wife had 5 children. He moved to New Jersey in 1774. In 1775 he was sent to represent New Jersey in the Second Continental Congress, and as a member of Congress he signed the Declaration of Independence. He left Congress in November of 1776 in order to serve on the navel board of Philadelphia. He was appointed judge of the Admiralty Court of Pennsylvania in 1779, and he aided in the ratification of the United States Constitution in 1787. In 1789 President George Washington nominated Hopkinson to be the judge of the United States District Court for the District of Pennsylvania. The United States Senate confirmed the nomination. Only a few years into serving in this position Hopkinson died in Philadelphia from a sudden epileptic seizure. He was 53 years old. He is buried in the Christ Church Burial Ground. At one point Hopkinson claimed that he had designed the American flag, and he asked Congress for a bottle of wine for his efforts. Congress denied the claim so now every year on his birthday, the workers at Christ Church take a bottle of wine to his grave in remembrance of his contribution.

George Ross was born in New Castle, Delaware in 1730. He was named after his father who was a minister who presided over the local Episcopal church. As a young man he was educated at home. When he was 18, as was the norm for the times, he took up the study of law at a brother's law office in Philadelphia. He was admitted to the bar and with his sympathies at the time leaning toward England he became the Crown Prosecutor for 12 years and in1768 he was elected to the provincial legislature. It was during this time that his feelings toward England began to change and he soon became a strong supporter of the various colonial assemblies in their disputes with Parliament.

In 1774 he was selected to be one of Pennsylvania's delegates at the 2nd Continental Congress. As a member he became a signer of the Declaration of Independence. In 1776, he became a Colonel in the Continental Army. That same year he acted as Vice President of the State constitutional convention where he helped write a declaration of rights. He was re-elected to Congress in 1777 but due to poor health he resigned that position that same year. In

George Ross

1778 he began service acting as an admiralty judge and in 1779 he became Judge of the Admiralty Court of Pennsylvania. That same year he died in office and was buried in Christ Church Burial Ground in Philadelphia.

Benjamin Rush was born on January 4, 1746, in Byberry, Pennsylvania. His family included seven children and when Rush's father died it was up to his mother to

Benjamin Rush

care for the large family. Rush was five at the time. When he was eight Rush's mother sent him to live with an aunt and uncle in Maryland. His uncle, Samuel Finley, ran a private school and he was instrumental in convincing Rush to become a doctor.

In 1760, Rush graduated with a Bachelor of Arts degree from the college of New Jersey which is now Princeton University. In 1761 he began an apprenticeship under a Doctor

John Redman in Philadelphia. Redman convinced Rush to continue his medical studies at the University of Edinburgh in Scotland. He graduated in 1768 with a medical degree.

Rush returned to America in 1769 at the age of 24. He opened a medical practice in Philadelphia and became a professor of chemistry at the College of Philadelphia which is now the University of Pennsylvania. He would eventually publish the first American chemistry textbook.

Around this time Rush joined the Sons of Liberty and began writing essays in favor of American independence. As a result of these activities Rush was appointed to the Second Continental Congress in 1776. While serving in Congress he became a signer of the Declaration of Independence.

Rush was instrumental in encouraging Thomas Paine to publish "Common Sense." As a matter of fact Rush came up with the title. Rush was always worried about his reputation in Philadelphia and was therefore very happy that he had found someone else to pen such an anti-English essay.

Rush became surgeon general of the middle department of the Continental

This stone marks the grave of an American patriot and a signer of the Declaration of Independence.

This is the grave of a man who fought in the Continental Army after signing the Declaration of Independence.

This is the grave of Francis Hopkinson a talented musician and composer who also signed the Declaration of Independence.

Here is the final resting place of Benjamin Rush a signer of the Declaration of Independence whose many other achievements are largely unrecognized.

Army in 1777. In this capacity he clashed with Dr. William Shipman who was the director general of hospitals for the army. Rush believed that Shipman was responsible for the miserable health conditions the army faced. He filed a formal complaint against Shipman, but Congress investigated and found the complaint to be without merit.

In 1778, Rush made a mistake he would regret for the rest of his life. He sided with a group whose aim was to remove George Washington as commander in chief. Rush sent an unsigned letter to Patrick Henry urging Washington's removal. Though the letter was unsigned Rush was easily identified as the author due to his distinctive handwriting style. Rush was left with no choice but to resign from the army.

Rush returned to a very busy civilian life. In 1783, he was appointed to the staff of the Pennsylvania Hospital. Next he was elected to the convention to be held in Pennsylvania that would ratify the United States Constitution on December 12, 1787. In 1791, he became professor of medical history and clinical practice at the University of Pennsylvania.

Rush's accomplishments include the establishment of Dickinson College in Carlisle, Pennsylvania as week as the Philadelphia Society for Alleviating the Miseries of Public

Prisons and served as the treasurer of the U.S. Mint. He also acted as the intermediary in providing the reconciliation between John Adams and Thomas Jefferson.

In 1793 Philadelphia was hit by an outbreak of yellow fever. Rush was one of three doctor's available to treat the more than 6,000 people affected by the fever. He worked, often without proper rest, to halt the epidemic. Eventually he developed a new and improved treatment by combining calomel and jalap. This combination aided in curbing the spread of the fever.

Rush died in 1813 from an unspecified illness. He was laid to rest in the Christ Church Burial Ground.

If You Go:
The Christ Church Burial Ground charges a modest entrance fee. The money raised is used to cover the cemeteries maintenance costs. The man the authors consider the first American Benjamin Franklin (see page 221) is buried here along with a number of other important Americans. If you make the trip you are in the midst of Philadelphia's historic district. Independence Hall, the Constitution Center and the Betsy Ross House are within easy walking distance. In addition there are numerous restaurants in the area should you desire refreshments.

"The Surgeon General"
SAMUEL W. CRAWFORD

County: Philadelphia
Town: Philadelphia
Cemetery: Laurel Hill
Address: 3822 Ridge Avenue

"I must sustain with honor my flag and the reputation of the name I bear."
—*Samuel W. Crawford, delivering his lifelong motto while serving at Fort Sumter.*

Samuel Wylie Crawford was one of only two individuals who were present at Fort Sumter, the outbreak of the Civil War, and at Appomattox Court House for the surrender (the other was General Truman Seymour). Born in Fayetteville, Franklin County, Pennsylvania (just across South Mountain from Gettysburg) on November 8, 1829, Crawford pursued medical studies at the University of Pennsylvania, graduating in 1850. He subsequently joined the Army as a surgeon, serving as such until the outbreak of hostilities in Charleston Harbor in 1861. When the Confederates opened fire on Fort Sumter, commencing what would be a long and bloody war, Crawford commanded several of the cannon that returned fire. A month after this action, Crawford changed career paths, abandoning the surgeon role for a commission as major in the 13th U.S. Infantry.

By April 25, 1862, Crawford was promoted to brigadier general of volunteers, but had yet to see much action. On June 26, Crawford was assigned to Major General John Pope's newly constituted Union "Army of Virginia." The first action of the campaign was at Cedar Mountain on August 9, 1862. Crawford's brigade launched a surprise attack upon the Confederate left, routing a division that included the Stonewall Brigade. The Confederates counterattacked, however, and Crawford's brigade, which was unsupported by other units, was driven back with 50% casualties.

An interesting meeting occurred the day after Cedar Mountain. During a truce for burying the dead, Crawford met Rebel cavalry chief J.E.B. Stuart, whom he had known

Brigadier General Samuel Wylie Crawford

in the Old Army, on the field. Stuart bet Crawford a hat that the Federals would claim Cedar Mountain had been a Union victory. In due time, under a flag of truce, a hat had arrived at the outpost for Stuart and with it a copy of a New York paper that proclaimed a triumph for Pope in that action. That hat shortly gained notoriety when it was captured in a Union cavalry raid that nearly netted Stuart himself at the start of the Second Bull Run Campaign.

The following month, on September 17, 1862, during what is known as the 'bloodiest single day battle in American history,' Crawford was heavily engaged at the Battle of Antietam. When the commander of the XII Corps, Major General Joseph K. Mansfield, was killed early at Antietam, the next in line—General Alpheus S. Williams—was elevated and assumed temporary command of the corps. Inasmuch as Williams was Crawford's superior, Crawford was elevated to Williams' former position. His opportunity was short, however, as Crawford was soon shot in the right thigh, and bled profusely. He stayed on the field until he was weakened by the loss of blood and was carried off. Due to the nature of his wounds, he convalesced at his father's home for eight months.

In May of 1863, Crawford returned to the Army, following in the footsteps of Generals John F. Reynolds (see *Keystone Tombstones – Susquehanna Valley Region*, p. 134) and George G. Meade (see page 281) as the commander of the Pennsylvania Reserves Division. In late June, in response to Lee's invasion of the North, the Pennsylvania Reserves were added to the Army of the Potomac. On July 2, 1863, the second day of the battle, Crawford and his division arrived at Gettysburg, under the command of Major General George Sykes. Crawford was ordered to assist the brigade of Colonel Strong Vincent at Little Round Top, but did not arrive in time to see any action.

Meanwhile, General James Longstreet's Confederates had swept through the Devil's Den, driving the Union defenders back to the west of Little Round Top, to an area that became known to the soldiers as "the Valley of Death." Crawford's division swept down the slope of Little Round Top along with the brigades of Colonels William McCandless and David J. Nevin. While McCandless's brigade led the charge, Crawford seized the colors of the First Pennsylvania Reserves from a surprised Corporal Bertless Slot. After a brief struggle and with Corporal Slot running alongside his horse grasping his pant leg, Crawford led his division in a charge that cleared the Valley of Death and, in his estimation, saved Little Round Top.

The following is Crawford's report of the action on July 2:

Bronze statue of Crawford on the Gettysburg battlefield (photo by Tammi Knorr)

"The firing in front was heavy and incessant. The enemy, concentrating his forces opposite the left of our line, was throwing them in heavy masses upon our troops, and was steadily advancing. Our troops in front, after a determined resistance, unable to withstand the force of the enemy, fell back, and some finally gave way.

The plain to my front was covered with fugitives from all divisions, who rushed through my lines and along the road to the rear. Fragments of regiments came back in disorder, and without their arms, and for a moment all seemed lost. The enemy's skirmishers had reached the foot of the rocky ridge; his columns were following rapidly... Not a moment was to be lost. Uncovering our front, I ordered an immediate advance. The command advanced gallantly with loud cheers. Two well-directed volleys were delivered upon the advancing masses of the enemy, when the whole column charged at a run down the slope, driving the enemy back across the space beyond and across the stone wall, for the possession of which there was a short but determined struggle. The enemy retired to the wheat-field and the woods."

Although this was a relatively minor engagement and casualties were light, Crawford spent the remainder of his life basking in the glory of Little Round Top. The next day, the final day of battle, Crawford was again engaged in a heated struggle, this time with the troops from Georgia and Texas:

"The line was then formed, and, under the immediate direction of Colonel McCandless, dashed across the wheat-field and into the upper end of the woods. The enemy's skirmishers were driven back as he advanced, and the upper end of the woods was now cleared. The command then changed front to rear, and charged through the entire length of woods. One brigade of the enemy, commanded by Brigadier General Anderson and composed of Georgia troops, was encountered. It had taken position behind a stone wall running through the woods, and which they had made stronger by rails and logs. We fell upon their flank, completely routing them, taking over 200 prisoners, one stand of colors belonging to the Fifteenth Georgia, and many arms. The colors were taken by Sergt. John B. Thompson, Company G, First Rifles. Another brigade, under General Robertson, and composed of Texas troops, which lay concealed beyond the woods and near the foot of the ridge, ran, as reported by the prisoners, without firing a shot. The enemy's force at this point consisted of the division of Major-General Hood, and was composed of three brigades, under the rebel Generals Anderson, Robertson, and Benning. They very greatly outnumbered us, but the rapidity of the movement and the gallant dash of my men completely surprised and routed them. They fell back nearly a mile to a second ridge, and entrenched themselves. By this charge of McCandless' brigade and the Eleventh Regiment, Colonel Jackson, the whole of the ground lost the previous day was retaken, together with all of our wounded, who, mingled with those of the rebels, were lying uncared for. The dead of both sides lay in lines in every direction, and the large number of our own men showed how fierce had been the struggle and how faithfully and how persistently they had contested for the field against the superior masses of the enemy. The result of this movement was the recovery of all the ground lost by our troops, one 12-pounder Napoleon gun and three caissons, and upward of 7,000 stand of arms. Large piles of these arms were found on brush heaps, ready to be burned."

Though Crawford's men actually only attacked a small contingent of Longstreet's men on July 2, he later claimed that he had "completely surprised and routed" most of Hood's division. A few months after Gettysburg, Crawford had the nerve to ask George Sykes to confirm claims which overstated Crawford's division's achievements to the detriment of Sykes's old Regular Division. Sykes refused Crawford's request, blisteringly.

Crawford remained in command of his division through the Overland Campaign (May/June 1864) and the Siege of Petersburg, and was again wounded at the Weldon Railroad on August 18, 1864. Crawford was present for Robert E. Lee's surrender at Appomattox Court House in April 1865, making him one of the few soldiers to be present at both the beginning and the effective end of the Civil War.

After the war, Crawford was prominent in preserving the Gettysburg Battlefield and at one point attempted to raise money to cover the hill with a large memorial building and museum dedicated to his division. This plan was a

Crawford's grave (photo by Joe Farrell)

failure, and Little Round Top remains close to its original condition, although sprinkled with smaller monuments. Crawford also spent considerable effort politicking to get the official records of the war changed to acknowledge his role as the savior of Little Round Top, but he was also unsuccessful in that quest. Frank Wheaton commented wryly on Crawford's selfishness: "Crawford's innate modesty never prevented his appropriating his full share of all that was done by his own division and by [Nevins's Sixth Corps brigade] that afternoon at Gettysburg." Crawford's attempts to garner acclaim not due him reached a pathetic state when, after the war, he offered former Confederate Maj. Gen. McLaws "a grade in the army" in exchange for a written acknowledgment that the Pennsylvania Reserves had driven back his forces on July 2nd. McLaws declined.

Crawford was a man very full of himself, never shy about taking full credit for his own and others' achievements on the battlefield. He was "a tall, chesty, glowering man, with heavy eyes, a big nose and bushy whiskers," as one of his comrades remembered him, who "wore habitually a turn-out-the-guard expression." This description did not do justice to his spectacular sideburns, which reached all the way to his shoulders. He was quite showy, mounted on a handsome "blood bay" horse given to him by Major General William S. Rosecrans. Joshua Chamberlain described him with a slightly acid tone as:

> "a conscientious gentleman, having the entré at all headquarters, somewhat lofty of manner, not of the iron fiber, nor spring of steel, but punctilious in a way, obeying orders in a certain literal fashion that saved him the censure of superiors--a pet of his State, and likewise, we thought, of Meade and Warren, judging from the attention they always gave him--possibly not quite fairly estimated by his colleagues as a military man..."

Crawford retired from the Army on February 19, 1873, and was given the rank of brigadier general, U.S. Army Retired. He was the author of *The Genesis of the Civil War*, published in 1887. On November 3, 1892, he died in Philadelphia, and is buried there in Laurel Hill Cemetery.

If You Go:

Also buried in Laurel Hill Cemetery are four men who were brevetted brigadier generals in March or April 1865 for "meritorious service." They are:

Alexander Cummings: nicknamed "Old Straw Hat." He served as commander of the 19th Pennsylvania Volunteer Cavalry, and as the Superintendent of Colored Troops in the Department of Arkansas after the Union opted to allow black troops into the army.

Robert Thompson: commanded the 115th Pennsylvania Volunteer Infantry.

William Redwood Price: served in a variety of administrative posts in Washington, D.C.

William Delaware Lewis, Jr.: commanded the 110th Pennsylvania Volunteer Infantry.

"The First American"

BENJAMIN FRANKLIN

County: Philadelphia
Town: Philadelphia
Cemetery: Christ Church Burial Ground
Address: Corner of 5th and Arch Streets

It is not exaggerating to say that to this day, no Pennsylvanian is as well known or as well respected as Ben Franklin. The man excelled at so many things. He was an author, a political theorist, a scientist, an inventor, a diplomat and politician (though he might disagree), and a revolutionary. He truly earned the title "The First American."

Ben Franklin was born in Boston, Massachusetts on January 17, 1706. His father, Josiah Franklin, was born in England where he married his first wife in 1677. The couple arrived in America in 1683. By that time, they had three children, and after arriving in America, they had four more. Josiah made a living as a soap and candle-maker. After his first wife died, he remarried and had ten more children. Franklin was Josiah's 15th child and his last son.

Franklin's parents wanted a career in the church for him. He was sent to school with the clergy but after two years, his parents could no longer make the payments to allow him to continue. Franklin never graduated, but through his own reading, he continued what would be called a self-education. At the age of twelve he went to work for his brother James, a printer, who taught him the trade. James founded "The New England Courant," the first independent newspaper in the colonies. Franklin began to write letters to the paper under the name of Mrs. Silence Dogwood. The views expressed became the subject of conversation around Boston. When James discovered that Franklin was the popular author, he punished him. In addition to verbal abuse, his brother was known to beat Franklin. Having had enough, Franklin fled his apprenticeship at age seventeen, and according to the laws of the time, became a fugitive.

Franklin arrived in Philadelphia in 1723, seeking a fresh start. With his experience, he was able to find work

Benjamin Franklin

in printing shops. Pennsylvania's Royal Governor William Keith convinced Franklin to return to England to find the equipment needed to start a new newspaper in Philadelphia. When the Governor failed to provide the backing for the enterprise, Franklin found work in a printer's shop in London. He returned to Philadelphia in 1726, and went to work for a merchant as a clerk, shopkeeper, and a bookkeeper.

Franklin organized a group of men known as the "Junto" in 1727. The goal of the group was to engage in activities that would improve the members as individuals and at the same time benefit the community. The group created a library. Franklin came up with the idea to form a subscription library, in order to increase the number of books available. This was done by combining the funds of the members to buy additional books that would be available for all to read. Franklin hired the first librarian in 1732.

In 1728, Franklin's employer passed away and Franklin returned to the printing business. The next year, he became the publisher of a newspaper called "The Pennsylvania Gazette." The newspaper provided Franklin with a mechanism to make known his views on the important issues of the time. His observations were well received and his stature continued to grow.

In 1730, Franklin entered into what would be called a common law marriage with Deborah Reed. He could not marry Reed because she already had a husband, though he had abandoned her. One of the reasons that may have led Franklin to make this decision was the fact that he had recently acknowledged that he was the father of an illegitimate son named William, and he wanted to provide his son a family life. William's mother remains unknown. Ben and Deborah had two other children. The first was a son named Francis, who was born in 1732, and died in 1736. The second child, a daughter named Sarah, was born in 1743.

During this time period, Franklin also began a career as an author. In 1733, he began to publish "Poor Richard's Almanac." Franklin seldom published under his own name and in this instance the author was identified as Richard Saunders. Some of his witty adages such as "Fish and visitors stink in three days" are still quoted today. Though published under the name Saunders, it was common knowledge that Franklin was the author. His reputation continued to grow. The almanac itself was a tremendous success, selling about 10,000 copies per year. In today's world, that would translate to about three million copies.

Franklin founded the American Philosophical Society in 1743. The purpose of this organization was to provide a forum where scientific men, like himself, could discuss their projects and discoveries. It was around this time that

Franklin began studying electricity. That study would remain a part of his life until the day he died. The story of
the kite, the string, and the key is probably a false one. The
television show "MythBusters" simulated the supposed experiment and concluded that if Franklin had proceeded as
described, he would have been killed.

In addition to his scientific studies, Franklin was also
an inventor. Among his more noted inventions are the
Franklin stove, the lightning rod, and bifocal lenses.
Franklin, viewed his inventions as yet another way that life
could be improved for humankind.

In 1747, Franklin decided to get out of the printing
business. He formed a partnership whereby David Hall
would run the business and the two would share the profits. This provided Franklin with a steady income and also
gave him the time to pursue his studies and other interests. His writings, inventions, and discoveries had by now
made him well known throughout the colonies and in Europe.

As he grew older, Franklin became more and more interested in public affairs. He was drawn into Philadelphia
politics and was soon elected to the post of councilman. In
1749 he became a Justice of the Peace and two years later,
he was elected to the Pennsylvania Assembly. In 1753, he
was appointed to the post of joint deputy postmaster general of North America. In this role, he worked to reform the
postal system. Among his accomplishments was the adoption of the practice to deliver mail on a weekly basis.

During this time, Franklin founded the first hospital in
the colonies. Honors continued to come his way. In 1753,
both Harvard and Yale awarded him honorary degrees. In
1757, the Pennsylvania Assembly selected Franklin to go to
England to oppose the political favoritism that was being
shown to the Penn family who were descended from Pennsylvania's founder William Penn. The family was exempt
from paying any land taxes and retained the right to veto
legislation passed by the Pennsylvania Assembly. Franklin
worked on this mission for five years but it ended in failure
as the Royal government refused to turn their backs on the
Penn family.

During his stay in England, more honors came his way.
In 1759, the University of Saint Andrews awarded him an

honorary degree. Three years later, Oxford followed suit by awarding Franklin an honorary doctorate for his scientific achievements. It was as a result of this award that he became known as Doctor Franklin. To top it off, he also secured an appointment for his illegitimate son William. The younger Franklin was named Colonial Governor of New Jersey.

When Franklin returned to America, the feud between the Penn's and the Assembly was ongoing. Franklin became leader of the anti-Penn party known as the anti-propriety party. In 1764 he was elected Speaker of the Pennsylvania House. As speaker, Franklin attempted to change Pennsylvania from a propriety to a royal government. The move was not popular with the voting populous who feared that such a change would infringe on their freedoms. As a result, Franklin was defeated in the elections held in October of 1764. After his defeat, the anti-propriety party sent him back to England to try yet again to fight the influence of the Penn family.

While in London, Franklin spoke out in opposition to the Stamp Act of 1765, but the measure passed over his objections. This did not deter him, and he continued to fight the act. His efforts contributed to its eventual repeal. As a result, he became the leading representative for American interests in England.

During his time in Europe, Franklin decided to tour Ireland. This visit would have a profound effect on him. When he witnessed the poverty in Ireland, he became convinced that it was a result of regulations and laws similar to those through which England was governing America. He came to the conclusion that America would suffer a fate similar to Ireland's if England's colonial exploitation continued.

Franklin's common law wife never accompanied him overseas because of her fear of the ocean. While he was on this trip, she implored him to return to America. She claimed she was ill and blamed her condition on his absence. Franklin stayed in England and Deborah Reed died as a result of a stroke in 1774.

Franklin returned to America in May of 1775. By this time the American Revolution had already begun with the battles of Lexington and Concord. Pennsylvania selected him as one of their delegates to the Second Continental

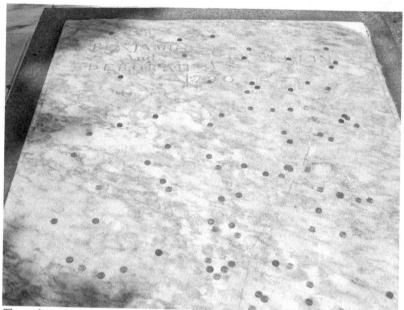

The authors consider this man to be Mister Pennsylvania and Mister America.

Congress. While serving in Congress, he was appointed to the committee chosen to draft the Declaration of Independence. Thomas Jefferson did the bulk of the work on the Declaration, though Franklin did make several minor changes to the draft Jefferson provided to the other members of the committee. As the Declaration was signed, the President of Congress, John Hancock, remarked "We must all hang together." Franklin replied, "Yes, we must, indeed, all hang together, or most assuredly we shall all hang separately."

In July of 1775, the Continental Congress appointed Franklin to the post of United States Postmaster General. He was the country's first postmaster. The appointment made sense based on Franklin's previous postal experience. The postal system that was established then evolved into the United States Postal Service that is still operational today.

In 1776, Franklin was sent to France to represent American interests. He was already well known in that country due to his writings, inventions, and scientific discoveries. His appointment bore fruit. Franklin succeeded in securing a military alliance between the United States and

France in 1778. This alliance was of critical importance to the Americans in their struggle against England. There are those who doubt that the American Revolution would have succeeded without the help of France. Franklin also played a key role in negotiating the Treaty of Paris in 1783. This treaty ended the American Revolution and established the United States as an independent country.

Franklin returned to the United States in 1785. His stature as a champion of American independence was exceeded by only one man, that man being George Washington. That same year, he was elected President of Pennsylvania, a post that would be similar to governor today. Franklin served in this position for just over three years.

In 1787 he was selected to serve as a Pennsylvania delegate at the Constitutional Convention in Philadelphia. For four months, the delegates met and argued over whether the country should establish a strong federal government. On the day the voting on the proposed constitution was to take place, many of the delegates believed it would be voted down. Prior to the voting, Franklin advised the Convention that he had a few comments to make. At the time he was too frail to deliver the speech himself so he had fellow Pennsylvania delegate James Wilson read it for him. In the speech Franklin spoke of his own misgivings about the Constitution. However in the end he said, "Thus I consent, sir, to this Constitution. The opinions I have of its errors, I sacrifice to the public good." He went on to say, "On the whole, sir, I cannot help expressing a wish that every member of the convention who may still have objections to it would, with me, on this occasion doubt a little of his own infallibility and make manifest our unanimity." When the vote was taken it was close to unanimous. Only three of the forty one delegates refused to sign the document and it was eventually ratified by all thirteen states.

Franklin died in his Philadelphia home on April 17, 1790. He was 84 years old. He is the only founding father who signed all four of the documents central to the establishment of the United States. These are the Declaration of Independence, the Treaty of Paris, the Treaty of Alliance with France, and the United States Constitution. His funeral was attended by an estimated 20,000 people.

He was laid to rest in the Christ Church Burial Ground in Philadelphia.

If You Go:

The Christ Church Cemetery charges a modest entry fee. This fee is used to cover the cemeteries maintenance costs. There are a number of other important Americans buried here and maps are available at the cemetery (again for a modest charge) that direct you to their gravesites. If you do make the trip, you are in the midst of Philadelphia's historic district. Both Independence Hall and the Constitution Center are within easy walking distance. In addition, there are many street vendors and numerous restaurants in the area if you desire refreshments. Finally, the Betsy Ross House, which includes her burial site is only about three blocks away.

"Smokin' Joe"
JOE WILLIAM FRAZIER

County: Philadelphia
Town: Philadelphia
Cemetery: Ivy Hill
Address: 1201 Easton Road

He was considered one of the greatest heavyweight boxers of all time. His three fights with Muhammad Ali have achieved legendary status. Howard Cosell's repeated cries of "down goes Frazier" during his fight with George Foreman is cemented as one of the greatest sportscasting performances of all time. He was known to boxing fans as "Smokin' Joe" Frazier.

Joseph William Frazier was born on January 12, 1944, in Beaufort, South Carolina. He was the 12th child born to his parents. His early life was lived on the ten acres of farmland owned by his family. In later years Frazier recalled that he was particularly close to his father who would carry him to the still where he made bootleg liquor. Frazier's parents worked the farm which had very poor soil. All they were able to grow was cotton and watermelon.

In the early 1950's Frazier's parents purchased a television. Frazier's family would get together and watch boxing matches. Frazier viewed bouts that featured fighters like Sugar Ray Robinson and Rocky Marciano. During this period one of Frazier's uncles, after taking note of his nephew's sturdy build said, "that boy is going to be another Joe Louis." The next day Frazier constructed his own heavyweight bag that for years he worked on almost every day. It's clear that by this time Frazier's toughness was already in evidence. His classmates would pay him a quarter to walk home with them so the bullies would leave them alone.

At the age of 15 Frazier found work on a farm owned by a white family named Bellamy. One of the Bellamy's was a tough man named Jim. One day a 12 year old black boy accidentally damaged a tractor on the farm. Jim was so angry that he used his belt to whip the boy. Frazier witnessed the beating, and he told other black workers on the farm

Joe Frazier

what he had seen. Later Jim Bellamy confronted Frazier and demanded to know why he told the other workers. Frazier denied he had done so, but Bellamy didn't believe him, and he threatened to take off his belt again. Frazier told Bellamy that he wasn't going to use that belt on him. Bellamy sized up Frazier and decided to settle things by telling Frazier to get off his farm. After this incident Frazier decided he had to leave Beaufort. He took a bus to New York where he lived with one his brothers.

Frazier then began his amateur boxing career. In 1962, 1963 and 1964 he won the Golden Gloves Championship in the heavy weight division. In the three years he fought as an amateur, he only suffered one loss and that was to Buster Mathis. In 1964 Frazier attempted to make the United States Olympic Boxing team. He fought his way to the final of the Olympic Trial where he was matched up against none other than Buster Mathis. Frazier was out to revenge his only loss, but at the end of the bout the judges declared Mathis the winner. Frazier disagreed with the judges and remarked, "all that fat boy had done was run like a thief, hit me with a peck and backpedal like crazy." The loss depressed Frazier, and he actually thought about giving up boxing. Fortunately his trainer, Yank Durham, talked him out of it and even convinced Frazier to go as an alternate to Tokyo where the Olympics would be held.

The decision to go to Tokyo turned out to be a good one. Mathis was injured, and Frazier replaced him on the American team. He won his first two fights by knock out. He was the only American boxer left entering the semi-finals. His next opponent was Vadim Yemelyanov from the Soviet Union. Yemelvanov was 6 foot 4 and weighed 230 pounds. Frazier was pounding the Russian and knocked him to the canvas twice in the second round. Late in that round, Frazier landed a left hook and felt a jolt of pain shoot through his arm. He had broken his thumb. Fortunately for Frazier the match was decided in his favor when Yemelvanov's corner men threw in the towel.

Frazier was determined to fight in the final, so he kept the news of his broken thumb to himself. His opponent in the final was Hans Huber who was representing Germany. Frazier relied mainly on his right hand during the bout. He threw very few left hooks, and his punches were not as powerful as they had been in his previous fights. After three rounds it was up to the five judges to decide the winner. Three of them voted for Frazier making him the gold medal winner. Frazier was the only United States boxer to win an Olympic gold medal.

Following the Olympics, Frazier turned professional in 1965. He won his first fight when he knocked out Woody

Goss in the first round. After that he won three successive
fights, and no opponent lasted longer than three rounds.
Then during training Frazier's left eye was badly injured, so
badly that he was declared legally blind in that eye. Somehow Frazier continued to pass pre-fight physicals in spite
of this condition. Frazier then fought Mike Bruce who actually sent Frazier to the canvas in the first round. Frazier
beat the referee's count and knocked Bruce out in the third
round.

It was about this time in 1966 that Frazier's trainer,
Yancey Durham, convinced Eddie Futch to join Frazier's
team as an assistant trainer. Futch was centered in Los
Angeles so Frazier went there to train. Frazier fought three
times on the west coast winning all three bouts. One of the
fights was against George Johnson who went a full ten
rounds with Frazier before losing a decision. Ring magazine
reported that Johnson bet his entire purse that Frazier
would not knock him out.

In 1967 Muhammad Ali was stripped of his heavyweight title when he refused to be inducted into the mili-

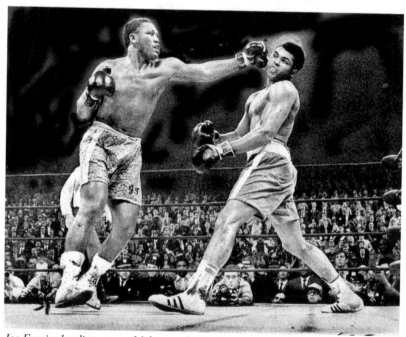

Joe Frazier landing one on Muhammad Ali

tary. A heavyweight elimination tournament was set up to crown a new champion. At the time Frazier was the number one contender but Futch convinced him to not participate in the tournament. Fitch was also instrumental in Frazier adopting a bob and weave style which made it more difficult for his opponents to land their punches. At the conclusion of the tournament Jimmy Ellis was crowned Heavyweight Champion.

On February 16, 1970, Frazier fought Ellis at Madison Square Garden for the undisputed heavyweight title. Ellis had never been floored in his career, but Frazier sent him to the canvas twice in the fourth round. When the bell sounded to start round five, Ellis remained in his corner, and Frazier was the new Heavyweight Champion.

In his first bout defending his title Frazier, who had won 26 straight fights, went up against the Light Heavyweight Champion Bob Foster. In the second round, Frazier sent Foster to the floor twice. The second knockdown came as a result of a powerful left hook, and Foster was unable to beat the count. This successful defense set up what would be called the "fight of the century" when Frazier would meet Muhammad Ali who was back in boxing after a three year suspension.

The fight took place in Madison Square Garden on March 8, 1971. Both Ali and Frazier were undefeated, and Ali as usual was predicting a victory. Once again Eddie Futch was a major factor in the outcome of the bout. Futch noticed that Ali had a tendency to drop his right hand prior to using it to deliver a powerful punch, and he instructed Frazier to watch that hand and when he saw it drop to deliver a left hook to Ali's face. Ali won many of the early rounds, but then Frazier began coming on and began pounding Ali to the body. In the 15th round Frazier saw Ali drop his right hand and Frazier, as instructed, delivered a left hook that sent Ali to the canvas. Frazier was declared the winner by unanimous decision. The contest saw both fighters head to the hospital afterward, and Frazier remained there for a week.

After defeating Ali, Frazier successfully defended his title against Ron Stander and Terry Daniels. Though he had won both fights, many observers felt that he hadn't been as dominant as he had been in previous bouts. In his next title defense Frazier was matched against George Foreman. Although Frazier was the favorite, there were boxing experts, including Howard Cosell on hand to broadcast the event, who were picking Foreman to win. Regardless of predictions nobody expected the fight to unfold the way it did. Frazier came out fast and landed his patented and powerful left hook, but it failed to faze Foreman. It could be that right then Frazier knew he was in trouble. The challenger responded with a combination followed by a right uppercut that sent the champion down. Howard Cosell screamed three times in a row "down goes Frazier." The moment is still remembered as one of Cosell's finest moments.

Frazier rose from the canvas only to be floored again before the round end-

Beautiful grave site of the great heavyweight champ Smokin' Joe Frazier. (& the reflection of the photographer—Joe Farley)

ed. Early in round two Foreman again connected with a right that sent Frazier to the canvas. Cosell described it as target practice for Foreman. Foreman didn't let up, and he floored Frazier three more times. After the 6th knockdown, the referee stopped the fight, and Foreman was the new champion.

Frazier continued to fight winning his next two bouts which set up a rematch with Ali. The fight was considered a letdown based on their earlier bout because there were numerous clinches. After 12 rounds, Ali was declared the winner though many disputed the decision. By the time Frazier and Ali would meet again, Ali would be the champion based on the fact that he knocked out George Foreman in 1974.

Here Rests One of God's Men
"Smokin' Joe Frazier"

Joseph Frazier entered this world on January 12, 1944, born to Ruben and Dolly Frazier in Beaufort, South Carolina. "Billy Boy," the nickname given affectionately to him by his dad, developed his signature "Left Hook" by being his dad's left hand man. Billy Boy knew at a young age that he wanted to be the Heavyweight Champion of the world.

He moved to New York, then to Philadelphia, worked at a meat packing company, trained at the Police Athletic League gym and won three National Golden Glove titles. In 1964, after fighting at least three fights with a broken thumb, he won the Olympic Gold Medal in Tokyo, Japan as a Heavyweight Boxer.

He received the name "Smokin' Joe" from his trainer Yancey Durham. Smokin' Joe won the Heavyweight titles for NABF, NYSAC, WBA and WBC. He was inducted into the Boxing Hall of Fame in 1980 with a boxing record of 32-4-1 with 27 knockouts.

Joe Frazier was a loving father who enjoyed attending church, fixing cars and listening to music. He was a great humanitarian and was involved in numerous charitable causes. He had a big heart and loved his family and community. He opened a gym in North Philadelphia in the 1960's where he mentored many men and women who became great boxers and citizens of the world.

"May the Work I've Done Speak for Me"
Thank you for life. We will truly miss you, and you will never be forgotten.
Love, Your Children

Monument at the grave of Smokin' Joe.

It can be argued that the third Ali – Frazier fight was the greatest heavyweight championship bout of all time. It took place on October 1, 1975 in the Philippines and became known as the "Thrilla in Manila." Before the fight Ali consistently referred to Frazier as "The Gorilla." From the beginning, the fight was intense and punishing. Early in the bout Ali said to Frazier, "They said you were through Joe." Frazier responded, "They lied, pretty boy." After the 14th round Frazier's eyes were swollen shut, and Eddie Futch refused to let him answer the bell for the final round. Ali emerged the winner, but he commented later that the fight was the "Closet thing to dying that I know of."

Frazier fought a few more bouts before announcing his retirement. He made a brief comeback in 1981 fighting one time before he retired for good. His final record as a professional was 32 wins, 4 losses and 1 draw.

In his later years, Frazier lived in Philadelphia where he owned and managed a boxing gym. He and Ali continued their rivalry. When Ali lit the Olympic flame in 1996, Frazier said that he would have liked to have thrown Ali into the fire. It wasn't until 2009 that Frazier said he no longer had bad feelings about Ali. Frazier was diagnosed with liver cancer in September of 2011. He died on November 7th of that year. Ali was among those who attended his funeral.

If You Go:

Others buried in Ivy Hill Cemetery include Willie Anderson, Franklin Gowen and Bill Tilden. Anderson was the first golfer to win four U.S. Open Championships (see page 188). Gowen was famous for leading the prosecution, some would say persecution, of the Molly Maguires in the 1870s (see page 246). Tilden was a tennis great who dominated that sport in the 1920s and 30s (see page 324). Both Harold Melvin of Harold Melvin and the Blue Notes and Marion Williams the famed gospel singer are also buried at Ivy Hill, but they are in unmarked graves. You can still visit their gravesites as the folks working in the cemetery office will be glad to provide you with their locations. In addition if you are at Ivy Hill, you are about a mile away from Holy Sepulcher Cemetery. Frank Rizzo and Connie Mack are buried there. Rizzo was a colorful and controversial Mayor of Philadelphia (see page 319). Mack was a legendary major league baseball manager (see page 273).

"General Controversy"

ALFRED SULLY
JOSHUA T. OWEN
FRANCIS ENGLE PATTERSON
HENRY MORRIS NAGLEE

County: Philadelphia
Town: Philadelphia
Cemetery: Laurel Hill
Address: 3822 Ridge Avenue

There are many Civil War generals buried in Philadelphia and many of them at the beautiful, historic Laurel Hill Cemetery. This chapter will feature four who generated some controversy then and now. All are buried in Laurel Hill Cemetery.

ALFRED SULLY
Alfred Sully was involved in controversy in both the Civil War and the Indian Wars. He was born on May 22, 1821 in Philadelphia, the son of a famous portrait painter, Thomas Sully. Thomas (who is also buried at Laurel Hill) is famous for his portraits of John Quincy Adams, Marquis de Lafayette, Thomas Jefferson, George Washington and many other famous people of the early 18th century. Alfred, like his father, was also a noted watercolorist and oil painter. He graduated from West Point in 1841 and served in the Seminole Wars, the Mexican War and on the American frontier in the West against the Cheyenne in the 1850's.

In February 1862, Sully was appointed colonel of

Alfred Sully

the 1st Minnesota Volunteer Infantry and commanded them in the Peninsula Campaign and the Seven Days Battles. After again commanding his regiment at the Battle of Antietam in September 1862, he was promoted to brigadier general.

He commanded a brigade in the II (Second) Corps of the Army of the Potomac at the Battle of Fredericksburg in December 1862. On May 1, 1863, just before the Battle of Chancellorsville, Sully was removed from his brigade by division commander Major General John Gibbon. According to historian Stephen Sears in his book "Chancellorsville," six companies of the 34th New York under Sully's command had stacked their arms and were refusing to serve any longer. The dispute was about exactly when their two-year enlistment was up. John Gibbon had no patience or sympathy with such protests. He told Sully to deal with it but Sully replied that he was unable to. Gibbon went to the 34th camp, accompanied by the 15th Massachusetts regiment with rifles in hand, and confronted the protestors. He called the protest a mutiny and said that unless they returned to duty he would order the 15th Massachusetts to open fire "and kill every man it could." He then asked every man now ready to do his duty to step forward. By ones and twos protestors stepped forward, then more followed and finally every man stood on the new line. That ended the mutiny of the 34th, whose members would serve faithfully until they were mustered out the next month.

The grave of General Alfred Sully

Gibbon remembered trembling at the thought of what might have happened, but still thought the action he took should have been taken by Sully earlier. He relieved Sully of his command on the spot. A court of inquiry would find Gibbon's action unjustified, but Sully never again served in the Army of the Potomac. He was transferred to the District of Dakota where he was again involved in controversy at the Battle of Whitestone Hill against the

Joshua T. Owen

Sioux in September 1863. Sully's troops killed, wounded or captured 300 to 400 Sioux (including women and children) while losing 20 men and having 38 wounded. Whether this was a battle or a massacre is an ongoing debate.

Alfred Sully died in 1879 while in command of the U.S. Army Post at Fort Vancouver in the Washington Territory.

JOSHUA T. OWEN

Joshua Thomas Owen was born in Wales in 1822. At the age of nine, he emigrated to the United States and settled in Baltimore. He studied and practiced law, established the Chestnut Hill Academy for boys in Philadelphia, and served in the Pennsylvania legislature. He also served as a private in a local militia unit in Philadelphia.

When the war erupted, Owen was elected colonel of the 24th Pennsylvania Volunteer Infantry regiment. When the 24th enlistment expired after three months, he helped organize and was placed in command, of the 69th Pennsylvania Volunteers. The 69th was a predominantly Irish regiment that was part of the Philadelphia Brigade. He saw action at Seven Pines and Glendale during the Seven Days Battles and then at Antietam. Owen was promoted to brigadier general for his service on June 30, 1862 at the Battle of Glendale.

At the Battle of Fredericksburg, he led his command in one of the futile Union assaults on Marye's Heights, where they suffered heavy losses. He led the brigade at Chancellorsville where it took no active part. After Chancellorsville, Owen was arrested during the march into Pennsylvania and relieved of command for reasons that are unclear. His replacement, Brigadier General Alexander Webb, would be awarded the Medal of Honor commanding the brigade during Pickett's Charge at Gettysburg.

Owen's grave

Owen was returned to command his brigade at the Wilderness, Spotsylvania, and Cold Harbor, where he was again arrested. Ironically, the arrest was made by General John Gibbon (who one year earlier had relieved Alfred Sully of his command). Owen was charged with "disobedience of orders" in failing to support another brigade, the 164th New York. He was allowed to be honorably mustered out of the service in July 1864.

After leaving the army, Owen returned to the practice of law and founded the "New York Daily Register," a law journal which became the official publication of the New York court system. In 1866, he was elected recorder of deeds in Philadelphia, where he died on November 7, 1887.

FRANCIS E. PATTERSON

Francis Engle Patterson was born in Philadelphia on March 7, 1821 to Irish-American army officer Robert Patterson and Sarah Engle. He came from a family with a military background. His father served as a general with distinction in the Mexican War. He also served briefly in the Civil War but received an honorable discharge in July 1861 after being widely criticized for his performance against Stonewall Jackson at the Battle of Hoke's Run. Francis' brother, Emmet Patterson, and his brother-in-law, John Joseph Abercrombie, were both generals in the Civil War.

Francis Engle Patterson

Francis entered the army during the Mexican War and wound up a first lieutenant in the artillery. He transferred to the infantry, was promoted to captain, and resigned in 1857. He returned to service when the Civil War started and was commissioned a colonel in the Pennsylvania militia serving under his father. The militia unit's enlistment was for 90 days, after which Patterson was appointed as Brigadier General of Volunteers and given command of the 2nd New Jersey Brigade. He led his brigade in the Battles of Williamsburg and Fair Oaks.

In November of 1862, he led his unit in an unauthorized withdrawal near Catlett's Station, Virginia, due to unconfirmed reports about nearby Confederate forces. He was criticized by fellow general Daniel Sickles, who called for an inquiry on the matter. Before an investigation could be started, on November 22 Patterson was found dead in his tent near Occoquan, Virginia, either due to an accidental weapon discharge or suicide. His father and brother are buried next to him at Laurel Hill.

Patterson's grave

HENRY M. NAGLEE

Henry Morris Naglee was involved in controversy before and after his service in the Civil War. He was born in Philadelphia on January 15, 1815, and graduated from the United States Military Academy in 1835. He came to California in 1846 as a captain in the 1st New York Infantry Regiment and led troops in the last clash of the Mexican War in 1848, known as the Skirmish of Todos Santos.

Henry Morris Naglee

His men called him "Black Jack" and after the Skirmish he and about 50 men pursued the enemy. During this pursuit, Naglee ordered the shooting of two men who they had captured, an act that was in direct violation of military orders. The military governor of Alta California ordered Naglee arrested but he escaped punishment when President Polk granted him a pardon.

After his discharge from the army in 1849, Naglee became the first commanding officer of the 1st California Guards (which would become the California National Guard). He also entered into a career in banking, real estate and brandy making.

In 1861, Naglee reentered the army as a lieutenant colonel and in 1862 was made a brigadier general of volunteers. In May, he commanded a brigade in the Army of the

Naglee's grave (Photo by Joe Farley)

Potomac during the Peninsula Campaign, where he was wounded at the Battle of Fair Oaks, Virginia.

He was again involved in controversy when—after returning to California—he was involved in two very public scandals. The first involved a San Francisco actress named Mary Schell, a young lady with whom Naglee corresponded during the war. When Naglee broke off their relationship to pursue Marie Antoinette Ringgold, the spurned actress tried to blackmail him by threatening to print some of his passionate love letters. Naglee refused to pay, and Miss Schell published a book entitled "The Love Life of Brigadier General Henry Naglee, Consisting of a correspondence on Love, War and Politics." The book was quite popular and is still available.

Naglee married Miss Ringgold, who sadly died during the birth of their second daughter. He employed a nurse-maid, Emily Hanks, in 1871 to take care of his children. When Hanks became pregnant, she insisted the general was the father. When Naglee refused to marry her she filed a "breach of promise" suit. She won a settlement of $27,500 in a trial but the award was over-turned on appeal. The affair was headlines in local papers for three years.

Naglee died in San Francis-co in 1886 at the age of 71. There is a memorial to him in St. James Park in San Jose, California.

If You Go:
There are so many Civil War officers buried at Laurel Hill that it seems the entire city must have gone to war. Below are four major generals and three brigadier generals who are also buried in historic Laurel Hill.

Charles Ferguson Smith: served with great distinction in the Mexican War, first with

Smith's grave

Zachary Taylor and later with Winfield Scott. In the Civil War, he served under Ulysses S. Grant (one of his former students at West Point) in the Union capture of Forts Donelson and Henry. Smith personally led the charge that forced the surrender of Fort Donelson. Just prior to the Battle of Shiloh, he slipped while boarding a rowboat, scraping his shin. The wound got infected, ultimately resulting in his death on April 25, 1862.

Edgar M. Gregory: a prominent pre-war businessman who participated in helping runaway slaves escape to Canada. As commander of the 91st Pennsylvania Volunteer Infantry he was wounded at the Battle of Chancellorsville and missed Gettysburg while recuperating. He received a first brevet promotion for his gallant conduct at Poplar Spring Church and a second one for the Battle of Five Forks. After the war, he served in Texas as an assistant commissioner of the Freedman's Bureau. His grave was unmarked for over 100 years until a standard issue government marker was placed there.

Samuel Gibbs French: a Confederate major general who was New Jersey-born and served with distinction in the Mexican War. He married a southern woman and moved to the South. He fought at Jackson, Atlanta, Nashville and Mobile, Alabama. He wrote an autobiographical account of his war services entitled "Two Wars," which is still available. He is actually buried in Pensacola, Florida, but a cenotaph stands for him in his family's plot at Laurel Hill. (*See* Chapter 34, "Rebels Among Us").

Thomas Jefferson Cram: a topographical engineer and 1826 graduate of West Point.

Caldwell Hall: commanded the 14th New Jersey Volunteer Infantry and was severely wounded during the Battle of Monocacy, preventing him from ever returning to field service.

General French, CSA

Joseph Roberts: commanded the 3rd Pennsylvania Heavy Artillery regiment.

Charles Mallet Prevost: served as a U.S. Marshall in Wisconsin before the war. He commanded the 118th Pennsylvania Volunteer Infantry and was severely wounded at Shepardstown (West) Virginia. He returned for the Battle of Chancellorsville where he led his men while his injured arm was strapped to his side. He later commanded Camp Butler Military Prison in Springfield, Missouri.

"The Molly Maguires"
BLACK JACK KEHOE and FRANKLIN GOWEN

Counties: Schuylkill, Philadelphia
Towns: Tamaqua, Philadelphia
Cemeteries: Old Saint Jerome's, Ivy Hill
Addresses: Corner of High and Nescopeck Streets, 1201 Easton Road

In Pennsylvanian history, there are few groups as interesting or as controversial as the Molly Maguires. Some historians view them as an Irish Catholic terrorist organization, while to others, they are no more than an organized labor movement created as a response to the persecution of Irish coal miners. Still, there are some who argue that the organization never existed. Undeniable, however, is the fact is that between June 21, 1877, and October 9, 1879, twenty Irish catholic men were hanged for murder and accused of belonging to a secret society known as the Molly Maguires. Ten of these men were hanged on June 21, 1877, a day that would become known as "Black Thursday" or "The Day of the Rope."

The Molly Maguire story began in the early 1860's and ended in 1879 when the last hanging took place. The center of action was the anthracite coal region in northeastern Pennsylvania. The alleged Mollies were most active in two counties Carbon and Schuylkill.

As a result of the potato famine in the late 1840's, many Irish immigrates landed in America. Those who settled in the Pennsylvania coal region found that the only jobs available to them were in the mines. The work was difficult and dangerous. In addition, the miners were forced to live in coal company provided housing and could only shop at the company store where prices were so inflated that it was not unusual for a miner to find himself in debt to the company as his wages could not cover his rent and other expenses. These conditions led to the beatings and murder of mine owners, foreman and superintendents. The mine owners and newspapers believed these beatings and

John "Black Jack" Kehoe, "King of the Mollies," soon before his execution in 1878.

killings were part of an organized conspiracy headed by Irishmen who called themselves the Molly Maguires.

During the Molly era, the miners were forming a union under the leadership of John Siney. The union was known as the Workingmen's Benevolent Association and through Siney, and the leadership of the organization as a whole, they sought to seek concessions through negotiations. At

The tombstones in this old cemetery have been destroyed due to vandalism. Two alleged Molly Maguires are buried here including Alec Campbell. Almost all historians agree that one of the two interned here, placed their handprint on his cell wall prior to his execution. The print remains to this day as a sign of his innocence.

times, they used strikes as a tool. In December of 1874, what was called the long strike began in the coalfields. The strike lasted for just under six months and when the miners broke they were forced to return for lower wages than they had previously earned. The person responsible for this settlement was Franklin B. Gowen, the President of the Philadelphia and Reading Coal and Iron Company.

Gowen was born in Mount Airy, Pennsylvania on February 9, 1836. He was the fifth child of an Irish Protestant immigrant who made his living as a grocer. Franklin attended a boarding school, John Beck's Boys Academy, starting at age 9 and ending when he was 13. After serving an apprenticeship to a Lancaster merchant, he decided to study law and worked under an attorney in Pottsville, Pennsylvania which happened to be the county seat of Schuylkill County. In 1860 he was admitted to the County Bar and in 1862 he was elected District Attorney of Schuylkill County. He held this position until 1864 when he resigned in order to pursue a private practice. Among his clients was the Philadelphia and Reading Railroad. He soon left private practice to head that company's legal department. It proved to be a wise move for in 1869, Gowen was appointed acting President of the company.

By this time, Gowen already had the Molly Maguires in his sights. In 1873, he hired the Pinkerton Detective Agency for the purpose of infiltrating the Mollies. Several Pinkerton operatives were sent into the coalfields, including James McParlan, who arrived in Schuylkill County on October 27,1873, using the alias of James McKenna. In April of 1874, McParlan was initiated into the Ancient Order of Hibernians (AOH), a legal Irish Catholic organization. It was Gowen's belief that the Molly Maguires operated within this organization. It is worth noting that violence on both management's and labor's side increased once the Pinkertons arrived in the area.

The Pinkertons were not the only weapon used by Gowen in his attacks on the Mollies. He had his own private police force known as the Coal and Iron police. An 1868 act of the legislature authorized the creation of this private army. A deputy commissioner for Pennsylvania's Bureau of Labor Statistics held the opinion that the coal operators were their own personal government in the middle of a republic. There was no limit to the number of Coal and Iron policemen that could be hired by the Reading Coal and Iron Company, nor were there any background checks on those who applied to join the force. This police force patrolled the coal region unmolested by local authori-

On June 21, 1877, within the walls of the Schuylkill County prison (pictured above) in Pottsville six alleged Molly Maguires were executed by hanging.

ties. In May of 1875, Pinkerton sent Captain Robert Linden to the coal fields. He immediately received an appointment as a Coal and Iron policeman. The power of this police force was absolute. They were more powerful than the civil authorities. Linden was instrumental in investigating the crimes that led to the arrests of the alleged Molly Maguires.

One of the most important murders in the Molly Maguire story took place in Tamaqua during the evening hours on July 5, 1875. The Tamaqua police force consisted of two men: Barney McCarron and Benjamin Yost. Yost had a history of running into trouble with an Irish minor named James Kerrigan. Yost had arrested Kerrigan on several occasions for public drunkenness, and in at least one instance subdued Kerrigan with his billy club.

One of the duties of the Tamaqua police force was to extinguish the gas street lights. As Yost was climbing a ladder to shut off one of the light, shots rang out, and Yost fell to the ground. McCarron Turned towards the sound of the shots and saw two forms running away. McCarron gave chase but the assailants escaped. Yost died several hours later and word spread that the murder had been carried out by the Molly Maguires.

The first Mollies that ended up on the gallows were arrested in September of 1875 for the murder of mine superintendent John P. Jones. Jones was shot and killed at a railroad station in Lansford while on his way to work by two men who quickly left the scene. A witness to the murder quickly made the trip to Tamaqua and spread the news. In addition, this man claimed to have seen a man waving something white in the woods outside Tamaqua an apparent signal that brought two other men to him. A posse was formed to investigate. The three men arrested for the crime were found in those same woods having a meal. The men were identified as Edward Kelly, Michael Doyle, and Jimmy Kerrigan. Both Kelly and Doyle carried documents that identified them as members of the AOH. The three were taken to the Carbon County jail in Mauch Chunk, now known as Jim Thorpe.

These initial arrests provided the break the Pinkertons were waiting for, and they quickly took advantage of it. The accused men requested separate trials, and Michael Doyle was the first to be tried. Meanwhile Kerrigan and Kelly were kept in solitary confinement in the county jail.

This initial trial set the tone for the ones that would follow. The jury would have no Irish or catholic members and would be made up largely of Germans, including some who spoke little or no English. The District Attorney, while present, did not try the case. This duty fell to attorneys who worked for the railroad and coal companies. In the Doyle trial the prosecution was headed by General Charles Albright who worked for the Lehigh and Wilkes-Barre Coal Company. The general wore his civil war uniform, including his sword, throughout the trial. One has to wonder how he would have gotten past security today.

The prosecution called more than 100 witnesses that established that Doyle was seen in Lansford on the day of the murder. While no one testified that they had seen Doyle murder Jones, he was described as walking quickly toward the murder site and observed running away with a pistol in hand. The defense did not call a single witness in the case. In their summation the defense conceded that

Doyle was in Lansford that day, but he was simply looking for work.

The prosecution case was at its weakest when it came to providing a motive for the murder. Detective McParlan's reports to his superiors laid out a scenario that would have provided a motive. According to the detective, Kerrigan (the head of the Mollies in Tamaqua) had been beaten by the policeman Yost. Another Molly, Hugh McGehan, had been blacklisted by the mine foreman, Jones. Kerrigan initiated contact with James Roarity, the head of the Mollies in Coaldale, in order to exact revenge for these perceived wrong-doings. Kerrigan and Roarity decided that McGehan and a man by the name of James Boyle would murder Yost with the assistance of Kerrigan. Doyle and Kelly, again with Kerrigan's help, would take care of Jones.

The only way the prosecution could introduce this evidence would be to call McParlan as a witness. Because Mc-Parlan was still gathering information and the use of his testimony would have exposed his identity as a detective, the prosecution went on without him. It didn't matter. On February 1, 1876, the jury pronounced Doyle guilty and on the 23rd he was sentenced to be hanged.

At later trials, McParlan claimed that it was a common practice among the Mollies to trade jobs. This was done to make it difficult for the townspeople to recognize the out of town assailants.

Something of greater importance to the Molly Maguire story took place during the trial. Jimmy Kerrigan confessed. In fact, he produced a 210 page confession and agreed to testify against his fellow Irishmen in return for immunity. This action earned "Powder Keg" Kerrigan a new nickname, he would henceforth be known as "Squealer" Kerrigan.

Based on McParlan's reports and information supplied by Kerrigan, a unit of the Coal and Iron Police led by Captain Linden made a series of arrests. On February 4th this group set out and arrested James Carroll, James Roarity, Thomas Duffy, Hugh McGehan, James Boyle and Alexander Campbell for the murders of Yost and Jones. Six days later the Coal and Iron Police arrested Thomas Munley as a suspect in the murders of Thomas Sanger and William

Uren. Another alleged Molly, Dennis Donnelly, would be arrested later for his part in the murders.

Sanger and Uren were shot and killed on September 1, 1875. On that morning Sanger, who was a mine boss, left for work accompanied by Uren who worked for him. While on the road, the duo was attacked by five heavily armed men who shot and killed them both. Sanger had been targeted for evicting Irishmen. Uren was simply in the wrong place at the wrong time.

Following these murders, a one page handbill titled "Strictly Confidential" began circulating in the coalfields. The paper claimed to present facts to be considered by the

Joe Farrell stands in front of Jack Kehoe's grave holding the key supplied by a local resident which allowed us entrance to the aged cemetery. Kehoe has been called the "King of the Mollies" but he was almost surely innocent of the crime that sent him to the gallows.

*Here is Jack Kehoe's Hibernian House looking much as it did the day he was
arrested. It is still in operation and run by Kehoe's great-grandson.*

Vigilance Committee of the Anthracite Coal Region. The
document goes on to list a number of murders that had occurred in the region and named the murderers and their
residences. In terms of the Sanger and Uren case the
handbill states, "On September 1st, 1875 at about 7 A.M.
Thomas Sanger, a mining boss, and William Uren, a miner

of Raven Run, were shot and fatally wounded by James O'Donnell, alias "Friday," and Thomas Munley, as the un-suspecting victims were on their way to work. Charles O'Donnell, Charles McAllister, and Mike Doyle were present, and accessories to this murder." The information in the handbill was almost certainly based on reports from Detective McParlan, and it is just as probable that it was distributed by the Pinkerton's.

The handbill began circulating in the fall of 1875, on December 10th of that year it would bear fruit. At about 3 in the morning of the 10th Charles and Ellen McAllister were asleep in their home in Wiggans Patch. A small child lay between them and Ellen was pregnant. Ellen's mother was also in the house along with her unmarried sons James "Friday" O'Donnell and Charles O'Donnell. Four borders were also asleep in the house including James McAllister who was the brother of Charles.

Charles McAllister was awakened by a crashing noise: the kitchen door being smashed in. He told his wife to stay in bed and ran to the cellar where he made his way to his neighbor's through a door that connected the residences. His wife did not obey; she got up and opened a door that led to the kitchen and was shot and killed. Now pairs of men began searching every bedroom in the house. They brought James McAllister down the stairs into the yard where he freed himself and ran. Shots were fired, and he was hit in the arm but escaped. James O' Donnell also managed to escape. Charles O'Donnell was not so lucky; he was taken outside, and when he struggled free, he was downed by gunshots. Men gathered around his fallen body and emptied their pistols. The shots were fired so close to the body that they burned the flesh. The next day a note was found on the property that stated "You are the killers of Sanger and Uren." Black Jack Kehoe, the man Gowen considered to be the King of the Mollies, was the broth-er-in-law of both Charles McAllister and Ellen McAllister.

To this day no one knows who the men were who par-ticipated in what became known as the Wiggans Patch massacre. What we do know is that Detective McParlan felt responsible. Upon hearing of the killings, he sent a letter of resignation to the Pinkerton office in New York City. In the letter he states, "Now I wake up this morning to find that I

am the murderer of Mrs. McAllister." His resignation was
not accepted.

Events moved quickly as a series of Molly Maguire trials
commenced. The second trial, that of Edward Kelly, began
on March 29th. Again, there were no Irish on the jury and
the prosecution team was the same. The jury returned a
guilty verdict on April 6th, and six days later Kelly was
sentenced to be hanged.

After these first two convictions, the Pottsville Court-
house in Schuylkill County was the scene of the next trial.
Leading the prosecution in this case would be Franklin
Gowen, President of the Philadelphia and Reading Coal and
Iron Company. Gowen was well acquainted with the
Pottsville Courthouse. As stated previously, he had served
as Schuylkill County's District Attorney. The trial started
on May 4 and involved the killing of the Tamaqua police officer Benjamin Yost. James Boyle, James Roarity, Hugh
McGehan, Thomas Duffy and James Carroll stood accused
of the murder.

This trial marked the first appearance of the detective
James McParlan as a witness for the prosecution. The in-
former, Jimmy Kerrigan, would also testify. Just as the trial
was getting underway, news spread that the coal and iron
police had arrested ten more Mollies in Schuylkill County.
Among the ten was Black Jack Kehoe. Kehoe was a respected man active in community affairs who had written to local
newspapers denying the existence of an organization known
as the Molly Maguires. He was also active in the leadership
of the Hibernians. In addition, he had worked his way out of
the mines and had much to lose if his leadership of such a
group as the Mollies could be proven.

Detective McParlan was the main witness at this trial,
and through his testimony, the prosecution was able to
leave the impression that the AOH and the Molly Maguires
were one and the same. McParlan detailed secret signs and
sayings that members used to identify each other. He stated that the chief purpose of the organization was to protect, and, when necessary, seek revenge for members who
felt they had been wronged in some manner. In this way he
tied the murders and beatings of the mine owners and
bosses to the organization. Jimmy Kerrigan also testified
and supported McParlan's account.

On the Day of the rope four alleged Mollies were hanged together at the same time in the old jail in Jim Thorpe. The gallows were built in the middle of the cell block so the condemned men were able to hear the construction prior to their execution.

The defense did call several witnesses in this case including Mrs. Kerrigan who testified that her husband told her he had murdered Yost. She also condemned him for allowing innocent men to take the blame for his crime. While she was being cross examined, one of the jurors became ill. On May 18th the trial was suspended pending his recovery, however his condition did not improve and on May 25th he died of pneumonia. All the work that had gone into the case was lost. The jury was dismissed, and the prisoners returned to the county jail to await a new trial.

Before the second Yost trial began, Alexander Campbell was brought before the court in Mauch Chunk for the murder of John P. Jones. Campbell, like many of the accused Mollies, was born in Ireland. He arrived in Pennsylvania in 1868 where he opened a saloon in Tamaqua. He later moved to the Lansford area where he operated another saloon, the Columbia house. Campbell was viewed by many to be the leader of the Mollies in Carbon County. What made the Campbell trial important was that all agreed he was not present when Jones was killed. He was charged as an accessory before the fact, accused of being involved in the planning of the murder. The prosecution alleged that Kelly, Doyle and Kerrigan spent the night before the killing at Campbell's tavern. The defense countered with several witnesses who said they had been at Campbell's that night and had not seen the three men. After an eleven day trial the jury quickly returned with a guilty verdict and on August 28th Campbell was sentenced to be hanged. Clearly, an Irishman owning a public tavern was a dangerous business to be involved in at the time.

Before Campbell's trial was over, another had begun in Pottsville where Thomas Munley was tried for the murders of Thomas Sanger and William Uren. The prosecution case rested entirely on the testimony of McParlan. Several of Munley's family members testified that he was at home on the day of the murder. Despite this testimony, Munley was found guilty and sentenced to death.

By then, the second Yost trial was underway with the accused being Boyle, Carroll, McGehen and Roarity. Thomas Duffy had requested and was granted a separate trial. McParlan and Kerrigan repeated their testimony and all four men were found guilty. They too were sentenced to be hanged. In addition, the separate trial did not help Duffy as he was also found guilty and received the same sentence.

The Pinkertons continued to investigate past murders including that of mine boss Morgan Powell who had been killed in 1871. Three men, John Donahue, Thomas Fisher and Alec Campbell, were arrested and tried for this murder. All three were convicted and sentenced to death. This was Campbell's second conviction.

The first ten executions took place on June 21, 1877, Black Thursday, or the Day of the Rope as it was referred to by locals. Four of the convicted Irishmen would be hanged in the Mauch Chunk jail. The other six would face the hangman in Pottsville.

The Mauch Chunk hangings occurred first. The gallows had been constructed so that all four men could be hanged at the same time. At around 10:30 in the morning, Alexander Campbell took his place on the gallows. In his final statement, he forgave his executioners. Michael Doyle was next, and he took his spot on the gallows. He said that he had come to this point because of his failure to follow the advice of his church on secret societies. John Donahue took his place and declined comment. Edward Kelly was the last to take his place and, led by his priest, forgave everyone and added that if he had listened to his priests, he would not have found himself on the gallows. The men were then readied for execution and at approximately 10:45, the trap was sprung and the four hurtled to their death. After the bodies were cut down and their hoods removed, the sheriff invited the spectators present to inspect the bodies.

In Pottsville, the authorities had decided to hang the prisoners two at a time. Between 8 and 10 AM, those with official passes were allowed into the prison where they scurried to find the best spots to watch the executions. Meanwhile, the area around the prison, including the hills, were packed with people.

Around 11 AM, the first two prisoners, James Boyle and Hugh McGehan emerged from the jail and made their way to the gallows. Both asked for forgiveness, and Boyle pardoned those who were about to hang him. Ten minutes later, the two were dead. The pair to follow were James Carroll and James Roarity. The latter had been convicted primarily based on the testimony of Jimmy Kerrigan who claimed that Roarity had paid him to have Yost killed. On the gallows, Roarity insisted that this was not so, and he added that Thomas Duffy had nothing to do with the Yost murder. Carroll simply stated that he was an innocent man. Both men were hung at around 12:20. Thomas Duffy and Thomas Munley were the last to the gallows. Neither said much beyond that it was no use and at 1:20, both were sent falling to their death.

At this point the Mollies, if they ever existed, were finished as a power in the coal region. Ten more would be hanged, and others would serve long prison terms. This was not enough to satisfy Franklin Gowen. He wouldn't be happy until he saw Jack Kehoe, who was already serving a seven year prison term, at the end of a rope.

Kehoe was a man who worked his way out of the mines. By 1873, he opened a tavern and rooming house in Girardville called the Hibernian House. He ran this business for three years and during this time became active in local politics. He was elected to the post of Constable in Girardville and was also named Schuylkill County delegate in the AOH. When local newspapers, based on information supplied by the Pinkertons, began linking the Hibernians to the Molly Maguires Kehoe publicly denied such charges. It was Kehoe's view that the Mollies were the fictional invention of the mine owners. Based on information supplied by Detective McParlan, Kehoe was arrested in 1876 and charged with conspiracy to commit murder. This charge did not carry a death sentence, but Gowen resurrected a murder that occurred in 1862 and named Kehoe one of the killers.

Frank Langdon was a mining boss in Audenried where Kehoe lived and worked. On June 14, 1862, he was assaulted by at least three men. He was able to return home, but he died three days later as a result of the beating. In January of 1877, Kehoe was tried for his murder. The evidence presented at the trial was murky at best. Kehoe was said to have threatened Langdon weeks before he was beaten, but other witnesses claimed to have seen Kehoe on a hotel porch at the time Langdon was assaulted. In his summation, Gowen described Kehoe as a man who made money by his traffic in the souls of his fellow men. Despite the lack of evidence, Kehoe was found guilty and sentenced to death.

Kehoe's lawyers fought the conviction to the State Supreme Court which denied the appeal. Next they petitioned the Board of Pardons where they produced sworn statements from John Campbell and Neil Dougherty (both of whom had been convicted of second degree murder in the matter) admitting their participation in the beating and swearing that Kehoe was not present. In September 1878, the Board voted 2-2 on the petition. A tie vote meant the conviction was upheld.

On December 18, 1878, Kehoe waited in his cell with one of his lawyers, Martin L'Velle. He told L'Velle that he was prepared to die. Shortly thereafter, Kehoe took his place on the gallows in Pottsville. Given the opportunity to speak, he proclaimed his innocence, adding that he had not even seen the crime being committed. After making his statement, Kehoe nodded to the sheriff signifying that he was ready. He was quickly shackled and strapped, and at 10:27 a.m., the trap door was sprung. Four other men would be hanged as Mollies after Kehoe, but public interest in the story and in the hangings was never the same. In

September of 1978, the Governor of Pennsylvania, Milton Shapp, released a statement that included the following; "It was Jack Kehoe's popularity among the workingmen that led Franklin Gowen to fear, despise, and ultimately destroy him." On January 12, 1979, Shapp signed a posthumous pardon for Jack Kehoe. This is the only posthumous pardon issued in the history of Pennsylvania.

Kehoe is buried in the old Saint Jerome's Catholic Cemetery in Tamaqua. The two victims of the Wiggans Patch massacre, Ellen McAllister and her brother, Charles O'Donnell, were also laid to rest here. The cemetery is located on the corner of High and Nescopeck streets, and it is fenced in and locked. A neighbor who lives on that corner has a key that he is happy to share with visitors. When we were looking for a way in, he appeared and asked "You here to see Kehoe?" That's how we found our way into the cemetery. Two other alleged Mollies, Thomas Duffy and Jack Donahue, are also buried there in unmarked graves. Another place worth visiting in relation to Kehoe is his Hibernian House in Girardville, which is now run by his great grandson. Among the artifacts that can be viewed at this location is Kehoe's cell door from the Pottsville prison.

Alec Campbell is buried in Saint Joseph's Catholic cemetery on Ludlow Street in Summit Hill. There are no grave markers in this cemetery due to acts of vandalism. A mock trial of Campbell was held in Jim Thorpe recently using the transcripts from his trial. A relative portrayed Campbell, and he was found innocent. Another alleged Molly, Thomas Fisher, lies there as well.

The Schuylkill County jail in Pottsville where many of the hangings took place is still in operation, but aside from plaques noting what happened, there is little to see. There is one interesting plaque that is on the wall at the jail's main entrance. The plaque notes that the largest mass execution in Pennsylvania history took place inside this prison. It also references the four executions that took place in Mauch Chunk that same day. What is striking is it ends by stating that the pardon of Jack Kehoe reflects "the judgment of many historians that the trials and executions were part of a repression directed against the fledgling mine workers union of that historic period."

The Carbon County jail, however, is now a museum where regular tours are conducted. A replica of the gallows stands where the original one once stood. In addition, visitors can view the mysterious handprint in cell 17. According to legend, as one of the Mollies (either Alec Campbell or Thomas Fisher) was about to be taken to the gallows, he put his handprint on the wall of his cell saying that it would remain forever as a sign of his innocence. Despite efforts to remove the print, it remains to this day.

Things went well for one of the other main characters in the Molly story. James McParlan was named manager of the Pinkertons' office in Denver Colorado. He passed away in Denver in 1919.

Franklin Gowen eventually lost his leadership position in the Philadelphia and Reading Coal and Iron Company. He returned to private practice. On December 13, 1889, according to the coroner who investigated the death, Gowen shot himself while staying in a hotel in Washington D.C. Many of Gowen's family and friends believed he was murdered. In 2002, a book written by Patrick Campbell (a descendant of Alec Campbell) entitled "Who Killed Franklin Gowen," concludes that Gowen was a homicide victim. Gowen is buried in the Ivy Hill Cemetery just outside Philadelphia.

Final resting place of Franklin Gowen who was the man most responsible for the hangings of 20 alleged Molly Maguires during the 1870's.

In 1969, a highly fictionalized major motion picture called "The Molly Maguires" was released. It was filmed largely in Pennsylvania including several scenes that take place in Jim Thorpe. Much of the movie was filmed in Eckley, not far from Hazleton. Eckley in now a museum and visitors are most welcome. In the movie, Richard Harris plays Detective McParlan and Sean Connery stars as Black Jack Kehoe. It's worth a look.

If You Go:
In the center of downtown Jim Thorpe, you can always visit the Molly Maguire Pub where one can find good food and drink at reasonable prices. The pub has a large outdoor deck that is open weather permitting. That same section of Jim Thorpe is home to many antique and specialty shops that you might want to check out.

In addition, the town is quite close to the Pocono's, so white water rafting is available as well as skiing depending on the season. Finally, you can visit the Jim Thorpe Memorial which is the final resting place for that great athlete (see *Keystone Tombstones – Anthracite Region*, page 1).

"That Ball's Outta Here"
HARRY NORBERT KALAS

County: Philadelphia
Town: Philadelphia
Cemetery: Laurel Hill
Address: 3822 Ridge Avenue

"That ball is outta here" was Harry Kalas' home run call, and it has become one of the legendary baseball calls. Harry Kalas was a Hall of Fame broadcaster best known for his role as lead play-by-play announcer for the Philadelphia Phillies. He also was well known as the voice of NFL films from 1975 until his death.

Kalas was born in Naperville, Illinois on March 26, 1936. He graduated from Naperville High School in 1954. He made the University of Iowa his college choice, graduating in 1959. Soon after he left the university, he was drafted into the United States Army. He was stationed in Hawaii where he served until he was discharged in 1961. It was at this point that Harry began his illustrious broadcasting career, calling minor league baseball games for the Hawaii Islanders.

In 1965, he was hired by the Houston Astros to broadcast their games. He remained there until the Phillies hired him in 1971. Initially, his hiring was not met with the approval of a number of Phillies fans. The man he replaced, Bill Campbell, was extremely popular among the team's fan base. Kalas won the fans over quickly. His easy going style that would all of a sudden register great excitement when a Phillie made a great play in the field or delivered a key hit turned Campbell into a fond memory.

Kalas was the Master of Ceremonies at the opening of Veteran's Stadium. He also called the last game at the "Vet" and the first game at Citizens Bank Park. He was eventually paired up with Hall of Fame player Richie Ashburn (see page 94) and the duo became best friends as well as sports icons in Philadelphia. He and Ashburn broadcast together for 27 seasons until Ashburn's death in 1997.

During his Phillies career Kalas broadcast six no-hitters, six National League Championship Series, and three World Series. He missed broadcasting the 1980 World Se-

Tomb of Harry Kalas in Lauel Hill Cemetery

ries because of a Major League Baseball rule that prohibited local broadcasters from calling the series due to conflict with the networks. As a result of a public outcry the rule was changed. By now, Kalas had clearly made a national name for himself.

Kalas was nicknamed "Harry the K" by Phillies fans and loved the Frank Sinatra song "High Hopes" which he sang on many occasions. The year before his passing, Harry had the opportunity to broadcast the ultimate highlight: calling

Gravesite of the legendary Phillie and NFL announcer. Note grave goods behind box seats on right side of photo.

the game as his beloved Phillies won the World Series and became "the 2008 World Champions of Baseball." He then joined the on-field celebration, grabbing a microphone and belting out "High Hopes."

To a whole generation of football fans, Kalas was known as the voice of "Inside The NFL." He did the voiceover from 1977 through 2008. In addition to his work with the Phillies and NFL films, Kalas called various sports over the years for the Mutual Broadcasting System, CBS Radio, and Westwood One. This included NFL games, Major league Baseball, college basketball, and Notre Dame football. For many years, he narrated the "Alcoa Fantastic Finishes" in game highlight spots for use during NFL telecasts.

On April 8, 2009, the Philadelphia Phillies honored Kalas by having him throw out the first pitch before a game with the Atlanta Braves. The Phillies received their championship rings as part of the ceremony. It turned out to be the last home game Harry Kalas ever announced. Kalas collapsed in the press box as he was preparing to broadcast a game between the Phillies and Washington Nationals at National's Park. He died on April 13, 2009 at George Washington University Hospital at the age of 73. For the rest of the season, the Phillies wore a patch on their uniforms that bore the initials "HK."

Kalas received the Ford Frick Award from the National Baseball Hall of Fame in 2002. In June 2009, he was inducted into the National Radio Hall of Fame and Museum. He was named Pennsylvania Broadcaster of the Year 18 times.

Close-up of grave goods left by visitors to Harry the K's grave.

He is buried in historic Laurel Hill Cemetery overlooking the Schuylkill River. His tombstone is shaped like a giant microphone with the letters "HK" in the middle and a likeness of Kalas' autograph at the microphone's base which sits on top of a raised base shaped like home plate and is flanked on each side by a pair of seats from Veterans Stadium. In 2010, the grave was resurfaced with sod that originally came from Citizens Bank Park. When we visited his grave, visitors had left baseballs there, some autographed, and there were numerous coins as well.

If You Go:
There are several interesting and famous graves in Laurel Hill Cemetery (see George Meade on page 281).

Henry Deringer, who is interred here, was developer of one of the most famous American guns the derringer, designed to be compact and easily concealed. John Wilkes Booth used a derringer to assassinate Abraham Lincoln.

Boies Penrose is also buried nearby. He was a US Senator from 1897-1921. There is a prominent large statue of Penrose on the grounds of the Pennsylvania State Capitol, although it is hard to understand why. The statute shows Penrose with his hand in one pocket. Many from Pennsylvania claim it's not lifelike because Boies never had his hand in his own pocket.

The cemetery itself is located very near the Philadelphia Zoo and the city's art museum. Both deserve a visit. While it is hard to recommend where to stop and dine in Philly (there are so many great places), we had a great lunch at a spot close to the cemetery called the Trolley Car Café on S. Ferry Road. It featured delicious gourmet salads, sandwiches, and soups and offered a patio setting if you wished to move outside.

"An Unknown Hero"

OLIVER B. KNOWLES

County: Philadelphia
Town: Philadelphia
Cemetery: Laurel Hill
Address: 3822 Ridge Avenue

It is amazing how difficult it is to find information about Oliver Blatchy Knowles considering what he did in his short life. He entered the Civil War as a private at the age of 19 and ended the war four years later a brevet brigadier general at the age of 23.

Knowles was born on January 3, 1842 in Philadelphia. His father, Levi Knowles, was a prominent flour merchant who was heavily involved in civic and charitable organizations in Philadelphia. Oliver quit high school after two years and joined his father's business. He was tall (6'2") and through his love of horses he developed into an excellent horseman. When the war broke out, 19-year-old Knowles was recruited by William Henry Boyd of Philadelphia. Boyd was raising a company of cavalry which would become part of the First New York Cavalry (also called the "Lincoln Cavalry"). Boyd was a captain and young Oliver Knowles became his orderly as he quickly established a reputation for dedication to his duty and for following orders. Their colonel was a man named Carl Schurz, a former German Revolutionary of 1848 and confidant of President Lincoln.

The Lincoln Cavalry saw its first combat at Pohick Church, Virginia on July 22, 1861. It was a skirmish with Confederate cavalry, the first cavalry-against-cavalry action in the war. In the four years that followed, Knowles and the men of the Lincoln Cavalry never forgot the lesson of that first encounter: in a cavalry fight, the advantage is with the party that moves first. Knowles performed so well that in September 1861 he was promoted to corporal.

In January 1862, he was promoted again to sergeant and after the Peninsula Campaign he received a commission as a second lieutenant. The Lincoln Cavalry saw action at Antietam and then spent much of the early part of

Lee surrenders to Grant at Appamattox Court House, after which Knowles was promoted

1863 pursuing the troops known as Mosby's Raiders, a cavalry battalion commanded by John "Gray Ghost" Mosby. Mosby's Raiders were known for their quick raids and disappearances.

In April 1863, Knowles was made a first lieutenant and took a furlough. He rejoined the regiment in Harrisburg just in time to participate in the Battle of Gettysburg.

In August 1863, after much of the First New Yorkers' enlistments expired, the 21st Pennsylvania Cavalry was

The grave of General Knowles

formed and mustered in with Boyd as its colonel and
Knowles as a major. The regiment was dismounted and
served as infantry during the Overland Campaign in the
spring of 1864. In June, at the Battle of Cold Harbor, Boyd
was severely wounded and Knowles took command of the
regiment. He led the 21st in action during the siege of Petersburg. In October, the regiment was mounted and acting
as cavalry again, and Knowles was promoted to colonel. He
was 22 years old.

Knowles led the unit in various actions around Peters-
burg and then was sent to participate in the Appomattox
Campaign. They saw action at Dinwiddie Court House, Five
Forks, Sayler's Creek and Appomattox Court House, where

Lee would surrender on April 9, 1865. In June, Knowles received a brevet to brigadier general of volunteers for gallant and meritorious service. He left the army in July and returned home to Philadelphia.

Oliver Knowles moved to Milwaukee, Wisconsin, where he was in the grain trade. He was stricken with cholera and died on December 6, 1866, less than a month before his 25th birthday. His remains were returned to Philadelphia and buried in Laurel Hill Cemetery. His gravestone reads:

He was:
Gentle, yet courageous
Firm, but magnanimous
Beloved by all

His name is on the 21st Pennsylvania Cavalry Regiment monument on the Gettysburg Battlefield.

If You Go:
There are numerous Civil War generals buried in Laurel Hill Cemetery. The following six were all at the Battle of Gettysburg:

Louis Francine: fatally wounded in the Peach Orchard on July 2, 1863. The 7th New Jersey Infantry Monument on the Gettysburg battlefield stands on the spot where Francine was wounded.

Benezet Foust: led the 88th Pennsylvania Infantry and was wounded on the first day of the battle.

William Painter: was with Major General John Reynolds when Reynolds was killed on Day 1 (see Chapter 6).

John Hoffman: led the 56th Pennsylvania Infantry, which was the first Union infantry regiment to participate in the battle.

Langhorne Wister: assumed command of his brigade on Day 1, when the previous commander, Edmund Dana, was struck down.

George Alexander Hamilton Blake: was a cavalry officer who served with distinction during the Gettysburg Campaign.

A stone's throw from Laurel Hill is St. James-the-Less Episcopal Churchyard, which contains the graves of a number of Civil War generals and heroes. Among them is Robert Morris, Jr., the great-grandson of Revolutionary War patriot and Declaration of Independence signer Robert Morris. Morris, Jr. was captured by Confederate forces at the Battle of Brandy Station in Virginia, and died while imprisoned at the infamous Libby Prison in Richmond.

Also at St. James-the-Less Episcopal Churchyard are the graves of: John Grubb Parke, a major general who led his troops in the assault and capture of Vicksburg and fought in the Battles of Knoxville, Petersburg and Fort Stedman, Virginia; Benjamin Chew Tilghman, who commanded the 26th Pennsylvania Volunteer Infantry and later the 3rd United States Colored Troops; James Barnet Fry, who served as Provost Marshal General of the Union Army; and Medal-of-Honor recipient Anthony Taylor (see Chapter 35) who was awarded the Medal of Honor for his actions at the Battle of Chickamauga.

Libby Prison in Richmond, VA

"The Tall Tactician"
CONNIE MACK

County: Philadelphia
Town: Philadelphia
Cemetery: Holy Sepulchre
Address: 3301 Cheltenham Avenue

Cornelius McGillicuddy, better known as Connie Mack, was a professional baseball player, manager, and team owner. He played 11 years in the major leagues. As a player he had earned a reputation for being a smart student of the game. However in terms of actual talent, he was considered average at best. It was as a manager where Mack left his mark on the game. He was elected to the Baseball Hall of Fame as a manager in 1937.

Connie Mack was born on December 22, 1862, in East Brookfield, Massachusetts. His parents were Irish immigrants. His father's health had been ruined in the Civil War, and he became an alcoholic who no longer worked. As a result at age 14, after completing the eighth grade, Mack was forced to leave school to help support his family. By the age of 16 he was working in a shoe factory. By age 20 he had been promoted to the position of foreman. When he turned 21 Mack was offered $90 a month to play catcher in the Connecticut State League for Meriden which at that time was a very good salary. He had already acquired the nickname "slats" playing semi-pro ball, and now Meriden shortened his name to "Mack" to fit better on the scorecards.

In 1886, he was signed by the major league Washington D.C. team. In that first season he played in ten games for Washington and had a batting average of .361. In terms of hitting it was the high point of his career. The following season the league instituted a rule change that took away the batter's right to call for a high or low pitch. Word soon spread that Mack couldn't hit the low ball and by 1888, his batting average had fallen to .187. From this point forward it was only his skill as a fielder that allowed him to extend his playing career.

During this time frame Mack made some changes in his personal life. On November 2, 1887, he married Margaret

Connie Mack

Hogan. They had three children Earle, Roy, and Marguerite. Mack's wife died in 1902 as a result of complications that occurred during the birth of the third child.

In 1889, Mack jumped to the Buffalo Bisons of the new (and soon to be defunct) Players League. When the league folded, after one year, he then signed with the Pittsburgh Pirates in 1890. It was in Pittsburgh that Mack ended his playing career in 1896. During his last three years with the Pirates, Mack was the team's player-manager. With his playing career over, he signed on as Manager of the minor league Milwaukee Brewers and managed there for four seasons. It was during his stint in Milwaukee that he would sign the pitching great Rube Waddell, a man who would follow him to the big leagues.

Mack was one of the driving forces behind the creation of a second major league team in Philadelphia. In 1901, he became manager and part owner of the Philadelphia Athletics, a team that would play in the new American League. The league as a whole knew that to survive it would have to field a product that was at least equal to what was being delivered by the already firmly established National League. Mack was up to the challenge. He persuaded Benjamin Shibe, a manufacturer of baseball equipment, to become the president and the club's chief financier. Shibe Park was built to be the new team's home field. Some critics derided the new team as the city's "White Elephant" but Mack turned the insult into a logo, and for decades the team sported white elephants on its uniforms.

Under Mack's leadership the Athletics experienced immediate success. One of his first moves was to sign the hard throwing and aforementioned Rube Waddell. With Rube leading the way, winning 24 games and leading the league in strikeouts, Mack's 1902 Athletics won the American league pennant. They repeated the feat in 1905 and appeared in the first World Series. Mack's team faced John McGraw's New Giants in that initial series. With Waddell unable to pitch due a shoulder injury, the Giant's Christy Mathewson dominated the series winning three games and leading his team to the championship four games to one.

Mack's style of managing, which was described as intelligent and innovative, earned him another nickname: the Tall Tactician. He valued intelligence in his players and wanted them to be self-disciplined. Unfortunately for Mack, Rube Waddell turned out to be a character. Rube was anything but self-disciplined. He developed a habit of exiting the stadium during games to follow fire trucks. In the off-season he found employment as an alligator wrestler. On the mound he was distracted by opposing fans that would hold up shiny objects. When they caught his attention, it seemed as if he was in a trance. Waddell also had a drinking problem severe enough that the Sporting News called him "sousepaw." By early 1908, Mack could take no more, and he traded Rube to Saint Louis. Waddell was a tremendous talent as evidenced by the fact that he won six consecutive American League strikeout titles. He was unable, however, to deal with his personal demons. He died in 1914 in a sanitarium in Texas. Waddell was elected to the Baseball Hall of Fame in 1946.

In 1910, Mack married Katherine Hallahan. It was his second marriage. It appears to have been a success for the whole family. His sons from his previous marriage would become executives with the Athletics. His team would become a family business. Connie Mack was determined to remain as head of the family.

The Philadelphia Athletics won their first World Series for Mack in 1910. Mack's team repeated the feat in 1911, beating the Giants and getting revenge at the expense of John McGraw. Mack's team at the time included the future Hall of famers Eddie Collins and Frank "Home Run" Baker. Mack led the Athletics to a third World Championship in 1913. He had them back in the series the following year, but the Athletics were upset by the Boston Braves.

Starting in 1916, Mack's teams hit hard times. For seven consecutive seasons the Athletics finished in last place. It's hard to believe a manager could survive a showing like that today, but being an owner of the team probably helped. Mack remained at the helm and in the mid-1920's, the Athletics were once again competing for league titles.

During this time Mack recruited and developed some great players including catcher Mickey Cochrane (Mickey Mantle was named after Cochrane). Mack also signed the great pitcher Lefty Grove, and the power hitting outfielder Jimmie Fox. All three players were elected to the Baseball Hall Fame. From 1925 to 1933, the Athletics finished in third place twice, they were the runner-up four times and they won three American League titles. In 1929, they won another World Series and then repeated in 1930. They made it to the series in 1931 but were defeated. As the Great Depression worsened, attendance fell sharply and Mack was forced to sell his best players. While he would manage until 1950, he would not win another championship.

At the time of his retirement in 1950 he was 87 years old. His 50 year tenure is the most for a coach or manager with the same team in North American professional sports. He won nine pennants and appeared in eight World Series, winning five. Even during his dark final years his popularity not only endured but it grew. George M. Cohan (of Yankee Doddle Dandy fame) wrote a song about him. In 1944, he was voted favorite manager in the game by players and sportswriters. He never wore a uniform while managing, always wearing a suit. Fans came to games just to see him. By this time he was almost regarded as a holy relic by the game of baseball.

After he retired as manager, he remained owner and president, although his sons increasingly took over the running of the team. He remained president until 1954. He holds the records for both most wins and most losses. However no other manager has managed to get within 1,000 wins of his total. Mack resigned as president of the Athletics after the 1954 season. When he stepped down he sold the team to Arnold Johnson, who moved the Athletics to Kansas City.

The grave of one of baseball's greatest men and minds makes no mention of his contributions to the nation's national past time.

Even after leaving the game, more honors continued to come Mack's way. Shibe Park was renamed Connie Mack Stadium in 1953. In addition to his Hall Of Fame election, he was the first person inducted into the New York City based Irish American Baseball Hall Of Fame. He is also mentioned in Ogden Nash's poem "Line-up For Yesterday."

Connie Mack died on February 8, 1956. He was 94 years old. The priest at his funeral said, "It is not the custom in our church at requiem mass to preach a sermon." However according to the great sportswriter Red Smith (a close friend of Mack's) Father Cartin made an exception. He said, "Those who know the greatness of this man can pay tribute to his greatness far better than I... His memory is held sacred in the lives of our people in general, whose inspiration he was... He will indeed be missed by our American people, generations young and old." He is buried in Holy Sepulchre Cemetery in Cheltenham, PA. His grave says simply "McGillicuddy." There is no indication of his first name or any of his accomplishments.

If You Go:

Holy Sepulchre is a beautiful, well maintained cemetery with a number of noteworthy graves. Frank Rizzo, the controversial Police Commissioner and Mayor of Philadelphia, is buried there. (See page 319.)

Another interesting story is that of Billy Maharg whose real name was Graham or Maharg spelled backwards. Maharg had a strange Major League baseball history which consisted of appearing in two games, one game and one at-bat in each league. He appeared in 1912 as a replacement player for the Detroit Tigers when a group of Tigers refused to play as a protest to Ty Cobbs suspension for attacking a fan in the stands. The replacement Tigers lost to the Philadelphia Athletics 24-2. Maharg went 0 for 1 in that game and then played again in 1916 for the Phillies when he was given the chance to bat in the final game of the season. He was employed by the Phillies as a driver and assistant trainer. He is best known, however, for his role in the infamous Black Sox scandal of 1919. Maharg conspired with eight players to fix the World Series in exchange for $100,000. Maharg and his partner in crime, Sleepy Bill Burns, approached New York gambler Arnold Rothstein to

Here lies Billy Maharg (Graham spelled backwards) who was a main player in the 1919 world series scandal.

make a deal. Other gamblers got involved and Maharg and Burns suffered multiple double-crosses. A disgruntled Maharg gave the full details to a Philadelphia writer in 1920, and eight players were indicted. Maharg testified in the trial and the players were found not guilty but were banned from baseball for life. Actor Richard Edson played Maharg in the 1988 film *Eight Men Out*.

Also buried nearby is John H. McVeigh, a World War II Congressional Medal of Honor recipient. He was an infantry Sergeant who was awarded the CMOH for his bravery near Brest, France on August 29, 1944. In a savage hand-to-hand struggle with German troops, he was shot and killed at point blank range.

Holy Sepulchre also contains the grave of William "Bill" Hewitt, a Hall of Fame professional football player. Hewitt played for the Bears and Eagles in the 1930s.

Finally, if you visit Holy Sepulchre, you are about one mile away from the Ivy Hill Cemetery. For information on who you can visit at Ivy Hill, see Willie Anderson on page 188.

George Gordon Meade

"The Old Snapping Turtle"

GEORGE MEADE

County: Philadelphia
Town: Philadelphia
Cemetery: Laurel Hill
Address: 3822 Ridge Avenue

George Gordon Meade was a career United States Army officer and is best known for being the victor of the Battle of Gettysburg in 1863. He was born on December 31, 1815, in Spain. His father was serving there as an agent for the United States Government. In 1828, his father died and six months later the family, facing financial difficulties, returned to the United States. Initially George was educated at the Mount Hope Institution in Baltimore. In 1831, with financial considerations being a prime consideration, he entered the United States Military Academy at West Point. He graduated ranked nineteenth in his class of 56 cadets in 1835 and was transferred to Florida at the beginning of the Seminole Wars. He became ill with a fever in Florida and was reassigned to Massachusetts. He was very disillusioned with the military and resigned his commission in 1836. He went to work for a railroad company as an engineer to survey territory for new rail lines.

In 1840 he met Margaretta Sergeant and soon she became his wife. She was the daughter of John Sergeant who was Henry Clay's running mate in the 1832 presidential election. They had seven children together. With a family to support, Meade found it difficult to secure steady employment. Though he had never intended to make the army a career, he reapplied to the military in 1842 and was appointed a 2nd Lieutenant in the Topographical Engineers. He was assigned to General Winfield Scott's Army during the War with Mexico. He was brevetted to first lieutenant as a result of his conduct during the Battle of Monterrey.

After the war in Mexico was over, Meade moved back to Philadelphia where he worked on building lighthouses for the Delaware Bay. He was eventually promoted to Captain, and for the next ten years he spent time in surveying and design work for lighthouses on the east coast. He oversaw

General Meade's monument at Gettysburg.

the construction of lighthouses at Barnegat, Atlantic City, and Cape May, New Jersey. Among his accomplishments during this period was the design of a hydraulic lamp that was approved by the Lighthouse Board for use in American lighthouses. He also participated in the survey of the Great Lakes and tributaries.

He was promoted from Captain to Brigadier General in August 1861, just a few months after the start of the Civil War. The sectional strife took a personal toll on the Meades as his wife's sister was married to Governor Wise of Virginia who became a Brigadier General in the Confederate Army. Nicknamed "The Old Snapping Turtle," Meade gained a reputation for being short- tempered and obstinate. In March 1862, he was severely wounded at the Battle of Glendale. A musket ball struck him above his hip, clipped his liver, and just missed his spine as it passed through his body. He recovered from his wounds in Philadelphia and led his brigade at the Battle of Second Bull Run and at the Battles of South Mountain, Antietam, and Fredericksburg. Soon after Fredericksburg, Meade was assigned to command the Fifth Army Corps of the Army of the Potomac. His assignment as corps commander took him through the trial of the Battle of Chancellorsville in May 1863. Though the army had been soundly defeated there, Meade handled his corps with great skill and protected the important fords on the Rappahannock River.

Unhappy with the performance of the Army of the Potomac, President Lincoln changed command from McClellan to Burnside to Hooker to Meade. Meade assumed command just days before the monumental Battle of Gettysburg, which is considered the turning point of the War. Meade was not Lincoln's first choice as he asked John Reynolds to take command but Reynolds declined. In defending his decision to appoint Meade as commander of the union forces, Lincoln said, "Meade will fight well on his own dunghill."

Meade was fortunate to have such competent and brave officers as Reynolds, Buford, Hancock, Vincent, Custer, and Chamberlain with him at Gettysburg. Meade made the decision to fight a defensive battle and did well in deploying his forces. His forces repelled attacks on his flanks and on the final day of the battle, stood tall against an attack on the center of their lines. This disastrous attack became known as Pickett's Charge. Although Meade field-marshaled the Union victory at Gettysburg, he was criticized severely then and now for not pursuing the defeated Confederate forces after the battle. Meade infuriated Lincoln when he reported that the "invaders have been driven from our land." Reportedly, upon receiving the dispatch, Lincoln said angrily "Doesn't he understand it's all our land?" Lincoln was overwrought at the missed opportunity to perhaps end the war and ordered Meade to pursue and attack Lee's retreating Army. It was too late however, and Lee escaped to Virginia. In March, Lincoln put General Ulysses S. Grant in charge of all Union Armies.

When Grant was appointed, Meade offered his resignation. He wanted to give Grant the opportunity to appoint the general of his choosing for the position. Grant told Meade he had no intention of replacing him. While Meade stayed with the Army, he did not approve of Grant's tactics. Meade had become a cautious general while Grant was willing to attack and suffer losses, secure in the knowledge that he had replacements available and the confederates did not. By all accounts, Meade served Grant well during the remainder of the war. He received a promotion to Major

Final resting place of George Meade (the Old Snapping Turtle) who commanded the victorious Union Army at Gettysburg.

General at the war's end. He was outranked by only Grant, Halleck, and Sherman.

After the War, General Meade was a Commissioner of Fairmont Park in Philadelphia from 1866 until his death. Prior to his death he received an honorary doctorate in law from Harvard University. In addition, his scientific achievements were recognized by several institutions, including the American Philosophical Society and The Philadelphia Academy of Natural Sciences. He died on November 6, 1872 in the house where he lived at 1836 Delancey Place in Philadelphia from complications of his old wounds combined with pneumonia. He was 56 years old. Many felt his victory at Gettysburg had stopped a rebel invasion of the city. After his death, his widow accepted the house as a gift from the city of Philadelphia. To this day the house still has the word "Meade" over the door though now it has been converted into apartments. Meade is buried in a modest grave in Laurel Hill Cemetery in Philadelphia.

If You Go:
Laurel Hill is a large, well-kept cemetery rich in history with many interesting graves. Due to the size of this cemetery, the authors recommend that if you visit you should make an initial stop at the cemetery office to obtain directions to the sites you are there to see.

Among the graves are three officers who fought with Meade at Gettysburg:

Oliver Blatchy Knowles (see page 268): entered the war as a private and ended it as a brevet brigadier general after fighting in Antietam, Shenandoah, Gettysburg, Spotsylvania, Petersburg and the last campaign of Appomattox. Less than two years after the war ended, he died of cholera at the age of 25.

William Lovering Curry: fought at Gettysburg with the 106th Pennsylvania Volunteer Infantry and was stationed at the famed "Copse of Trees" during Pickett's Charge. He was wounded at Spotsylvania and died a month later.

Alexander Williams Biddle: fought at the Battles of Fredericksburg, Chancellorsville, Gettysburg, and Bristoe Station as a major and then lieutenant colonel. At Gettysburg, his unit was one of the first to see action on the first day of battle.

Also buried at Laurel Hill is Frank Furness, who served as a Civil War officer and was awarded the Medal of Honor for his bravery at Trevilian Station, Virginia, on June 12, 1864. However, he is better known for having been a major architect from 1870 to 1890. He designed over 400 buildings, including banks, churches, synagogues, rail stations and numerous mansions. His first major work, Philadelphia's Academy of Fine Arts, is still standing. His grave, however, is very modest and simple.

In addition to Furness, there are five other Civil War Medal of Honor recipients (see Chapter 35) at Laurel Hill: (1) Henry Harrison Bingham; (2) George J. Pitman; (3) John Hamilton Storey; (4) Pinkerton Vaughn; and (5) Robert Teleford Kelly.

Other Laurel Hill graves of interest are those of:

Brigadier General Henry Bohlen: recruited a regiment of mostly German emigrants at the outbreak of the war and became its colonel. He fought against Stonewall Jackson in the Shenandoah Valley, and was killed at the Second Battle of Bull Run.

Brigadier General James St. Clair Morton: a West Point-educated engineer, he was chief engineer of General Burnside's IX (Ninth Army) Corps at Petersburg, Virginia. He was killed while scouting on June 17, 1864.

Brigadier General Hector Tyndale: a prominent businessman and abolitionist in Philadelphia, he accompanied John Brown's wife to her husband's execution and escorted the body back from Harpers Ferry, Virginia to New York for burial. He was wounded twice at Antietam and had three horses shot out from under him.

William Brooke Rawle: who fought at Gettysburg and wrote two books about his experience. They are titled "The Right Flank at Gettysburg" and "With Gregg in the Gettysburg Campaign." Rawle fought against Maj. Gen. J.E.B. Stuart's cavalry on the third day of the battle. On Gregg Avenue, there is a memorial on the battlefield known as the William Brooke Rawle Flagpole, commemorating his action on that day.

"Founding Fathers"

ROBERT MORRIS and JAMES WILSON

County: Philadelphia
Town: Philadelphia
Cemetery: Christ Episcopal Church and Churchyard
Address: 20 North American Street (Second and Market Streets)

Both men were born in Europe. They both came to America because of the opportunities the new world had to offer. They both settled in Philadelphia. They were both successful: one as a businessman, the other as an attorney. Both men were also successful in the field of Pennsylvania politics. Both men signed the Declaration of Independence and the United States Constitution. Their names are Robert Morris and James Wilson, and they were truly Founding Fathers.

Robert Morris was born in Liverpool, England, on January 20, 1734. When he was thirteen years of age, he joined his father in Maryland. His father sent him to Philadelphia to stay with a family friend named Charles Greenway. Morris then became an apprentice for the Philadelphia merchant and Philadelphia mayor Charles Willing. Charles Willing died in 1854, and his son Thomas Willing made Morris a partner in the firm. On May 1, 1757 the two businessmen established the shipping and banking firm of Willing, Morris Company. The two would remain partners until 1779.

The new company's shipping business was involved in the slave trade. The company funded a slave trading voyage, but the trip turned out to be unprofitable. On a second voyage their ship was captured by French pirates. The company did handle several slave auctions for other importers. In 1765 they were involved in their last deal involving slaves when they advertised seventy slaves for sale. Records indicate the slaves were not sold in Philadelphia but sent to Jamaica. Both Willing and Morris supported non-importation agreements which resulted in the end of all trade with England including the importation of slaves.

In 1769 at the age of 35, Morris married the 20 year old Mary White. They would have seven children together: five

Robert Morris

sons and two daughters. White came from a well-respected family in Maryland; her brother was a well-known Bishop named William White. Morris worshipped at Saint Peter's Church in Philadelphia which was run by his brother-in law. As a matter of fact, both Morris and William White are buried in the churchyard. When the Continental Congress was in session, many of its members worshiped there including George Washington.

Morris first became involved in politics when England passed the Stamp Act of 1765-1776. Basically it imposed a tax on all legal documents. Morris served on a committee of merchants established to oppose the tax. In one instance he served as a mediator between a mass of protesters and the stamp tax collector. The protesters were threatening to tear down the home of the collector. Morris was able to resolve the dispute peacefully by getting the collector to agree not to collect the tax. Morris was still a loyal British subject, but he believed this tax constituted taxation without representation and in a short time the tax was repealed.

Morris was warden of the port of Philadelphia. When the tea tax was passed and a ship carrying tea entered the Delaware Bay, orders were issued that the ship should not be brought to port. The Captain of the ship followed another ship up the channel which set up a large public protest in Philadelphia. The captain was taken to the State house where he met with a group that included Morris. At the conclusion of the meeting, the captain agreed to leave the city and to take his tea with him.

Morris now became very active in Pennsylvania politics. He served in the Pennsylvania legislature from 1776 to 1778. He was also elected as a Pennsylvania representative to the Second Continental Congress where he served from 1775 to 1778. While in Congress he devised a system to enable the Americans to smuggle war supplies provided by France. He also sold his best ship, The Black Prince, to the Congress, and it became the first ship in the Continental Navy.

On July 1, 1776, Morris voted against the motion for independence which resulted in Pennsylvania voting against the measure. The following day when a similar vote was taken, John Dickinson and Morris abstained which put Pennsylvania in favor of independence as the motion passed unanimously. When Morris signed the Declaration of Independence he said, "I am not one of those politicians that run testy when my own plans are not adopted. I think it is the duty of a good citizen to follow when he cannot lead."

During the fight for independence, Morris became known as the "Financier of the Revolution." From 1781 to 1784, he was the Superintendent of Finance and it was his responsibility to manage the young country's economy. During the revolution he loaned the country $10,000 to pay the troops Washington had assembled. He also donated his own funds for the same purpose. Morris saw his own wealth increase during these times as a result of privateers who attacked and seized the cargo of British ships during the revolution. Morris owned at least an interest in many of the ships used by privateers and he also was involved in selling the goods seized from the British. Thomas Paine and others would later accuse Morris of war profiteering, but a congressional committee acquitted Morris of these charges in 1779.

Morris played an important part in getting Washington's army from New York to Yorktown, Virginia. He was with Washington the day the army went on the move, and he acted as quartermaster. He also used $1,400,000 of his own credit to move the army. This would not be the last time that he used his personal funds to aid in the war effort and the use of his personal fortune strained his finances.

While Morris was Superintendent of Finance he was assisted by a friend named Gouverneur Morris (they were not related). Together they proposed the creation of a national economic system. This proposal served as the basis for the system started by Alexander Hamilton when he became Secretary of the Treasury. Morris also pushed for the establishment of a national mint, a recommendation that was finally adopted in 1792 after being pushed by Hamilton and Thomas Jefferson.

In 1787 Morris was elected as a Pennsylvanian representative to the Constitutional Convention. He was also instrumental in getting Gouverneur Morris selected as a member of Pennsylvania's delegation. Robert Morris nominated his friend George Washington to be president of the convention. When the Constitution was adopted, both Morris and Gouverneur Morris were among the signers.

Washington wanted Morris to be his Secretary of the Treasury in 1789, but Morris turned down the offer and suggested the appointment of Alexander Hamilton, a man

James Wilson

who supported most of Morris's policies. Morris served as a United States Senator, representing Pennsylvania from 1789 to 1795. He supported the economic program set forth by the Federalist party that resulted in internal improvements such as canals to improve commerce.

Morris became heavily involved in unsuccessful land speculations. He invested heavily in the western territories and soon found that he was unable to sell the lands or afford to pay the taxes on them. Morris's rise in America had been spectacular and so was his fall. Hounded by creditors, he was arrested and placed in a debtor's prison in Philadelphia from February 1798 to August 1801. In 1800 the United States Congress passed a temporary Bankruptcy Act which once enacted resulted in his release from prison. Morris was in poor health and spent his remaining years in retirement. He died on May 8, 1806, in Philadelphia and was laid to rest in the Christ Episcopal Churchyard.

James Wilson was born on September 14, 1742, in Carskerdo, Scotland. He attended a number of Scottish universities, including Edinburgh and Saint Andrews, but never graduated with a degree. Wilson arrived in America in 1766 at the age of 21 and settled in Philadelphia. He found work teaching at The Academy and College of Philadelphia which is now the University of Pennsylvania. The University awarded him an honorary Master of Arts degree.

Wilson decided to study law, and he did so at the office of John Dickinson. After gaining admittance to the bar, he set up a law practice in Reading, Pennsylvania in 1767. His practice was very successful and soon he bought a small farm near Carlisle, Pennsylvania. He was soon handling law cases in eight counties while he continued to lecture at The Academy and College of Philadelphia. In 1771 he married, and he and his wife had six children together.

Wilson was quick to take up the revolutionary cause. In 1768 he authored *Considerations on the Nature and Extent of the Legislative Authority of the British Parliament*. The work was published in 1774, and it concluded that Parliament had no authority to pass laws governing the colonies because the colonies were not represented in Parliament. Wilson put forth his view that all power is derived from the people. He also had a very different view of what the English Empire could be. In describing his vision he wrote, "Distinct states independent of each other but connected under the same sovereign." Years later at America's Constitutional Convention he would raise this idea again.

Wilson was a member of the Continental Congress in 1776. In Congress he was considered one of the "cool devils," a name attached to representatives who worked to delay independence. This group angered John Adams. During this time Wilson caucused his district to determine where those he represented stood on the question of independence. After receiving this information he voted

Here is the grave of Robert Morris who helped fund the Continental Army during the American Revolution.

for independence. During his time in Congress he served on the Committee on Spies with Thomas Jefferson, John Rutledge, John Adams and Robert Livingston. Their committee defined what was considered treason for the young country.

In 1779, after the British left Philadelphia, Wilson successfully defended 23 people from property seizure in an action that was initiated by the government of Pennsylvania. As a result on October 4, 1779, a mob attacked Wilson's home. Wilson and 35 of his friends barricaded themselves in what would later be called Fort Wilson. During the fight that followed six people were killed and many more were wounded. The city's soldiers eventually drove the mob away. The rioters were pardoned by Joseph Reed who was then the president of Pennsylvania's Supreme Executive Council.

Wilson was considered to possess one of the great legal minds of his time. In addition the study of government had become a passion for him. As a result he was one of the most active delegates at the Constitutional Convention that began in May of 1787. Wilson addressed the convention 168 times on the numerous issues that the delegates had to address. He favored a single executive, and he wanted the president and senators to be elected through the popular vote. Doctor Benjamin Rush, who also attended the convention, described Wilson's mind as "one blaze of light." On the day of the vote to adopt the constitution, Benjamin Franklin had composed a speech urging its passage.

This is the grave of James Wilson signer of both the Declaration of Independence and the United State's Constitution.

Franklin did not feel up to giving the speech himself so he had Wilson read it on his behalf.

Wilson, like many of the delegates to the convention, was not fully satisfied with the Constitution. Despite his reservations he worked hard to make sure that Pennsylvania would accept the document. His efforts met with success when Pennsylvania became the second state to ratify the Constitution. Despite the ratification many Pennsylvanian's remained opposed to the new form of government. On December 27, 1787, an outdoor rally was held in Carlisle to celebrate the Constitution. A group of men armed with clubs attacked and began beating Wilson. Wilson later said he would have been killed if not for an old soldier who threw his body over Wilson's and absorbed many of the blows.

President Washington nominated Wilson to be a Justice on the United States Supreme Court on September 24, 1789. He was confirmed by the United States Senate and served on the court until 1798. During that time only nine cases were heard by the highest court in the land.

Much like Morris, Wilson's final days were filled with financial failures. He too found himself deep in debt as a result of land speculation. Wilson fled to North Carolina to escape his creditors. It was in North Carolina, while visiting a friend, that Wilson suffered a stroke and died at the age of 55. He was originally buried in North Carolina, but in 1906 he was re-interred in the Christ Episcopal Churchyard in Philadelphia.

If You Go:
See "Philadelphia Saints" (p. 5) and "Philadelphia Sinners" (p. 62). Also buried at Christ Episcopal Churchyard are two other signers of the United States Constitution, Pierce Butler who was a representative from South Carolina and Jacob Broom who represented Delaware.

"The Irish Commander"
ST. CLAIR AUGUSTINE MULHOLLAND

County: Philadelphia
Town: Philadelphia
Cemetery: Old Cathedral Cemetery
Address: 48th Street and Lancaster Avenue

St. Clair Augustine Mulholland was born on April 1, 1839, in Lisburn, County Antrim, Ireland. He and his parents came to the United States in 1846 and settled in New Jersey. Four years later they moved to Philadelphia, where Mulholland remained for the rest of his life. In Philadelphia he worked in a printing shop and later as a painter of window shades. However, even during these days before the Civil War he demonstrated an interest in military life. He joined the Pennsylvania militia and developed into an expert drill instructor.

When the Civil War began, Mulholland tried to recruit men for a unit he wished to be made part of the Irish Brigade. While he was unsuccessful initially, he did manage to recruit two companies of men that would form the 116th Pennsylvania Volunteer Infantry and be attached to Meagher's Irish Brigade. Mulholland was initially made lieutenant of the 116th in June of 1862, and then lieutenant colonel on September 1, 1862.

Mulholland was wounded during the attack of the Irish Brigade up Marye's Heights at the Battle of Fredericksburg on December 13, 1862. Though the wound was serious enough to require Mulholland to use a cane to walk, he returned to the field in 1863. By all accounts Mulholland was respected and admired by the men he commanded. He was also a personal favorite of Major General Winfield Scott Hancock (see page 133) and the two developed a lifelong friendship.

At the Battle of Chancellorsville on May 3-4, 1863, Mulholland and his men saved the guns of the 5th Maine Battery that had been abandoned to the Confederates. On the evening of May 4, General Hancock chose Mulholland to protect the army in a rear guard action. Hancock fully expected that his friend and his men would be captured, and

St. Clair Augustine Mulholland

so he told Mulholland that he would try to work out a prisoner exchange for him should that occur. Mulholland and 400 men protected the retreat of the Union Army. In addition, he avoided capture and was able to return with his men. For those actions, Mulholland was awarded the Medal of Honor.

In early 1864 Mulholland returned to Philadelphia to recruit enough men to return the 116th to full strength. He

Marye's Heights at Fredericksburg

was successful and was promoted to colonel. He was
wounded again during the Battle of the Wilderness and a
third time at Po River. After only 10 days in the hospital he
resumed his command, only to be wounded again at the
Battle of Totopotomoy Creek. After he recovered, Mulhollad
led his brigade in all the actions around Petersburg and
again demonstrated his bravery by leading an assault on a
fort on the Boydton Plank Road. He finally left the volunteer service on June 3, 1865. In 1866, upon the recommendation of General Hancock, President Johnson
nominated Mulholland for the brevet grade of brigadier

Final resting place of St. Clair Augustin Mulholland a true Civil War hero.

general of volunteers and the Senate confirmed the appointment that year. In 1869, he was nominated for appointment to the brevet grade of major general and the Senate also confirmed that nomination.

After the war, Mulholland was appointed Chief of Police in Philadelphia. President Grover Cleveland appointed him to the position of United States Pension Agent—a post he would continue to hold under Presidents McKinley and Teddy Roosevelt. He also lectured and wrote on the Civil War. He compiled a history of the 116th and another on the men who had been awarded the Medal of Honor. Mulholland died on February 17, 1910, in Philadelphia and was laid to rest in Old Cathedral Cemetery.

If You Go:
See the "If You Go" section of Dennis O'Kane on page 304.

SAINT JOHN NEUMANN

(See Saint Katherine Drexel and "Philadelphia Saints," p. 5.)

"The Fighting Irishman"
DENNIS O'KANE

County: Philadelphia
Town: Philadelphia
Cemetery: Old Cathedral
Address: 48th Street and Lancaster Avenue

He was born in Derry, Ireland in 1818. He left Ireland and came to America with a wife and two daughters. After settling in Philadelphia, he and his wife had their third daughter. On July 3, 1863, he found himself on Cemetery Ridge in Gettysburg commanding the 69th Pennsylvania Volunteers. His name was Dennis O'Kane.

The 69th Pennsylvania was part of the Philadelphia Brigade. It was made up largely of Irish immigrants or the children of Irish immigrants. The 69th had been involved in numerous battles including the Second Bull Run, South Mountain, Antietam, Fredericksburg , Chancellorsville and now Gettysburg.

O'Kane almost did not make it to Gettysburg. Nine months earlier he had faced a court martial. At the time, the 69th was at Harper's Ferry and O'Kane's wife and eldest daughter had come to visit him. O'Kane rented a carriage and horses and proceeded to show his wife and daughter around the town. During the trip, O'Kane's commanding officer, Colonel Joshua Owen, showed up drunk and on horseback. He proceeded to guide his mount against the carriage horses. When he repeated the maneuver, O'Kane called out to him to stop it. At that point Owen called O'Kane an Irish son of a bitch and then he invited O'Kane's wife to spend the night with him in his tent. O'Kane immediately jumped from the carriage, grabbed Owen, and pulled him from his horse. Owen's head bounced as it hit the ground. This led to O'Kane's court martial, but he was acquitted. It also led to the dismissal of Owen and O'Kane's rise to command the 69th.

O'Kane was present on the third day of the Battle of Gettysburg when the Confederate cannons began the bombardment that would precede Pickett's Charge. During the shelling, O'Kane observed General Hancock calmly riding

Dennis O'Kane

among the troops who had hit the ground for protection.
Hancock, who had presided at O'Kane's court martial,
waved to O'Kane and O'Kane responded with a salute.

When the shelling ended and the smoke lifted, O'Kane
could see the Confederates emerging from the woods on
Seminary Ridge making their way towards his troops.
O'Kane reminded the men of the 69th that they were fighting today to protect their own state. He ordered the 69th's
colors uncased and the green flag with a golden harp on
one side and the Pennsylvania coat of arms on the other
was soon in the air.

Currier and Ives print of the highwater mark at Gettysburg.

The Union artillery opened up on the advancing Confederates, opening holes in their lines that other rebel soldiers rushed to fill as the charge continued. The soldiers of the 69th watched from behind a stone wall as the Confederates drew nearer. When a section of the Union line manned by the 71st Pennsylvania retreated, the 69th was unprotected on its right side. The Confederate General Lewis Armistead, with his hat resting on the tip of his sword, led his men toward that very spot. O'Kane then ordered his men to turn to the right and face the enemy. During the fighting that followed, O'Kane saw General Armistead collapse after being wounded. Shortly thereafter, O'Kane himself was seriously wounded and had to be removed from the field but not before knowing that his troops had played a key part in repulsing the Confederate attack.

O'Kane died the next day, July 4, 1863. His funeral was held in Philadelphia at Saint James Church. His pallbearers were Union Army officers. After mass, his remains were transported to Cathedral Cemetery where he was laid to rest with full military honors.

O'Kane's grave

If You Go:

Civil War Brigadier General Richard Dillon is also buried at Cathedral Cemetery. Dillon lost an arm at the Battle of Chancellorsville. He was brevetted brigadier general on March 13, 1865, for gallant and meritorious service during the war.

Cathedral Cemetery is also the final resting place for Civil War Medal of Honor recipient Edmund English. He received this honor for his actions during the Battle of the Wilderness. His citation reads that "during a rout and under orders to retreat seized the colors rallied the men and drove the enemy back."

In addition, Civil War Union Brevet Major General and Medal of Honor recipient St. Clair Augustine Mulholland was also laid to rest at Cathedral Cemetery (see page 296).

"The Defender of Vicksburg"
JOHN C. PEMBERTON

County: Philadelphia
Town: Philadelphia
Cemetery: Laurel Hill
Address: 3822 Ridge Avenue

John Clifford Pemberton was best known as the Confederate major general who surrendered Vicksburg to Ulysses S. Grant in July of 1863, following a long siege. Pemberton was a career United States Army officer who fought in the Seminole Wars and with distinction during the Mexican War before joining the Southern cause during the Civil War.

Pemberton was born on August 10, 1814, in Philadelphia, Pennsylvania as the second child of John Pemberton (1783-1847) and Rebecca Clifford (1792-1869). As a student at the University of Pennsylvania, the young Pemberton decided he wished to have a career as an engineer. Believing the United States Military Academy the best way to gain this education, he applied to West Point, using his family's connection to President Andrew Jackson to secure an appointment. He was admitted to the Academy in 1833, where he was the roommate and close friend of George G. Meade (see p. 281). He graduated four years later, finishing ranked in the middle of his class.

Pemberton was commissioned a second lieutenant in the 4th U.S. Artillery Regiment on July 1, 1837. He served in the Seminole Wars in Florida and at various forts around the country before being stationed at the U.S. Army Cavalry School at Carlisle Barracks, Pennsylvania, in 1842 and 1843.

At the outbreak of the Mexican War, Pemberton was stationed at Fort Monroe in Virginia (from 1844 to 1845). Next, he was part of the occupation of Texas (1845 to 1846) after which his 4th Artillery Regiment was sent into Mexico under Zachary Taylor. He fought at most of the major battles in that war and was appointed a brevet captain "for Gallant Conduct in the several Conflicts at Monterrey."

After the war with Mexico ended, Pemberton married a Virginian, Martha Thompson. Due to the lack of records to

Confederate General John C. Pemberton

the contrary, many historians have come to believe Pemberton's marriage to this Norfolk native was the primary reason he later sided with the Confederacy. Pemberton again moved about the country for numerous assignments, including more action against the Seminoles (1856-1857), frontier duty at Fort Leavenworth, Kansas (1857-1858) and the Utah War (1858), returning to garrison duty at the Washington Arsenal in Washington, D.C. by 1861.

On April 24, 1861, just 12 days after the shots initiating the Civil War were fired at the Battle of Fort Sumter,

Pemberton tendered his resignation from the United States army. The resignation was not immediately accepted, however. First, Pemberton felt obligated to accept a meeting request he received from General Winfield Scott. Scott tried his best to persuade Pemberton to remain with the North. Scott felt he could convince Pemberton that he was making a bad decision, a stance that received a significant boost when Pemberton received unexpected news regarding two of his younger brothers, Andrew and Clifford. He learned that on the very same day he tendered his resignation, Andrew and Clifford had joined the Union cavalry (the Philadelphia City Troop). Despite that development, despite his Northern birth, and despite Winfield Scott's best persuasive efforts, Pemberton stuck to his decision and joined the Confederate cause.

He was appointed a lieutenant colonel in the Confederate Army on March 28, and was made assistant adjutant general of the forces in and around the Southern capital of Richmond, Virginia, on April 29. He was promoted to colonel on May 8, and the next day was assigned to the Virginia Provisional Army Artillery, with the rank of lieutenant colonel. Pemberton was then appointed a major in the Confederate Army Artillery on June 15 and quickly promoted to brigadier general two days later. His first brigade command was in the Department of Norfolk, leading its 10th Brigade from June to November.

Pemberton was promoted to major general on January 14, 1862, and given command of the Confederate Department of South Carolina and Georgia, an assignment lasting from March 14 to August 29, with his headquarters in Charleston. Many South Carolinians feared that the Northern-born general was not dedicated to an all-out defense of the department. Pemberton added to their fears by publicly declaring that, if faced with a situation where he had to make a choice between abandoning an area on the one hand, versus risk losing an outnumbered army on the other, he would choose to abandon the area. It was that public statement, combined with his generally abrasive personality and the distrust of his Northern birth that led the governors of both South Carolina and Georgia to petition Confederate President Jefferson Davis seeking Pemberton's removal. Fortunately for Davis, it just so happened that he needed a commander for a new department in Mississippi. He also needed to find a command post for Gen. P.G.T. Beauregard. Davis decided to send Pemberton west, and assigned the more popular Beauregard Pemberton's prior position in Charleston as commander of the Confederate Department of South Carolina and Georgia.

On October 10, 1862, Pemberton was promoted to the rank of lieutenant general, and assigned to defend the fortress city of Vicksburg, Mississippi, as well as the Mississippi River (that command being known as the "Department of Mississippi and East Louisiana"). Davis gave him the following instructions regarding his new assignment: ". . . consider the successful defense of those States as the first and chief object of your command." Pemberton arrived at his new headquarters in Jackson, Mississippi, on October 14.

His forces consisted of fewer than 50,000 men under the command of Major Generals Earl Van Dorn and Sterling Price, with around 24,000 in the permanent garrisons at Vicksburg and Port Hudson, Louisiana. John D. Winters described the men under Pemberton as "a beaten and demoralized army, fresh from the defeat at Corinth, Mississippi." Pemberton faced his former Mexican War colleague, the aggressive Union commander Major General Ulysses S. Grant, and over 100,000 Union soldiers in the Vicksburg Campaign.

Pemberton immediately set to work solving supply problems and improving troop morale. For several months he enjoyed remarkable success, defeating attempts by Grant to take Vicksburg in the winter of 1862-63.

In the spring, however, Grant confused Pemberton with a series of diversions and crossed the Mississippi River below Vicksburg practically unnoticed. Grant was free to maneuver because Pemberton's responsibility to hold Vicksburg at all costs. Davis complicated matters by sending General Joseph E. Johnston to Mississippi to try to reverse declining Confederate fortunes. Johnston ordered Pemberton to unite his forces and attack Grant, if practicable, even if that meant abandoning the defense of Vicksburg.

To make matters worse, Confederate General Joseph E. Johnston reassigned Pemberton's cavalry to the Army of Tennessee. Thus, in May of 1863, when Union General

Ulysses S. Grant's campaign to take the city began in earnest, the Confederate defender was deprived of vital intelligence about his enemy's whereabouts. Poor communication and lack of coordination with Johnston—as well as the Pemberton's own tactical errors—led to Confederate defeats at Champion Hill and Big Black River Bridge, and Pemberton was forced to back into the Vicksburg defenses. Two failed attempts to take the city by direct assault demonstrated the strength of the Vicksburg defenses and compelled Grant lay siege to the city. Despite constant pleas to Johnston for aid, Pemberton was completely isolated.

Pemberton held firm for over six weeks, while soldiers and citizens were starved into submission. He was boxed in with lots of unusable munitions and little food. The poor diet was showing on the Confederate soldiers. By the end of June, half were out sick or hospitalized. Scurvy, malaria, dysentery, diarrhea, and other diseases cut their ranks. At least one city resident had to stay up at night to keep starving soldiers out of his vegetable garden. The constant shelling did not bother him as much as the loss of his food.

Caves at Vicksburg

As the siege wore on, fewer and fewer horses, mules, and dogs were seen wandering about Vicksburg. Shoe leather became a last resort of sustenance for many adults.

During the siege, Union gunboats lobbed over 22,000 shells into the town and army artillery fire was even heavier. As the barrages continued, suitable housing in Vicksburg was reduced to a minimum. A ridge, located between the main town and the rebel defense line, provided a diverse citizenry with lodging for the duration. Over 500 caves were dug into the yellow clay hills of Vicksburg. Whether houses were structurally sound or not, it was deemed safer to occupy these dugouts. People did their best to make them comfortable, with rugs, furniture, and pictures. They tried to time their movements and foraging with the rhythm of the cannonade, sometimes unsuccessfully. Because of these dugouts or caves, the Union soldiers gave the town the nickname of "Prairie Dog Village." Despite the ferocity of the Union fire against the town, fewer than a dozen civilians were known to have been killed during the entire siege.

On the evening of July 2, 1863, Pemberton asked in writing his four division commanders if they believed their men could "make the marches and undergo the fatigues necessary to accomplish a successful evacuation" after 45 days of siege. With four votes of no, the next day Pemberton asked the Federals for an armistice to allow time for the discussion of terms of surrender, and at 10:00 a.m. on July 4 he surrendered the city and his army to Grant. The written terms (which in the first talks were simply unconditional surrender) were negotiated so that the Confederate soldiers would be paroled and: (1) be allowed to march out of their lines; (2) the officers permitted to take with them their side-arms and clothing; (3) the field, staff, and cavalry officers be permitted to take one horse each; and (4) the rank and file be allowed all of their clothing, but no other property.

Pemberton surrendered 2,166 officers and 27,230 men, 172 cannon, and almost 60,000 muskets and rifles to Grant. This, combined with the successful Siege of Port Hudson on July 9, gave the Union complete control over the Mississippi River, resulting in a major strategic loss for the Confederacy, and cutting off Lt. Gen. Edmund Kirby

Smith's command and the Trans-Mississippi Theater from the Confederacy for the rest of the war.

After his surrender, Pemberton was exchanged as a prisoner on October 13, 1863, and he returned to Richmond. There he spent some eight months without an assignment. At first Gen. Braxton Bragg thought he could use Pemberton, but after conferring with his own ranking officers he advised Davis that taking on the discredited lieutenant general "would not be advisable." Pemberton finally wrote Davis directly, asking he be returned to duty "in any capacity in which you think I may be useful." Davis replied that his own personal confidence in him remained unshaken, saying: I thought and still think that you did right to risk an army for the purpose of keeping command of even a section of the Mississippi River. Had you succeeded none would have blamed; had you not made the attempt, few if any would have defended your course.

Pemberton resigned as a general officer on May 9, 1864, and Davis offered him a commission as a lieutenant colonel of artillery three days later, which he accepted, a testimonial of his loyalty to the South and the Confederate cause. He commanded the artillery of the defenses of Richmond until January 9, 1865. He was appointed inspector general of the artillery as of January 7, and held this position until he was captured in Salisbury, North Carolina, on April 12. Along with Pemberton and his 14 remaining guns, the Federals rounded up about 1,300 men and nearly 10,000 small arms. There is no record of his parole after his capture.

John Pemberton might have made a positive contribution to the Confederate war effort had his talents been properly used. An able administrator, he was uncomfortable in combat. He had demonstrated his weaknesses in South Carolina, yet Davis had sent him to Mississippi anyway.

After the war, Pemberton lived on his farm near Warrenton, Virginia, from 1866 to 1876, and then returned to Pennsylvania. He died in Lower Gwynedd Township, Montgomery County, Pennsylvania, five years later, on July 13, 1881. He was interred in the Laurel Hill Cemetery in Philadelphia. Protests against his being buried there were made by the families of General Meade, Thomas McKean (Signer

Grave of Confederate General Pemberton

of the Declaration of Independence) and Admiral John Dahlgren (whose brother also served as a Confederate General). It was decided that Pemberton would be interred elsewhere; however, he ended up in an obscure area of the cemetery. A ground level plate notes he was a "Confederate General Staff Officer." A statue depicting Pemberton was erected in the Vicksburg National Military Park. His nephew, John Stith Pemberton, was also a Confederate soldier, and was later credited with inventing Coca-Cola.

If You Go:
See the "If You Go" sections of George Meade (p. 281), Samuel Crawford (p. 213), Oliver Knowles (p. 268), and "General Controversy," p. 237.

"The Youngest General"
GALUSHA PENNYPACKER

County: Philadelphia
Town: Philadelphia
Cemetery: Philadelphia National
Address: Haines Street and Limekiln Pike

Galusha Pennypacker was wounded seven times during the Civil War and became a brigadier general at the age of 20, making him the youngest person in United States military history to ever hold that rank, a record which stands to this day.

Pennypacker was born on June 1, 1844 in Valley Forge, Pennsylvania into a family with a history and tradition of military service. His father served in the Mexican War and his grandfather served in the Revolutionary War. Galusha and George Armstrong Custer were fifth cousins and two of the youngest generals in the Civil War. Pennypacker was also a cousin to General Benjamin Prentiss. Shortly after the Mexican War his father, Joseph, went to California in the Gold Rush and never returned. His mother died when he was three years old, and as a result Pennypacker was raised primarily by his grandmother.

At the age of 16, he enlisted in the 9th Pennsylvania Infantry Regiment from West Chester, Pennsylvania. When the war broke out in 1861, he was working as a printer's assistant at the Chester County Times newspaper and had been offered an appointment to West Point. He probably would have entered West Point in 1862, but events intervened. In April 1861, after Fort Sumter surrendered to the Confederates, President Lincoln called for volunteers and the 9th Pennsylvania answered the call as a body. In Harrisburg they were designated as Company A of the 9th Regiment. Pennypacker turned down the post of first lieutenant, believing he was too young for the responsibility. He was assigned to be regimental quartermaster and he excelled at it. The 9th, however, was a three-month regiment and served in the Shenandoah Valley suppressing secessionist activity. It was disbanded in July 1861 and Pennypacker set out to recruit a new regiment, the 97th, which served for the duration.

Galusha Pennypacker

In August 1861, Pennypacker entered "for the war" as captain of Company A, 97th Pennsylvania Volunteers. He was promoted to major in October. The 97th Regiment joined the X (Tenth Army) Corps in the Department of the South, and during 1862 and 1863 participated in all the engagements and sieges in which that corps took part. These included: the capture of Fort Pulaski (Georgia); the taking of Fernandina and Jacksonville (Florida); and actions against James Island, Charleston, and Forts Wagner and Gregg (South Carolina).

In April 1864, the regiment and the Tenth Corps were ordered to Virginia and became part of the Army of the James. Pennypacker was promoted to lieutenant colonel and was engaged in the Bermuda Hundred Campaign under Major General Benjamin Butler. During that campaign, Pennypacker was severely wounded in the right arm, left leg and right side at the Battle of Ware Bottom Church. He was hospitalized for three months and promoted to colonel. He returned to duty in August and during the Siege of Petersburg led his brigade and was again wounded at the Battle of Chaffin's Farm and New Market Heights.

On January 15, 1865, Pennypacker was severely wounded yet again at the Second Battle of Fort Fisher, North Carolina. Fort Fisher, which guarded the harbor of Wilmington, was the last coastal stronghold of the Confederacy and a haven for ships running the Union blockade. It was referred to as the Gibraltar of the South and was an important objective for General Alfred Terry. During the successful assault on Fort Fisher, the 97th's color bearer went down. Pennypacker personally picked up the banner and carried it onto a rebel parapet, where he planted it in the sand. He was almost immediately thereafter felled by a Confederate bullet. The wound was considered fatal and General Terry, calling him the "real hero of Fort Fisher" promised him a promotion to brigadier general.

Galusha Pennypacker did receive a brevet promotion to brigadier general dated January 15, 1865. He miraculously survived his wounds after 10 months in the hospital and on February 18, 1865 he received a full promotion to brigadier general of volunteers at the age of 20. To this day he is the youngest officer to hold the rank of general in the history of the U.S. Army. Later he would be awarded the Medal of Honor for his actions at Fort Fisher. His Medal of Honor citation reads: "Gallantly led the charge over a traverse and planted the colors of one of his regiments thereon, was severely wounded."

Pennypacker stayed in the army after the war, serving out west until he retired in July 1883. He settled down in a house on South 10th Street in Philadelphia. In 1991, on the 50th anniversary of the war, Pennypacker was interviewed by Phillip Dillon of the New York World. When asked if he had seen the man who shot him at Fort Fisher,

Pennypacker's grave (Photo by Joe Farrell)

Pennypacker responded that he had indeed, and proceeded to tell how after the Confederates surrendered, a Union soldier asked the assailant to turn over his blanket so they could use it to carry Pennypacker from the battlefield. According to Pennypacker, the man refused, saying "I won't give up my blanket; I'm a prisoner and entitled to my blanket." Hearing this remark sent Pennypacker's men into a rage. Immediately they began beating the Confederate. As Pennypacker recounted, "my men, with clubbed muskets, dashed out his brains," killing him instantly. "I closed my eyes and they carried me away in that blanket, but the horror of it has never gone out of my mind to this day," he told Dillon.

Pennypacker died in Philadelphia on October 1, 1916 and is buried in Philadelphia National Cemetery. There is a large, prominent (and somewhat bizarre) statue honoring him at 19th Street and Benjamin Franklin Parkway on the north side of Logan Square. His name is also inscribed on the Smith Memorial Arch in Philadelphia's Fairmount Park.

If You Go:
About eight miles south of Philadelphia National Cemetery, in Philadelphia's downtown historical district, is the famous Christ Church Burial (430 Arch Street, Philadelphia). There are two prominent Civil War generals buried there:

George Archibald McCall: commander of the Pennsylvania Reserve Corps. In June 1862, he commanded his corps in the victory at Dranesville, Virginia and at the Battle of Mechanicsville, Virginia. Later that month, McCall was wounded and captured at Frayser's Farm, Virginia and imprisoned at the infamous Libby Prison. He became ill from his wounds and confinement, and subsequently was prisoner-exchanged for a Confederate general, Simon Buckner, who would become governor of Kentucky in 1887. McCall's poor health forced him to resign from the army in March 1863.

Major General George Cadwalader: a hero in the Mexican War, he commanded the Department of Philadelphia during the Civil War. In that capacity, he oversaw the movement of thousands of Union troops and wounded men through the city of Philadelphia.

While in Philadelphia, you might find yourself craving an Irish pub. There are many to choose from, but we had a terrific experience at two that were only blocks apart in the shadow of City Hall. McGillin's Olde Ale House at 1310 Drury Street (an alley connecting 13th & South Juniper Streets, between Chestnut & Sansom Streets, in Center City) threw open its doors

George Cadwalader

the year Lincoln was elected president, making it the oldest continuously operating tavern in Philadelphia. As we partook of our cold, delicious brew served by friendly, enthusiastic staff surrounded by interesting historical artifacts, we wondered how many of the men we are writing about had been there quenching their thirst and discussing the issues of the day. We also wondered how McGillin's survived Prohibition, but that's for another book.

We also had a great time at nearby Fadó Irish Pub & Restaurant, situated at 1500 Locust Street. Fadó offers beautiful, modern decor with friendly, prompt service and a wonderful menu which includes many Irish favorites. So many good places . . . so little time.

"The Cop That Would Be King"

FRANK RIZZO

County: Philadelphia
Town: Philadelphia
Cemetery: Holy Sepulchre
Address: 3301 Cheltenham Avenue

Francis "Frank" Lazarro Rizzo was an American police officer and politician. He served two terms as mayor of Philadelphia from January 1972 to January 1980. He served as Police Commissioner for four years prior to becoming mayor. Mr. Rizzo was one of those seemingly larger than life figures, destined to be a hero to some and a villain to others.

He was born October 23, 1920 in Philadelphia to a police family. After a brief stint in the US Navy and three years working in a steel mill, he became a policeman in 1943, rising through the ranks to become Police Commissioner in 1967. He served in that role during the turbulent years of 1967-1971. Known as a cop's cop, he showed his mettle when, with a nightstick protruding from the cummerbund of his tuxedo, he left a black tie affair in order to lead "my men" to break up a riot. While serving as Commissioner, he expanded the police force, won the loyalty of his men, and kept the crime rate below that of any other major city. He was, however, accused of racism and police brutality. Supporters noted that in his five year tenure, Philadelphia had the lowest crime rate of the nation's ten largest cities. His detractors said the price for that order was intolerable. In 1970, shortly before he resigned to run for mayor, the police deeply embittered Philadelphia blacks by raiding the Black Panther headquarters, herding them into the street, and ordering them to strip naked in front of TV cameras and reporters. "Imagine the big Black Panthers with their pants down," Mr. Rizzo gloated at the time.

In 1971, Rizzo ran for mayor using "Firm but Fair" as his slogan and won as a law and order Democrat. As Mayor Rizzo continued to support the strong-arm tactics of the police department, he himself made use of them, forming a secret police force that investigated his political opponents. His rough edges and penchant for bombastic statements

Statue of Frank Rizzo

frequently inflamed his enemies. Two of his most famous quotes are: "Just wait until after November, I'm gonna make Attila the Hun look like a faggot" and "a liberal is a conservative who hasn't been mugged yet."

Rizzo had a controversial relationship with the media including Andrea Mitchell, who was one of the first female urban beat reporters. Almost immediately after he had been elected Mayor, *The Philadelphia Inquirer* began running a series of articles detailing Rizzo's years as police commissioner. The articles did not compliment the new mayor. In addition, Richard Dilworth, a former Philadelphia mayor, went public with allegations that Rizzo had used the police force for his own political purposes. Rizzo, by this time, had few supporters in the press, as he had hired about two dozen reporters who had written about him while he was commissioner in a positive manner. What Rizzo accomplished was the removal of his biggest supporters from the media.

Rizzo's problems with the press did not ease as he went further into his first term. In one incident, Rizzo was accused by the Democratic Party Chairman, Peter Camiel, of offering jobs in exchange for choosing certain candidates for other city offices. Rizzo responded by calling Camiel a liar. A reporter from the Philadelphia Daily News asked Rizzo if he would take a polygraph test to prove Camiel was lying. Both men agreed to take the test. "If this machine says a man lied, he lied," Rizzo said before taking the test. The test results showed that Rizzo appeared to be lying and Camiel appeared to be truthful. The scandal was widely reported and severely damaged his reputation and chances of becoming Governor. At this point, Rizzo severed his relationship with the media and didn't hold a press conference for almost two years.

Campaigning for a second term in 1975, Rizzo's slogan was, "He held the line on taxes." Almost immediately after his victory in the election, he convinced city council to raise the taxes. The move angered fiscal conservatives who had supported Rizzo during the campaign. Another development during his second term was the taking over by the city of the Philadelphia Gas Works. Formerly considered one of the best managed municipal utilities in the country, it soon became a long-running fiscal and management embarrassment to the city due to generous municipal labor contracts and the expansion of patronage hiring. Rizzo himself would serve as a security consultant at the Gas Works from 1983-1991.

Rizzo's actions during his second term resulted in a well organized effort for a recall election. As a matter of fact, the organizers of the effort collected well over the

250,000 signatures required to force the recall. Rizzo supporters responded by challenging the validity of the signatures and the constitutionality of the recall procedure. Polls showed that Rizzo would lose a recall election by a wide margin, but he managed to survive when the Pennsylvania Supreme Court, by a single vote, declared the recall process unconstitutional. The Supreme Court decision was written by Chief Justice Robert Nix. Nix had been elected to the court in 1971 with Rizzo's support.

As mayor, Rizzo continued to champion the idea that strong and severe law enforcement methods were necessary in light of rising crime rates. By 1979, the issue had been moved into the courtroom. The Justice Department filed suit in the United States District Court, charging Mayor Rizzo and other high ranking city officials with committing or condoning "widespread and severe" acts of police brutality. A federal judge later dismissed the suit saying the government had no grounds to have filed it in the first place.

Rizzo wanted a third consecutive term in 1979 but was facing a two term consecutive term limit in the City Charter. He got the City Council to place a question on the ballot that would have allowed him to run. In a record turnout, Philadelphians voted two to one against the change, thus blocking him from running in 1979. He ran again for Mayor

Hizzoner Frank Rizzo.

in 1983 but lost the Democratic nomination to Wilson Goode. In 1985, he switched to the Republican Party and ran again in 1987, but lost the general election again to Wilson Goode. He was running for Mayor again in 1991 when on July 16, Frank Rizzo died of a massive heart attack. Frank Rizzo's funeral was large and carried on live television. He is buried with family members in Holy Sepulchre Cemetery in Cheltenham.

A statue of mayor Rizzo waving one of his arms in greeting, stands in front of Philadelphia's Municipal Services Building. A book by Joseph Daughen and Peter Binzen titled "The Cop Who Would Be King" is considered an authoritative account of Rizzo's rise to power.

If You Go:
See the "If You Go" section of Connie Mack on page 278.

BILL TILDEN

County: Philadelphia
Town: Philadelphia
Cemetery: Ivy Hill
Address: 1201 Easton Road

Many have called the 1920's the Golden Age of Sports. Athletic heroes appeared from the beginning of the decade. In baseball, the big names included Babe Ruth, Lou Gehrig, and Ty Cobb. In football, Knute Rockne and his Four Horsemen along with Red Grange commanded the attention of the masses. Bobby Jones and Walter Hagen ruled the golfing world. In men's tennis, one man dominated the game like no one ever had. His name was Bill Tilden.

William (Bill) Tatem Tilden II was born on February 10, 1893 in Philadelphia. His family was wealthy, but they had been stung by the death of three of Bill's older siblings. His mother died when he was 15, and though his father could have easily looked after Tilden, he was sent to live with an aunt who lived in the same neighborhood. When he was 19, he lost his dad and an older brother. He suffered from severe depression for months.

Encouraged by his aunt, he began to concentrate on tennis. Compared to many of his peers, who had been playing for years, 19 was a bit old to begin taking the game seriously. He was not considered good enough to make his college team, which may explain why he dropped out of the University of Pennsylvania to work on his game. That is exactly what he did, not only practicing, but studying the game. By the early twenties, Tilden was ready to make his move.

In 1920, Tilden was 27 years of age and relatively unknown. All that was about to change. Starting in 1920, Tilden led the United States team to seven consecutive Davis Cup Championships. As of today, no other nation has equaled that record. In 1920, Tilden won his first United States National Championship (what would now be considered the United States Open). He would go on to win five more in succession. In 1929, Bill won the tournament

"Big Bill" Tilden

again, giving him a total of seven titles. He also participated in the men's doubles event, winning that five times, and
mixed doubles where he won four titles. Tilden competed
abroad as well. He competed at Wimbledon six times and
won in 1920, 1921, and 1930. After his 1930 win, needing

Big Bill in action.

money, Tilden turned professional. His career record as an amateur was 71-7 which equates to an incredible winning percentage of .910.

Tilden's professional career began in 1931 when he was 37 years old. The professional tennis tour was in its infancy, having only just begun in 1927. For the next 15 years, Tilden traveled across the United States and Europe competing against other professionals. He was no longer able to win matches whenever he wanted. His opponents included Ellsworth Vines and Don Budge, both of whom had been ranked number one in the world far more recently than Tilden. He was able to hold his own with these young players, but more importantly, he was the number one box office draw on the tour. To give you an idea of how competitive he was, in 1945, he teamed up with Vinnie Richards and won the professional doubles championship. At the time he was 52 years old.

How good was Tilden? Nicknamed "Big Bill" (he stood at six feet one inch), he was a tennis master. He possessed what was described as a cannonball serve. Many who saw him play believed that he often took a little something off his initial service because he disliked short volleys. He was a superb backcourt player, using multiple types of shots to outwit and overpower his opponents. Jack Kramer, who became the number one player in the world in the early 1950's, played against Tilden when he was a teenager and Bill was in his late 40's. Kramer later recalled that Tilden's service was good, and he had a forehand that couldn't be stopped. Kramer said Bill could put the ball anywhere he wanted it.

Tilden was also a student of the game. He even wrote a few books on the subject including, "Match Play and the Spin of the Ball." For years, this book was the tennis player's bible, and it is still in print and available today. Bill was a master of tennis tactics, and he had no equal in recognizing an opponent's strengths and using them to his benefit.

Tilden was also a showman. As a professional, he felt it was his job to sell tickets. Many believed he would deliberately lose the opening set of a match to peak the audience's interest. Sometimes when he was serving to win a match, he would pick up four balls in one hand and quickly fire four aces at his opponent.

Tilden's life off the tennis court was not nearly as successful. He was never known to have a sexual relationship with a woman. As he grew older, he appeared more feminine. Rumors about his homosexuality were both public and well known. In 1946, he was arrested in Indiana for soliciting an underage male prostitute. While in the custody of police, he signed a confession. Some stories claim that he never read the confession because he didn't have his glasses with him. It has been said that he was so vain, he didn't like to wear them. As a result of this arrest, he was sentenced to one year in prison (he served a little over seven months) and five years of probation. In 1949, he was arrested again. In this instance he had picked up a 16 year old hitchhiker who later sued him, claiming the incident had harmed him physically and emotionally. This case concluded with Tilden spending 10 months in jail. He emerged from prison a pariah in the tennis world. Clubs would not give him access to their courts to provide tennis lessons. In addition, he was not invited to play in many tournaments. To aid him in securing an income, his good friend Charlie Chaplin permitted Tilden to use his private court to provide lessons.

In spite of the above incidents, Tilden had his defenders. These people noted that he had never made sexual advances aimed at other players or any of his students. It was their view that Tilden was the victim of the rumors that surrounded him at the time.

Despite his problems, tennis honors continued to come his way. In 1950, the Associated press released a poll citing the greatest athletes of the first half of the 20th century. Among those named in their respective sports were Jim Thorpe, Jack Dempsey, Babe Ruth, and Bobby Jones. Tilden was named the greatest tennis player by a wider margin than any other athlete named in the poll. In 1958, he was inducted into the Tennis Hall of Fame. In addition, when Jack Kramer released his autobiography in 1979, he named Tilden one of the six greatest tennis players of all time.

In 1953, while getting ready to leave for Cleveland where the United States Professional Championship was being held, Tilden suffered a stroke and died. He is buried in a very modest grave in Ivy Hill Cemetery in Philadelphia.

If You Go:
See the "If You Go" section of Willie Anderson on page 188.

A modest tombstone lies over the greatest tennis player of his time.

"A Business Pioneer"

JOHN WANAMAKER

County: Philadelphia
Town: Philadelphia
Cemetery: St. James The Less Episcopal Churchyard
Address: 3227 West Clearfield Street

John Wanamaker is the founder of Wanamaker's Department Stores and a pioneer in marketing and advertising. He was born in Philadelphia on July 11, 1838. Not much is known about his early life except that his father and grandfather were brick makers, but young John took jobs at a bookstore and a number of clothing stores. In 1860 he married Mary Erringer Brown in Philadelphia, and they had six children.

John was unable to join the Army during the Civil War due to a persistent cough and ventured into business with his brother-in-law opening a men's clothing store in 1861 in Philadelphia. Business grew substantially based on his principle "one price and goods returnable." Soon he opened a second store on Chestnut Street and then published the first copyrighted advertisement by a retailer. In 1875 he purchased an abandoned railroad depot and converted it into a large store called "the Grand Depot." It is considered to be the first department store in Philadelphia.

He was an innovator and guaranteed the quality of his merchandise in writing. His store was the first with electrical illumination, the first with a telephone, and the first to have a restaurant inside. He invented the price tag and allowed his customers to return purchases for a cash refund. In 1878 he offered the first "white sale" with special prices on linens and other white products.

He gave his employers free medical care, education, recreational facilities, pensions and profit sharing plans before such benefits were popular. He was, however, a fierce opponent of unionization and fired the first twelve union members he discovered in 1887 during an organizing drive by the Knights of Labor.

John Wanamaker opened his first New York store in 1896 and continued to expand his business abroad with

John Wanamaker

Houses of Wanamaker's in London and Paris. A large, grander store in Philadelphia was completed in 1910 on the site of "The Grand Depot" encompassing an entire block at the corner of thirteenth and Market Streets across from City Hall. The store houses a large pipe organ called the Wanamaker Grand Court Organ and was dedicated by President William Howard Taft. The organ is still in use today for daily recitals and all sorts of special event concerts. The store's "Grand Court" also houses the "Wanamaker Eagle," a 2500 pound bronze eagle that became a famous meeting place.

After so much success in business, Wanamaker developed an interest in politics and gave $10,000 to the campaign of Benjamin Harrison in the 1818 presidential race. When Harrison won, despite receiving fewer popular votes than his opponent Grove Cleveland, he appointed John Wanamaker as United States Postmaster General. During his term as Postmaster he achieved many reforms such as extending mail serviced to rural areas and establishing the first parcel-post system. He issued the first commemorative stamps at the World Columbian Exposition in Chicago in 1893. He believed the stamps, which commemorated Columbus' discovery of the New World, would generate revenue. Many in Congress were critical of the idea and thought it an unnecessary expense. Wanamaker was proven right when more than two billion stamps were sold at a value of forty million dollars.

John Wanamaker's Grand Depot Store, Philadelphia, PA, circa 1880. Opened in 1876, John Wanamaker's massive Grand Depot sprawled over the site of the former Pennsylvania Railroad Freight Depot. One of the great innovators in American retailing, Wanamaker introduced a number of innovations in this store. The Grand Depot was the first American department store to have electrical illumination (1878), telephone service (1879), pneumatic tubes to transport cash and documents (1880), and elevator service (1884).

He also instituted the practice of sorting mail on a moving train to improve delivery time.

Wanamaker ran for the Republican nomination for the United States Senate in 1896 but lost to Boise Penrose and then for the gubernatorial nomination in 1898 but lost again this time to William Stone.

Throughout his life, Wanamaker was a devout Presbyterian and worked for many years with the Bethany Sunday School and founded several Presbyterian Churches. He was also able to maintain ties with the YMCA during his career and helped with the development of YMCA buildings all over the world.

Thomas Nast, ca. 1888. "$10,000 compliments of Pious John to help carry Indiana." Nash suggest that department-store magnate "Pious John" Wanamaker gave away some of his fortune to support the campaign of candidate Benjamin Harrison, who is wearing the too-large hat of his grandfather, President William Henry Harrison.

This mausoleum houses the remains of the innovative store owner John Wanamaker.

John Wanamaker died in his home in Philadelphia on December 12, 1922. Thomas Edison, a close friend, was pallbearer at his funeral. He is commemorated by a statue in front of Philadelphia's City Hall and buried in a large tower in the St. James the Less Episcopal Churchyard in Philadelphia. We were denied entrance into the tower by a caretaker who commented on not offending the family by allowing us to see inside.

If You Go:
Also buried at St. James the Less Episcopal Churchyard is Robert Morris Jr., the grandson of the Revolutionary War Patriot and Declaration of Independence signer, Robert Morris. He was a Union Civil War Officer captured at the Battle of Brandy Station Virginia on June 9, 1863. He was imprisoned at the infamous Libby Prison where he died on August 13. 1863.

The cemetery also contains the grave of Civil War Congressional Medal of Honor Recipient Anthony Taylor who enlisted as a private and was mustered out as a Captain. He was awarded his Medal of Honor as a Lieutenant for his bravery at the Battle of Chickamauga, Georgia on September 20, 1863.

Also buried there is Benjamin Chew Tilghman who served as an officer in the Civil War, was wounded at Chancellorsville and upon recovery accepted the role of Colonel and commander of the 3rd United States Colored Troops. After the War he became famous for a variety of inventions including the process of sandblasting.

Nearby St. James the Less at St Timothy's Episcopal Church Cemetery in Roxborough section of Philadelphia is the grave of Orlando Henderson Petty. Petty was awarded the Congressional Medal of Honor for his "extraordinary heroism" in the Battle of Belleau Wood, France. He was also awarded the Distinguished Service Cross and the Croix de Guerre with palm from France and the Croce di Guerre from Italy.

INDEX

Cemeteries

Cities and Towns

Pubs and Restaurants